A
BIOGRAPHICAL
DICTIONARY
of
ANCIENT
EGYPT

by

Rosalie and Antony E. David

University of Oklahoma Press
Norman

Oklahoma Paperbacks edition published 1996 by the University of
Oklahoma Press, Norman, Publishing Division of the University, by
special arrangement with B A Seaby Ltd., an imprint of
B T Batsford Ltd., 4 Fitzhardinge Street, London W1H 0AH.

Library of Congress Cataloging-in-Publication Data
David, A. Rosalie (Ann Rosalie)
    A biographical dictionary of ancient Egypt / by Rosalie and Antony
E. David.
        p.   cm.
    Originally published: London: Seaby, 1992.
    Includes bibliographical references.
    ISBN 0 8061 – 2822 4 (pbk.: alk. paper)
        1. Egypt—History—To 640 A.D.—Biography.   I. David, Antony E.
II. Title.
DT83.D2   1996
932—dc20   95-36539
                                                        CIP

Printed in Great Britain

Contents

Introduction

The history of ancient Egypt extends from c.3100 BC down to c.AD 600, although during the later period it had become part of the Roman Empire. Prior to the unification of the country in c.3100 BC, there were perhaps two thousand years when the civilisation gradually developed but since written records of this earliest period have never been discovered, the names of individual rulers or persons of historical importance have rarely survived. Therefore, it has been decided to incorporate here only the major figures between c.3100 BC and c.AD 600, although during the period of Roman rule only those Roman Emperors who had a marked association with or interest in Egypt have been included.

The main aim of the book is to make more easily available to the student and general reader a dictionary of biographical references which relate to the important historical and cultural figures and also to a selection of other less well-known individuals. There is a selection of maps showing the major sites in Egypt and Nubia, as well as other areas of the ancient Near East and the Classical world.

Over such a considerable timespan, clearly more historical persons are known than it is possible to accommodate in the space of this dictionary. Therefore, it has been necessary to omit some names, but in order to provide further information, in addition to the Biographical Dictionary, there is an index of persons who are mentioned in the main entries but do not warrant their own reference. As well as Egyptians, some foreigners are included in the Biographical Dictionary; these are the people with whom the Egyptians came into contact, either as the rulers or inhabitants of other states, such as the Mitannians or the Hittites, or as the conquerors of Egypt (the Assyrians, Persians, Greeks or Romans), or those writers such as the Classical historians who have left vivid descriptions of Egypt.

The spread of entries attempts to cover all the major periods of Egypt's history, although some dynasties are much more fully documented than others. Not only rulers and significant members of their families are included (although the list of rulers is not comprehensive), but non-royal persons who owned particularly impressive or interesting tombs, who are accredited with special literary or other skills, or who showed great military prowess are also mentioned. However, there are problems: the First, Second and Third Intermediate Periods are much less well-represented in terms of archaeological and inscriptional evidence than the Old, Middle or New Kingdoms, and since the artistic achievements of all periods are mostly anonymous, produced by nameless artisans organised into State or temple workshops, it is impossible to credit many individuals for some of the civilisation's most dynamic works of art. The Egyptians sought their ideal of perfection by attempting to retain and copy the earliest art-forms, so there was relatively little opportunity for individual expression or innovation on the part of the artisans and craftsmen.

Other problems centre around the chronology of ancient Egypt. In some periods, a relatively accurate sequence of rulers and their dates can be produced, but at other times, the evidence is scanty and even contradictory. The Chronological Table given in this book includes the dynasties provided in Manetho's original chronicle, arranged into the 'Kingdoms' and 'Periods' which are generally accepted today in Egyptology. The list of rulers includes all those entered in the Biographical Dictionary, as well as a few other relatively significant kings, but it does not attempt to provide a comprehensive table and further information on this should be sought in the Cambridge Ancient History. Generally, in addition to Egyptian historical inscriptions and the accounts of Egyptian history given by *Manetho and other Classical writers, additional information about certain periods of the country's history is provided in other contemporary sources, including Hebrew, Near Eastern and Classical historical and literary texts.

Egypt's own historical evidence comes from a variety of sources. These include the monuments – tombs, temples, pyramids and settlement sites; the inscriptions which occur on the walls of the buildings as well as those found on papyri, stelae, statues and many small artifacts; and the physical evidence of the mummified remains.

Entries in the Biographical Dictionary are arranged alphabetically. Each heading consists of a name, brief identification and a date; for the rulers, the dates of the king's reign are given, but for other entries, where the person achieved significance within a particular reign (for example, queens and royal officials), then the reign and dates of the relevant king are provided. Within each entry, cross-references are indicated by an asterisk placed at the beginning of the name under which the person is classified. At the end of most entries, there is at least one bibliographical reference, and in some cases, these refer to an ancient source whereas in others, they supply book references for further reading. In addition, the General Bibliography provides a small selection of general works, and also a list of all the abbreviations used in the main text.

There is also a Glossary which explains some of the terms in the text which have a special meaning or interpretation with reference to Egyptology.

Finally, a brief comment on the spelling of the kings' names: there were five main names in the Pharaoh's royal titulary and the two most important were inscribed inside cartouches (a stylised loop of rope). In the entries, the practise is adopted of using the one name by which the ruler is best known, and of retaining the Graecised rather than the Egyptian version of the name. Thus, entries occur under 'Cheops' rather than 'Khufu', 'Amenophis' rather than 'Amenhotep' and 'Ammenemes' instead of 'Amenemhet'.

OUTLINE HISTORY c.3100 BC-Fourth Century AD

The history of ancient Egyptian civilisation covers a period from c.3100 BC to the conquest of the country by Alexander the Great in 332 BC. Before the Dynastic Period (beginning c.3100 BC), the communities laid the foundations for the later great advances in technological, political, religious and artistic developments; this is generally referred to as the Predynastic Period (c.5000-3100 BC). After *Alexander the Great conquered Egypt in 332 BC, the country was ruled by a line of Macedonian Greeks who descended from *Alexander's general, Ptolemy (who became *Ptolemy I). The last of this dynasty, *Cleopatra VII, failed to prevent the absorption of Egypt into the Roman Empire in 30 BC, and subsequently Egypt was ruled by Rome as a province.

The basis of the modern chronology of ancient Egypt rests upon the work of the priest *Manetho (323-245 BC), who wrote a chronicle of the Egyptian kings (c.3100-332 BC), dividing his king-list into dynasties. Historians still retain these thirty-one dynasties, further subdividing them into major periods. These are: the Archaic Period (First and Second Dynasties); the Old Kingdom (Third to Sixth Dynasties); the First Intermediate Period (Seventh to Eleventh Dynasties); the Middle Kingdom (Twelfth Dynasty); the Second Intermediate Period (Thirteenth to Seventeenth Dynasty); the New Kingdom (Eighteenth to Twentieth Dynasties); the Third Intermediate Period (Twenty-first to Twenty-fifth Dynasties); and the Late Period (Twenty-sixth to Thirty-first Dynasties).

In the Predynastic Period, two kingdoms developed in Egypt, a northern one situated in the Delta and a southern one in the Nile Valley. They shared many features of a common culture. The appearance of writing, monumental brick architecture and advances in arts and crafts around 3400 BC may have been set in motion by the arrival of a new group of people (the so-called *Dynastic Race), and two kingdoms were subsequently established. The southern rulers ultimately set out to conquer the north; *King Scorpion made some military advances but the unification of the two kingdoms was finally achieved by *Narmer (c.3100 BC). In the following Archaic Period his descendants ruled a unified state, and the political and social organisation of the country was established. Great advances were also made in technology and building techniques, with the construction of substantial mudbrick mastaba-tombs for the aristocracy.

The Old Kingdom was the first great era of Egyptian civilisation. Although mastaba-tombs were retained for the nobility, and the mass of the population continued to be buried in the sand, the concept of a pyramid as the king's burial place was introduced. The first pyramid was built for *Djoser at Saqqara. This was designed as a step pyramid by *Imhotep, his vizier and architect, and formed one feature of an elaborate funerary complex. In the Fourth Dynasty, pyramid-building reached its zenith at Giza with the funerary complexes of *Cheops, *Chephren and *Mycerinus. The pyramid form was probably closely associated with the worship of the sun-god Re, and was intended to provide the dead king with a magical means of access to the heavens. However, the construction and maintenance of the pyramids and the employment of staff to service them became an increasing economic drain on Egypt's resources, and by the Fifth Dynasty, there was a reduction in the size and quality of the pyramids. The sun-cult now became omnipotent and the kings devoted their resources to building temples for the sun-god, at the expense of their own pyramids. As the pyramids declined, the kings sought eternal life by magical means, inscribing the interior walls of their pyramids with spells, known collectively as the Pyramid Texts.

In general, art, religion and literature flourished in the Old Kingdom, and an important literary genre - the Instructions in Wisdom - now emerged, which provides a unique insight into the contemporary moral and social values. A great gulf divided the king from his subjects. This was based on the assumption that he was half-divine, the offspring of the sun-god and the Chief Queen. Only he was expected to attain individual eternity; his subjects could only hope to experience immortality vicariously, through the god-king's personal beneficence. There was a rigid social hierarchy - below the king were the nobles who were usually related by family ties to the king; then came the state officials, the craftsmen and the peasants, who comprised the largest section of the population, and whose patient agricultural labours provided food for the whole society.

The nobility built mastaba-tombs near to the king's pyramid and equipped them lavishly for the hereafter with articles of everyday use. The interior walls were decorated with scenes which showed many aspects of daily existence; at Saqqara, there are some particularly famous examples such as the tombs of *Ti and *Ankhmahor which provide detailed information about the people's daily lives. Pyramids, tombs and temples were built of stone to last for eternity whereas houses, palaces and towns were constructed of mudbrick and consequently have survived less well. From the literature and the goods placed in the tombs, it is evident that the Egyptians had already achieved a high level of civilisation.

Towards the end of the Old Kingdom, economic, political, religious and social factors began to contribute to the decline of this centralised bureaucracy. After the end of the Sixth Dynasty, when *Pepy II's long reign accentuated some of the problems, there came a time of anarchy, known as the First Intermediate Period. Centralised government collapsed and Egypt returned to a political situation which reflected the times of the Predynastic Period, when local princelings ruled their own areas and fought against each other. Many of the monuments were desecrated and tomb-robbers ravaged the graves. Poverty, famine and disease quickly followed, and these disastrous conditions may be described in some of the most famous literary works such as the 'Prophecy of *Neferti' and the 'Admonitions' of the prophet *Ipuwer.

In the Eleventh Dynasty, the princes of Thebes who carried the name *Mentuhotep managed to restore some order in the country and there was a return to more settled conditions. During the First Intermediate Period, craftsmen were no longer concentrated at the capital city, Memphis, as they had been in the Old Kingdom. Provincial rulers were now buried in tombs in their own localities. These tombs were cut deep into the cliffs and were decorated with painted wall-scenes by local artists who also produced a wide range of goods which were placed in the tombs.

The next period – the Middle Kingdom – saw Egypt united again under a strong ruler, *Ammenemes I, who seized the throne and inaugurated a time of great prosperity. He moved the capital city north from Thebes to Lisht and revived the practice of building traditional pyramid complexes. His powerful descendants – *Amenemmes II, *Ammenemes III, *Sesostris I,*Sesostris II and *Sesostris III – tackled the major problems of ruling Egypt and re-established centralised government. They introduced the political concept of a co-regency: during his lifetime, the king associated his chosen heir with him upon the throne, thus ensuring a smooth succession when he died. This dynasty had no claims to royal antecedents and it was therefore necessary to establish an uncontested succession by political means.In addition, *Sesostris III abolished the powers of the great provincial nobles who had threatened the king's absolute supremacy since the last years of the Old Kingdom.

These dynamic rulers also established their contacts outside Egypt, restoring their dominion over *Nubia in order to gain access to the gold and hard stone of the region. Here, they pursued a policy of force, building a string of fortresses which were garrisoned by Egyptians. However, to the north, they followed a non-aggressive policy, re-opening or establishing trading contacts with the Aegean Islanders, the people of *Byblos, and the inhabitants of *Punt. Egypt once again enjoyed a high standard of living at home and prestige abroad as a major power.

After the collapse of the Old Kingdom society, the role of the king underwent some changes and Re, the royal patron deity, no longer enjoyed unrivalled supremacy. Another god, *Osiris, gained widespread support, since he could promise the chance of immortality not only to the king but to all believers who could demonstrate pious and worthy lives. This new democratic concept of the afterlife profoundly affected religious beliefs and customs and brought about widespread changes in building and equipping burial places. Although the kings continued to be buried in pyramids, many wealthy provincial nobles continued the practice of the First Intermediate Period and were buried in their own localities in rock-cut tombs, rather than return to the custom of building mastaba-tombs around the pyramid. The rock-cut tombs had a pillared hall and burial chamber cut out of the solid rock, and the internal wall surfaces were decorated with registers of scenes showing daily life activities.The sculpture, jewellery, art and literature of the Middle Kingdom all reflect a period of wealth and stability, but again, this was not to last, and in the Second Intermediate Period, Egypt again suffered a decline. The period consists of five dynasties; some have lines of native rulers (and some of these were contemporary, with 'kings' ruling in different parts of the country), while the Fifteenth and Sixteenth Dynasties are comprised of foreigners who conquered Egypt and established themselves as kings. These are known as the *Hyksos, and although it is uncertain how far their rulership extended in Egypt, they certainly claimed authority over much of the land. They were probably of *Asiatic origin, although the location of their homeland and the extent of their influence in Egypt have been disputed. An account of them is given in the writings of *Josephus and *Manetho.

The native princes of Thebes who comprised the Seventeenth Dynasty eventually drove the *Hyksos from Egypt and pursued them into southern Palestine. The *Hyksos ruler *Apophis I and the Theban princes *Kamose and *Seqenenre Ta'o II came into conflict, and *Amosis I finally defeated the Hyksos and established the

Eighteenth Dynasty, becoming the founder of the New Kingdom. The Hyksos intrusion profoundly affected Egypt's attitude towards foreign policy. Previously, they had shown little interest in colonising lands other than *Nubia, and had preferred to gain access to the commodities found in neighbouring countries through avenues of trade. However, once the Hyksos had been expelled, they began to adopt a more positive foreign policy particularly with regard to Palestine and Syria, to prevent any further invasions into Egypt.

During the early years of the Eighteenth Dynasty, the Egyptian kings (particularly *Tuthmosis I, *Tuthmosis III and *Amenophis II) sent major military expeditions to Palestine, Syria and Asia Minor. They sought to subdue the petty states in Palestine and to bring them under Egyptian influence; this policy brought them into direct conflict with another great power, *Mitanni. By the later Eighteenth Dynasty, this conflict had been resolved, with neither state an outright victor, and Egypt and *Mitanni became friends and allies. However, *Mitanni was replaced as a great power by the *Hittites who then posed a new threat to Egypt's dominance of the area. During the Nineteenth Dynasty, *Sethos I and *Ramesses II renewed Egypt's claims in Syria and Palestine and campaigned against the *Hittites, but this conflict was also ultimately resolved by a diplomatic alliance which included a Treaty and royal marriages.

By establishing her influence over the petty princedoms in Palestine, Egypt created the world's first empire which, during the Eighteenth Dynasty, stretched from the River Euphrates in the north down to the possessions in *Nubia. It was less rigidly organised than the later empires of the *Assyrians, *Persians, *Greeks and *Romans, and relied on a policy of allowing those princes who were loyal to Egypt to remain as the rulers of their own cities and states, giving allegiance and tribute to Egypt. When Egypt was strong, the vassal princes benefitted from this system, but when, as in the Amarna Period, the Pharaoh showed little interest in the empire, they became easy prey for other ambitious powers.

The military expeditions brought extensive booty back to Egypt and the vassal states paid handsome tribute into Egypt's royal coffers. However, a major recipient of this vast wealth was the great state-god, Amen-Re, whose principal shrine was at the Temple of Karnak at Thebes. The Theban princes of the Seventeenth Dynasty remembered their debt to their local, family god, Amun, and when their descendants, the Eighteenth Dynasty kings, became world conquerors, they associated Amun's cult with that of the old sun-god, Re, and, as Amen-Re, their god became the supreme deity of the pantheon and of the empire. His priesthood at Karnak became extremely wealthy and powerful; ultimately, when it was accepted that their support for a particular candidate in the event of a disputed succession would guarantee him the throne, their power came to rival that of the king.

Thebes was now not only the state capital of Egypt and the empire but also the religious capital. The kings had their Residence there and they selected a new burial site on the west bank of the river, opposite Thebes. They now abandoned the pyramid as the royal burial monument and chose instead to be interred in concealed rock-tombs in the vain hope of defeating the tomb-robbers. A remote and barren region situated in the cliffs on the west side of the Nile was selected for these burials; it is known today as the Valley of the Kings.Rock-tombs were cut deep into the mountain, with a series of chambers and descending passages which attempted to defeat the robbers. There was now no room to build a mortuary temple adjoining the tomb, where the burial service and continuing mortuary rites could be performed (the pyramid and temple had been adjacent in the pyramid complexes), so the temples were now located on the cultivated plain which lay between the cliffs and the Nile. Over sixty tombs have been discovered so far in this valley, but, with the exception of *Tutankhamun's tomb, all had been extensively ransacked in antiquity. Many of the royal mummies were re-buried by the ancient priests, in an attempt to protect them from further desecration and to ensure their eternal life, and in modern times, these have been discovered in two caches.

In the Valley of the Kings, the interior walls of many of the tombs are decorated with sculptured and painted scenes taken from the funerary books, which gave the king magical protection and assisted his passage through the dangers found in the underworld. Nearby, in the Valley of the Queens, some of the royal wives and princes occupied rock-cut tombs decorated with scenes which showed them in the presence of the gods. The courtiers and officials also possessed rock-cut tombs, scattered across the barren cliffs of this area, but by contrast with the royal tombs, these were decorated with wall-scenes which show a wide range of daily activities and which provide a remarkable insight into the lives of rich and poor during that period. Some of the finest are those of *Rekhmire, *Ramose and *Sennufer.

Not far away from the royal tombs the archaeologists discovered the town of the royal necropolis craftsmen, known today as Deir el-Medina. This was founded at the beginning of the Eighteenth Dynasty and was occupied for some four hundred years. The houses and the domestic rubbish heaps have provided the archaeologists with a wealth of information relating to the workmen's lives and working conditions. In the nearby cemetery, the tomb of a chief workman, *Sennedjem, supplies evidence of the quality of decoration carried out in their own tombs.

Towards the end of the Eighteenth Dynasty, the conflict between the king and the priests of Amen-Re reached a climax.*Amenophis III and, even more radically, his son *Akhenaten (Amenophis IV) took measures to limit the god's power. Akhenaten's reforms involved the promotion of a monotheistic cult of the sun's disc (the Aten) and the closure of the temples of the other gods. During this time of upheaval (known today as the Amarna Period), *Akhenaten, his queen *Nefertiti, and their daughters played important roles, but the experiment was doomed to failure.Under kings *Tutankhamun and *Horemheb, a counter-revolution took place which restored the traditional beliefs. *Horemheb, with no heir, left the throne to his old friend, Ramesses I; his son, *Sethos I, and his grandson, *Ramesses II, sought to restore Egypt's stability and prestige abroad, campaigning once again in Palestine and Syria. It is possible that the Exodus occurred during *Ramesses II's reign.

By the Nineteenth Dynasty, Egypt faced a new threat on her western front, where the *Libyan tribes were already attempting to infiltrate and settle. Although the Egyptians successfully repelled them for many years, the descendants of these *Libyan tribesmen finally became the kings of Egypt during the Twenty-second Dynasty. During the Nineteenth and Twentieth Dynasties, under *Merneptah and *Ramesses III, the Egyptians faced the combined attacks of the *Sea-peoples, who joined cause with the *Libyans.

By the Third Intermediate Period, Egypt's great days were over. In the Twenty-first Dynasty, the kingdom was again divided, with the legitimate line of kings ruling the north from the city of Tanis while a succession of High-priests of Amun controlled Thebes and its surrounding district. The rulers of the Twenty-second and Twenty-third Dynasties were of *Libyan origin, the descendants of those tribesmen who had infiltrated and settled at Bubastis in the Delta. *Shoshenk I was the most able of these and he briefly attempted to revive Egypt's internal and external powers. The Twenty-fifth (the so-called 'Ethiopian') Dynasty was also of foreign origin. These rulers came from the south and included *Piankhy, *Shabako and *Taharka; eventually, however, they were driven back to their homeland by the *Assyrians who invaded Egypt from the north.During the Late Period, Egypt's decline continued, although the native Saite rulers of the Twenty-sixth Dynasty (*Psammetichus I, *Necho I, *Psammetichus II, *Apries, *Amasis and *Psammetichus III) briefly revived the country and there was a resurgence of former glory, when arts and crafts again reached a high level of excellence and a marked nationalism was evident.

After this short respite, Egypt was once again under foreign domination in the Twenty-seventh and Thirty-first Dynasties, when she became part of the *Persian empire. The *Persian kings, *Cambyses and *Darius I, both took some interest in Egypt, although the overall influence of both the *Assyrians and the *Persians on the Egyptian civilisation was probably minimal. The kings of the Twenty-sixth Dynasty had pursued an active foreign policy, but in these last years, Egypt became increasingly marginalised as the centre of world events moved elsewhere.

In 332 BC, the king of Macedon, *Alexander the Great, added Egypt to his conquests and her dynastic history came to an end. When *Alexander died, his empire was divided with Egypt falling to Ptolemy, one of *Alexander's generals, who as *Ptolemy I Soter declared himself king of Egypt. He and his descendants ruled Egypt until 30 BC. Since twelve of these kings bore the name Ptolemy, this is often referred to as the 'Ptolemaic Period'.

Large numbers of *Greeks now settled in Egypt, ensuring that the Hellenistic culture prevailed there, with the official introduction of the Greek language, customs, religion, and legal system. Alexandria, the city that *Alexander the Great had founded on the Mediterranean coast, now became Egypt's capital as well as a beautiful and wealthy centre of learning. The native Egyptians continued to use their own customs and language but the country was effectively colonised by the *Greeks. The old traditions were only officially continued in the Egyptian temples, since the *Ptolemies built new temples of the same type, to establish and emphasise their divine right to rule Egypt as heirs of the Pharaohs. Heavy taxes and general dissatisfaction led to native opposition and rioting but in 30 BC, with the death of *Cleopatra VII, the country passed to the *Romans and became a mere province of the Roman Empire and the personal possession of its conqueror, *Augustus.

The *Romans retained many features of Ptolemaic rule, including the administrative system and the custom of representing themselves as Pharaohs which endowed them with divine authority to govern Egypt and exact taxes. Thus they completed and made additions to several of the Egyptian temples which the *Ptolemies had founded. Heavy taxation and declining standards in the lives of the native population characterised this period, and now Egypt's main purpose was to produce grain for Rome.

Under this domination, Christianity became widespread throughout Egypt and, as the result of the Edict of *Theodosius I, which proclaimed Christianity to be the official religion of the Empire, the temples of the gods were finally closed. The Egyptian Christians (described by the name '*Copts' from the sixteenth century onwards) rejected the doctrine that Christ combined a divine and a human nature; they adopted the monophysite heresy and broke away from the rest of Christendom.

In the fourth century AD, when the Roman Empire was partitioned into east and west, Egypt passed into the control of Byzantium, and, with the Arab conquest in the seventh century, the country gradually embraced Islam, although a substantial minority of Egyptians remained Christian.

GLOSSARY

AMULET

We use this term, derived and corrupted from the Arabic hamulet (meaning 'something which is worn or carried') to describe the sacred, magical charms which the Egyptians possessed to ward off evil and attract good luck. They were incorporated in jewellery, used in rituals, sewn on to clothing, or placed between the bandages of a mummy; both living and dead made use of them as a protective measure against illness, natural disasters and the evil wishes of enemies. They took the form of hieroglyphs, animals, plants, figures of deities, parts of the body, and other devices. The ankh-sign ('life'), the scarab ('eternal renewal') and the djed-pillar ('stability') were especially potent and widely employed.

ANIMAL WORSHIP

Many Egyptian gods had animal forms and characteristics, and some localities worshipped particular animals. They probably revered the animals' strength, beauty and usefulness to mankind, and also, because in some cases they feared them, they may have sought to placate them through deification. In some temples, there was a cult-animal (the god's manifestation) which was revered. At death, the cult-animals were mummified and buried; there were also vast cemeteries containing animals that pilgrims to sacred sites had purchased to honour the god.

APIS BULL

Worshipped at Memphis as a god of procreation and rebirth, the Apis also had close associations with Osiris, god of the dead. At death, the sacred bull, which had been kept in a special stall at Memphis, was mummified and buried in a sarcophagus (stone coffin) in the Serapeum (a series of subterranean galleries) at Saqqara. The priests then searched for the god's reincarnation in another bull (identified by distinctive body markings), which they installed at Memphis. Mnevis of Heliopolis was another god who was incarnate in a bull.

BOOK OF THE DEAD

The best known of the funerary 'books' of the New Kingdom. These were written on papyrus or leather rolls and placed in the tombs of the wealthy, providing them with a series of spells to ensure their safe passage into the next world. The magical potency of the words was reinforced by illustrations – coloured vignettes in the New Kingdom and line drawings in the Late Period. In addition to the Book of the Dead, other texts included the 'Book of Gates' and the 'Book of Amduat ('that which is in the underworld'). Ultimately, all these texts had been derived from the Pyramid Texts – the magical spells inscribed on the interior walls of some of the Old Kingdom pyramids.

BIRTH-HOUSE

This was an annexe added to temples in the later historical periods where the annual rites associated with the birth of the god-king were performed. Scenes of the divine marriage and king's birth occur around the interior walls. Egyptologists refer to these annexes as 'mammisi' – a term derived from the Coptic 'place of birth'.

CANOPIC JARS

Vessels (usually four to a set) used as receptacles for the viscera of the dead removed during mummification. Each jar was distinguished by its lid which represented one of the demi-gods known as the 'Four Sons of Horus': human-headed Amset, baboon-headed Hapi, jackal-headed Duamutef, and falcon-headed Qebehsenuef. They protected the viscera. Europeans used the term 'Canopic' for these jars, derived from Canopus, the name of the Egyptian port where Osiris (god of the dead) had been worshipped in the form of a jar with a god's head.

CARTOUCHE

A word used by Egyptologists for the oval in which were written the two most important of the five names of the king. This made the names readily distinguishable in hieroglyphic texts. The cartouche was probably derived from the hieroglyph representing 'that which the sun encircles' (i.e. the universe), depicted as a loop of rope with a knot at the base. By placing the king's name inside this loop, it indicated his domination of the whole world.

COLOSSUS, COLOSSI

Enormous statues of divinities or royal persons found in some of the temples: in the temple of Ramesses II at Abu Simbel (in front of the facade and as columns in the form of the god Osiris); as columns in the form of *Akhenaten in his Aten temple at Thebes; and as the Colossi of Memnon which once flanked the entrance to *Amenophis III's Theban mortuary temple.

CONSUL

In republican Rome, two consuls (the highest-ranking magistrates) were elected each year to carry out the chief functions of the State, and particularly to command the legions. Under the Empire, the office became largely honorific.

CULTS

Divine: offered by the priests on behalf of a god in his temple, this took the form of rituals that included the daily care and preparation (including the presentation of food-offerings) of the god's statue, and the regular festivals celebrating major events in his mythology. The temples specifically designed for this purpose are termed 'cultus temples'.

Funerary (or mortuary): offered by special priests on behalf of the deceased king or tomb-owner, this cult was designed to ensure the individual's continued existence after death. The rituals included the presentation of food-offerings. The royal funerary cult was performed in the mortuary (funerary) temples, while the rites for non-royal tomb-owners were carried out in their funerary (tomb) chapels.

CUNEIFORM

A writing system used for the ancient inscriptions of Babylonia, *Assyria, *Persia and elsewhere, cuneiform is distinguished by its wedge-shaped or arrow-headed marks.

CYLINDER SEALS

Ownership of documents, jars of oil and wine, and other precious commodities was indicated by means of a clay seal. Papyrus rolls were each folded in two and tied with a thread which was fastened with a clay seal, and the owner's special impression or seal was marked on the lump of clay that secured jar stoppers or box lids.

Various devices were used as seals including scarabs (set in rings or pendants), as well as flat or cylinder seals. On the latter, the design or owner's title was cut on to the outer surface, and when the cylinder was rolled over wet clay, the impression was transferred to the clay.

DEMOTIC

A cursive script developed from business Hieratic and introduced towards the end of the seventh century BC, demotic also had a distinctive grammar and new vocabulary. Mainly used for legal and administrative documents but also for some literary works, it replaced hieratic (now employed mainly for religious literature) and hieroglyphs (now confined to inscriptions on stone). For almost a thousand years, it was the only widespread writing form in general use.

DICTATOR

This was a magistrate appointed by a Consul to be in charge of the Roman State for a maximum period of six months; at first the office was introduced to cope with a military crisis, but later the holder performed religious or political functions.

DIVINE WIFE OF AMUN

This title was carried by the king's chief wife during the earlier New Kingdom, and she enacted the role of consort to the chief god Amun in religious ceremonies. Later, the title became an instrument of political policy to ensure that the king gained control over Thebes and that no male rival seized power there (as had occurred in the Twenty-first Dynasty). The title was now transferred to the king's daughter who became a priestess – the Divine Wife of the god Amun at Thebes – with great religious and political power which was nevertheless limited to Thebes. Also, she was not allowed to marry, but was obliged to adopt the daughter of the next king as her 'daughter' and the heiress to her title and position.

DOUBLE CROWN

Crowns were worn by gods and kings, to whom they conveyed powerful magical properties. As rulers of a united Egypt from 3100 BC, the kings wore the Double Crown which combined the Red Crown (the royal headdress of the Delta or Lower Egypt) with the White Crown of the south (Upper Egypt).

DYNASTY

*Manetho's chronicle divided his Egyptian king-list into thirty-one dynasties. A dynasty was usually but not always a family of rulers; in some cases rulership was passed from one dynasty to another by peaceful means (through marriage or appointment), but other dynasties seized the throne from their predecessors

FUNERARY CHAPEL

Sometimes known as the 'tomb-chapel', this was the area of the tomb complex where the burial rites and continuing rituals to ensure the survival of the deceased owner were performed. Unlike the burial chamber which was sealed after interment, the chapel remained open to give the family and funerary priest access so that they could continue to carry out the rites. The interior walls were decorated with carved and painted scenes showing everyday activities which the deceased hoped to perpetuate for himself in the afterlife.

GREAT ROYAL DAUGHTER

The eldest daughter of the ruling king and queen, she often became the next king's Great Royal Wife. Descent passed through the female line, so marriage to the Great Royal Daughter conferred the kingship on her husband. He was often her full- or half-brother, but other contenders could achieve the throne or consolidate a doubtful claim by such a marriage. The Egyptians preserved the fiction that each king was the offspring of the union between the king's Great Royal Wife and the chief state-god.

GREAT ROYAL WIFE

The king's chief queen, usually the mother of his heir, the Great Royal Wife was often the king's full or half-sister (the eldest daughter of the previous king and queen). Marriage to her enabled the king to inherit the throne, since descent passed through the female line. However, in some cases (for example, *Tiye, queen of *Amenophis III), the queen attained this status and position for other reasons.

HIERATIC

A cursive script developed from hieroglyphs and regularly used for business and everyday matters, from the earliest dynasties until the New Kingdom (about two thousand years). Hieratic was particularly employed for writing on papyrus: official, administrative and legal documents and also literary and scientific works.

HIEROGLYPHS

A pictographic system of writing used for the language of Egypt from c.3100 BC down to the fourth century AD. Mainly employed in inscriptions on monuments and for sacred, formal and historical texts.

HYPOSTYLE HALL

In the Egyptian temple, the pylon (gateway) gave access to open courts behind which lay one or two roofed and pillared halls, which provided a processional route to the sanctuary.

Egyptologists use the term 'hypostyle halls', from the Greek 'hypostylos' ('resting on pillars'); the halls were constructed so that the roof was supported by rows of columns.

MUMMY

Reputedly, 'mumia' was originally a substance that flowed down from the mountain tops and, mixing with the water that carried it down, coagulated like mineral pitch. The 'Mummy Mountain' in Persia was famous for the black, bituminous material that oozed forth and was credited with medicinal properties. Because the preserved bodies of ancient Egypt often have a blackened appearance, they were likened to 'mumia' and credited with similar properties, thus leading to their use in medieval and later times as medicinal ingredients. The use of the term 'mummy' for these bodies, although erroneous, has continued. Although 'mummies' (bodies preserved either intentionally or unintentionally by various means) have survived in several parts of the world, the term is most frequently used with reference to the ancient Egyptians.

NOME

The ancient Greeks first used this term to describe the great administrative districts of Egypt (and their term 'nomarch' for the official who governed the district), and Egyptologists have retained these words. Probably based on the prehistoric tribal divisions, the country was divided into thirty-eight or thirty-nine districts by the Old Kingdom, and by the Late Period, these had increased to forty-two.

NSW-BIT NAME

One of the five great names of the royal titulary, this literally means 'He who belongs to the Reed and the Bee', symbols respectively of Upper Egypt (the south) and Lower Egypt (the Delta). It is translated as 'King of Upper and Lower Egypt', and symbolised Pharaoh's rulership, since 3100 BC, over a united kingdom.

OBELISK

An upright stone topped by a gilded pyramidion, the obelisk caught the first rays of the rising sun. In its original squat form, as the Benben, it was present as the sun-god's cult symbol in his first temple at Heliopolis. Later, in the New Kingdom, obelisks were placed in pairs on either side of the main gateways to the temples. They were cut from the granite quarries at Aswan. Today, many of them stand in public squares in the world's great cities.

PALETTE

Slate palettes were originally employed to grind the substances (malachite and galena) used as eye-paint, and were placed in the early graves to meet the owner's needs in the next world. Much larger, ceremonial versions were discovered in early historical contexts, such as foundation deposits in temples, and some of these are finely carved with scenes of great importance. The most famous example is the Narmer Palette which depicts events at the time of Egypt's unification in c.3100 BC.

PAPYRUS

The writing material 'papyrus' was made from the plant *Cyperus papyrus L.*; this industry was a royal monopoly in Egypt. However, when Egyptologists refer to 'Papyrus X', this describes a named or numbered document, inscribed on papyrus, which is held in a particular museum or other collection.

The plant itself, with its green and vigorous growth, was regarded as a sacred symbol of rebirth and renewal. It was also used as a material for boat-building, ropes, sandals, mats and baskets.

Medical Papyrus: a document which usually preserves various medical diagnoses and treatments as well as a series of magical formulae designed to cure the sick. Twelve major medical papyri have so far been discovered, but it is probable that many more existed.

PHARAOH

A king of Egypt. The term (used only from the first millenium BC) was derived from the two hieroglyphic words 'Per' ('house') and 'aa'('great'); it meant the 'Great House' (i.e., the king's residence) and came to be applied also to the king's person. Even the *Ptolemies and *Romans adopted the title, which gave them wide-ranging powers when they ruled Egypt.

PREFECT OF EGYPT

Governor of Egypt, a position established by *Augustus.

PYLON

The gateway to an Egyptian temple, the pylon consisted of two massive stone towers which flanked the doorway that gave access to the courts and *hypostyle halls. On the facade of the pylon there were sunken recesses to hold wooden flagstaffs. The pylon interior was hollow; it often contained a staircase which led to the top. The pylon protected the temple interior and hid it from view.

PYRAMID

The earliest form was the Step Pyramid, and the first example was built by

*Imhotep for King *Djoser, at the beginning of the Third Dynasty. The true pyramid form reached its zenith with *Cheops' monument at Giza, which dates to the Fourth Dynasty. With the decline of the kingship towards the end of the Old Kingdom, the pyramid was discontinued, although it was revived in the Middle Kingdom. The rulers of the Twenty-fifth Dynasty reintroduced it in its final form, in their southern kingdom.Essentially, the pyramid was a royal burial-place; it was probably also regarded as a place of ascension to permit the king to join his father Re (the sun-god) in the sky. It formed part of a complex that also included a Valley Temple, Causeway and Mortuary Temple.

SATRAP

A Persian title for a Viceroy. The *Persian empire was divided into satrapies, each ruled by a satrap. Egypt was placed under a satrap during the period of *Persian domination; also, when *Alexander the Great conquered Egypt, he appointed a Greek viceroy with the title of satrap.

SCARAB

The dung-beetle which the Egyptians called 'Kheper'; they also used this symbol to represent the verb 'kheper', meaning 'to come into existence' or 'to become'. It came to symbolise spontaneous creation and rebirth, and to be regarded as the manifestation of Khepri, the creator-god who personified the rising sun.

Scarabs were produced as amulets (to give magical protection to the owner) and, in rings and pendants, to act as seals: the flat underside usually bears an inscription or design and many carry the names and titles of officials.

The kings also issued historical scarabs (rather like medals) to commemorate events of the reign. Large heart scarabs were often placed between the layers of bandages around the mummy; these were often inscribed with a spell from the Book of the Dead to prevent the heart testifying against its owner at the Day of Judgement.

SERDAB

A cell-like chamber in a funerary chapel attached to a tomb or pyramid; the serdab contained the statue of the deceased owner which his spirit could enter at will in order to partake of the essence of the food-offerings placed at the tomb.

SPHINX

The name given by the ancient *Greeks to the divine lions of Egypt, with the heads of pharaohs. 'Sphinx' is probably derived from their original Egyptian name 'shesep ankh', meaning 'living image'. In Egypt, the sphinx was almost always the male representation of royal power, in contrast to the Greek sphinx which was female and had an evil function.

The most famous Egyptian example is the Great Sphinx at Giza, reputed to possess the facial features of King *Chephren, which in antiquity guarded the ancient necropolis. At the Temple of Amun at Karnak, the entrance is guarded by two lines of ram-headed, lion-bodied sphinxes which incorporate the powers of the lion and of Amun's cult-animal, the ram.

STATE-GOD

Egyptologists divide the deities of ancient Egypt into three main groups: state-gods, local gods and household gods. State and local gods had temples and received worship through divine rituals; people addressed their prayers to household gods, in the privacy of their own homes; whereas local gods had limited importance in their own town or district, state-gods had responsibility for the well-being of the king, country and (at times) the empire. Some state-gods were always important, but others were elevated by royal patronage from the ranks of the local gods, with new dynasties sometimes promoting the deity of their own original locality.

STELA (pl. STELAE)

Monolithic slabs, usually of limestone, stelae are rectangular in shape with the upper part curved in a semi-circle or decorated with a cavetto cornice. Each is decorated with a picture and an inscription, usually in sunk relief, and they were either set into a wall or put up beside it.

Boundary: King *Akhenaten used stelae to mark the boundary of his new city, Akhetaten (Tell el Amarna).

Funerary: Placed in the funerary (tomb) chapel, this acted as the point of contact between this world and the next. Funerary stelae usually show the deceased in the gods' company, and in receipt of offerings from his family; they give his names, titles and the offering formulae to provide food for the deceased in the next world.

Royal: These large stelae were official proclamations set up in public places, and often provide important historical information. They show the king presenting a rite to a god, and the inscription eulogises the king and proclaims his decree, or recalls an event in his reign, such as victory in battle, the restoration of a holy monument, or a major trading expedition.

TEMPLES

Mortuary (Funerary) Temple: attached to the royal burial-place. Originally part of the pyramid complex, in the New Kingdom the mortuary temple became separated from the tomb (the kings were now buried in rock-cut tombs in the Valley of the Kings) because of lack of space and were built on the nearby plain. These temples accommodated the burial rites and the perpetual mortuary cult (including the eternal food offerings) to enable the dead king to continue his existence and rule in heaven. For non-royal people, the funerary chapel accommodated rites to ensure the deceased's continuation after death.

Solar Temple: these sun-temples were built in the Fifth Dynasty by the kings who wished to promote the cult of Re, the sun-god. Unlike the other temples, these were open to the sky; the main element was the Benben – a squat obelisk which was Re's cult-symbol. In the late Eighteenth Dynasty, *Akhenaten revived a special type of sun-temple for the worship of the Aten (sun's disc).

Valley Temple: this was part of the pyramid complex, adjacent to the river, where the king's body was first received on the occasion of burial. Preliminary rites (and possibly mummification) were performed here, and the body then passed along the covered causeway into the mortuary temple to receive the final rites before burial in the pyramid.

TOMBS

Mastaba: From c.3400 BC, these were built for the ruling classes; they consisted of an underground substructure (a brick-lined pit to accommodate the burial), and a superstructure (to mark the grave above ground and to provide storage for funerary possessions). They were built of mudbrick and, later, of stone. Egyptologists use the term 'mastaba' because the superstructure has the shape and appearance of the mastaba (Arabic 'bench') placed outside Egyptian village houses. The pyramid, built as a burial-place for royalty, probably developed from the mastaba tomb, but the nobility retained this structure for their own burials throughout the Old Kingdom.

Rock-cut: later, in the Middle Kingdom, rock-cut tombs replaced mastaba tombs for the nobles' burials. These were cut in the cliffs in the various nomes (provinces), and incorporated burial chambers and offering chapels. By the New Kingdom, the kings abandoned pyramids in favour of rock-cut tombs in the Valley of the Kings; their queens and princes were similarly buried in the nearby area now called the Valley of the Queens, while the high officials occupied rock-cut tombs scattered across the area.

TRIUMVIR

A member of the Roman Triumvirate (a board of three men) which was established to carry out a specific duty.

URAEUS

The word used by Egyptologists for the cobra-goddess who personified the burning eye of the sun-god Re. Represented as an enraged cobra with a dilated throat, the uraeus appears on the front of the king's headdress and, in association with the solar disc, on the heads of solar deities. In this form, the goddess spat fire at the enemies of the king or god.

VIZIER

The supreme chief of the government administration, who received his orders directly from the king. He was not only Minister of Justice, but was in charge of various departments including the police, public works, chancellery, treasury, judgement of appeals and river transport. He was also involved in advising councils of war and, as the king's delegate, the vizier reported back to him on all matters of importance. Translated as 'vizier', the ancient Egyptian word for this office is 'tjaty'.

EGYPT AND THE CLASSICAL WORLD

PANNONIA

DALMATIA

MOESIA

R. Danube

BLACK SEA

THRACE

Constantinople
(Byzantium)

PONTUS

●Rome

MACEDONIA

Chalcedon

●Nicaea

Hellespont

●Caesarea

Straits of Messina

●Pergamum

LYDIA

CAPPADOCIA

SICILY

Athens

Ephesus

Tarsus

Salamis

CARIA

●Antioch

ACHAEA

Halicarnassus

CILICIA

SYRIA

LYCIA

CRETE

Rhodes

CYPRUS

●Palmyra

●Beirut

MEDITERRANEAN SEA

●Damascus

Tyre

●Cyrene

PALESTINE

●Jerusalem

Alexandria●

Gaza

EGYPT

●Thebes

RED SEA

R. Nile

CLASSICAL LEVANT

Kara Tepe

Sindjtell

Adana

Tarsus

Antioch

Aleppo

Al Mina

Alalakh (Atchana)

R. Orontes

Ugarit

Nicosia

Salamis

Enkomi

CYPRUS

Larnaka

Paphos

Curium

Amathus

Hamath (Hama)

Antaradus (Tartus)

Amrit

Lake of Homs

Kadesh

Tripolis

Byblos (Gebeil)

P h o e n i c i a n s

Nahr al Kelb

Anti-Lebanon

Berytus (Beirut)

Sidon (Saida)

Sarepta

Damascus

MEDITERRANEAN SEA

Tyre (Sur)

Hazor

▲ *Mt Carmel*

Atlit

Megiddo

Dor

R. Jordan

Betshan

Plain of Sharon

Samaria

ISRAEL

Shechem

Jaffa (Joppa)

AMMON

Jericho

Jerusalem

Ascalon

JUDAH

MOAB

Gaza

Hebron

Philistines

Tell Beit Mirsim

DEAD SEA

Tell Fara
(Bethpelet)
(Sharuhen)

Beersheba

EDOM

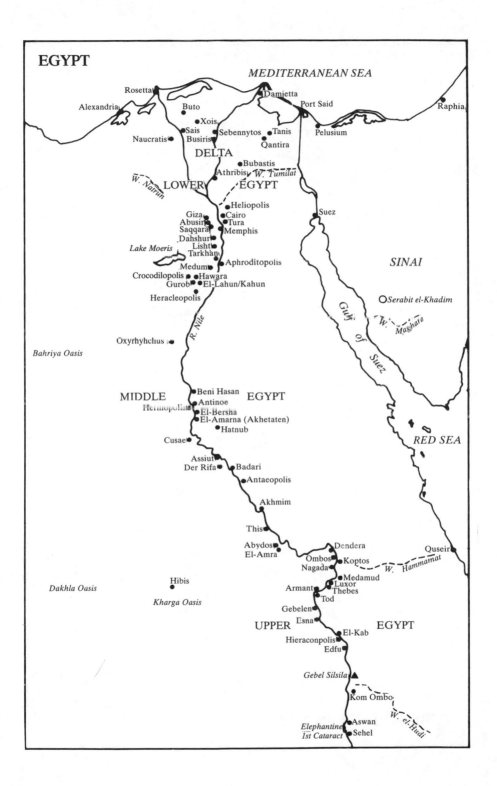

EGYPT

MEDITERRANEAN SEA

Rosetta
Damietta
Alexandria
Buto
Port Said
Raphia
Xois
Sais
Sebennytos
Tanis
Pelusium
Naucratis
Busiris
DELTA
Qantira
LOWER
W. Tumilat
Bubastis
Athribis
W. Natrun
EGYPT
Heliopolis
Giza
Cairo
Suez
Abusir
Tura
Saqqara
Memphis
Dahshur
Lishti
Lake Moeris
Tarkhan
SINAI
Medum
Aphroditopolis
Crocodilopolis
Hawara
Gurob
El-Lahun/Kahun
Heracleopolis
Serabit el-Khadim
W. Maghara
R. Nile
Oxyrhynchus
Bahriya Oasis
Gulf of Suez
MIDDLE
Beni Hasan
EGYPT
Antinoe
Hermopolis
El-Bersha
El-Amarna (Akhetaten)
Hatnub
RED SEA
Cusae
Assiut
Der Rifa
Badari
Antaeopolis
Akhmim
This
Abydos
Dendera
El-Amra
Quseir
Ombos
Koptos
Nagada
W. Hammamat
Hibis
Medamud
Dakhla Oasis
Armant
Luxor
Thebes
Kharga Oasis
Tod
Gebelen
Esna
UPPER
EGYPT
Hieraconpolis
El-Kab
Edfu
Gebel Silsila
Kom Ombo
W. el-Hudi
Elephantine
Aswan
1st Cataract
Sehel

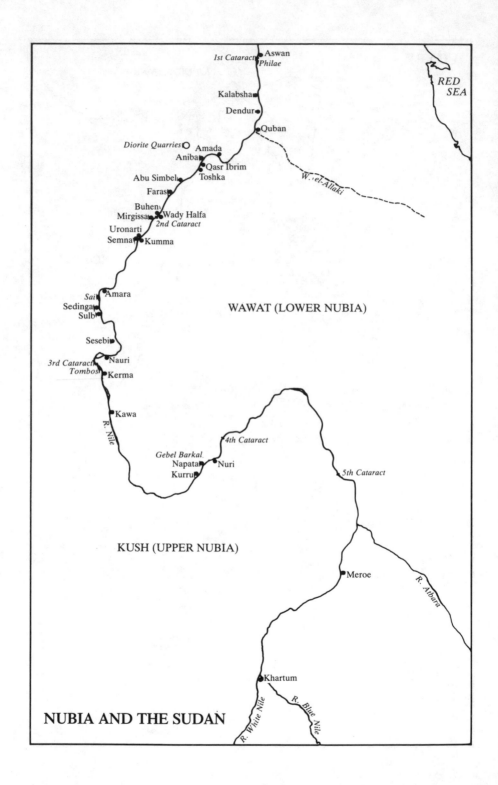

1st Cataract
Aswan
Philae
RED
SEA
Kalabsha
Dendur
Quban
Diorite Quarries ○
Amada
Aniba
Qasr Ibrim
Abu Simbel
Toshka
Faras
Buhen
Mirgissa
Wady Halfa
2nd Cataract
Uronarti
Semna
Kumma
W. el-Allaki

WAWAT (LOWER NUBIA)

Sai
Amara
Sedinga
Sulb
Sesebi
Nauri
3rd Cataract
Tombos
Kerma
Kawa
R. Nile
4th Cataract
Gebel Barkal
Napata
Nuri
Kurru
5th Cataract

KUSH (UPPER NUBIA)

Meroe
R. Atbara

Khartum

R. White Nile
R. Blue Nile

NUBIA AND THE SUDAN

A

Achthoes (Akhtoy) King c.2160 BC.
During the troubled period from the Eighth to the Tenth Dynasty, the only ruler whom *Manetho mentions by name is Achthoes; he places him in the Ninth Dynasty. This man was originally the governor of the Twentieth Nome of Upper Egypt which had its district capital at Heracleopolis. He managed to subdue opposition from neighbouring governors and came to be recognised as king throughout Egypt as far south as Aswan, although the eastern Delta may have remained outside his control. His throne name was Meryibre and he established the Heracleopolitan Dynasty; *Manetho's history claimed that he was more cruel than any of his predecessors and that he eventually became insane and was killed by a crocodile.

He was succeeded by seventeen kings who comprised the Ninth and Tenth Dynasties. One was Achthoes II, who was probably mentioned in the famous story of 'The Eloquent Peasant'; another king with literary connections was Wahkare, Achthoes III (the owner of a finely decorated coffin from el Bersha) who was accredited as the author of the Wisdom Text 'The Instruction of King *Merikare'.

*Merikare inherited the throne and died before the Theban rulers, under *Mentuhotep II (Nebhepetre), reached Heracleopolis, but his successor (who is not identified in the records) was overcome by the Thebans.

The Heracleopolitan rulers brought some stability to those areas they controlled and had a special alliance with the governors of Assiut. Funerary inscriptions and goods found in the tombs of the governors of Middle Egypt (Assiut, Beni Hasan and Akhmim) provide the primary material for the study of this period.

BIBL. Winlock, H. E. *The Rise and Fall of the Middle Kingdom in Thebes.* New York, 1947; *AEL* i. pp. 97-109, 169-83.

Africanus Sextus Julius Historian c. AD 220.
A Christian chronographer, the writings of Africanus (together with those of the Jewish historian *Josephus and the Christian writers *Eusebius and *Syncellus) have preserved in an incomplete form the major work of *Manetho, his *History of Egypt (Aegyptiaca).*Manetho's facts as they are stated in Africanus are often at variance with the details that *Eusebius provides.

BIBL. *Manetho* (transl. by Waddell, W. G.) London, Camb. 1945.

Ahhiyawa, Kingdom of, c.1400 BC onwards.
Mention of the kingdom of Ahhiyawa and its people occurs in the *Hittite records and it is evident that, at least for a period of time, the relationship between the *Hittite and the Ahhiyawan royal families was close. The facts also indicate that Ahhiyawa was a powerful sea-going nation and that its ships reached Syria (Amurru). The exact location of Ahhiyawa is uncertain; it has been argued that these people could be identified with the Achaeans (the Mycenaean *Greeks) who occur in Homer's writings and that Ahhiyawa might be either the kingdom of Mycenae itself or, perhaps more probably, one of the semi-independent island kingdoms of Crete, Rhodes or Cyprus. Although this identification has been challenged, it retains considerable support.The Achaeans have also been tentatively identified with the *Akawasha who are mentioned as one of the *Sea-peoples who attacked Egypt in the later New Kingdom; this theory is based on the similarity of the names.

BIBL. *CAH* ii, ch xxviii; Huxley, G. L. *Achaeans and Hittites*. Oxford: 1960; Gurney O. R. *The Hittites*. Harmondsworth: 1964, pp. 46-58.

Ahhotpe Queen c.1575 - c.1560 BC.
Ahhotpe was one of the powerful royal women who wielded great influence at the beginning of the New Kingdom. She was a member of the family of Theban princes who drove the *Hyksos from Egypt and established the Eighteenth Dynasty.
Consanguineous royal marriages at this period probably underlined the women's role in transmitting sovereignty in this new dynasty. Ahhotpe married her brother, *Seqenenre Ta'o II and they were the offspring of Ta'o I and his wife Tetisheri (whose parents were commoners). Ahhotpe's son, *Amosis I, founded the Eighteenth Dynasty and in an inscription on a stela at Karnak, which praises *Amosis I, Ahhotpe's contribution is also emphasised; she rallied the soldiers in Egypt and stopped a rebellion which probably occurred in the difficult period when the Theban rulers were establishing their power.
She was widely revered and had a long life, although her influence waned when *Amosis I's queen, *Ahmose-Nefertari, came to power. Nevertheless, she was given a magnificent burial, for her coffin and mummy case were discovered in the vicinity of the Valley of the Kings and the fine jewellery and ornaments which once adorned her mummy (mostly given to her by *Amosis I) are now in the Cairo Museum.

BIBL. von Bissing, F. W. *Ein Thebanischen Grabfund aus dem Aufang des Neuen Reichs*. Berlin: 1970.

Ahmose-Nefertari Queen c.1570 - c.1535 BC.
Ahmose-Nefertari was a 'King's Daughter' and a 'King's Wife'; her father was probably *Kamose, the Theban prince who helped to drive the *Hyksos from

Egypt and she married *Amosis I, the founder of the New Kingdom, who was probably her uncle.She continued the tradition of powerful royal women who played a major role in the early years of the Eighteenth Dynasty, but her influence was even greater than that of her predecessors. Together with her husband, she received widespread acclaim; he gave her the title of 'Second Prophet' in the temple of Amun at Karnak and when he died, Ahmose-Nefertari retained her powerful influence throughout the reign of her son, *Amenophis I.

Only rarely were humans deified in Egypt, but Ahmose-Nefertari and her son received their own cult; they were worshipped in the Theban necropolis and were adopted by the royal necropolis workmen of Deir el Medina as their special patrons and protectors.

Painted representations of the queen show her with a black or even a blue skin colour but the significance of this is not clear. Her mummy and coffin were discovered in the cache of royal mummies; she may originally have been buried in the tomb of her son, *Amenophis I, at Dira Abu'n Naga at Thebes and she also received a funerary cult in his Theban mortuary temple.

BIBL. Cerny, J. Le culte d'Amenophis Ier chez les ouvriers de la Necropole thebaine. *BIFAO* 27 (1927), pp. 159-203.

Akawasha,   One of the *Sea-Peoples   c.1236 BC.

The Akawasha ('Ikws) were one element in the alliance of *Sea-peoples who supported the *Libyans in attacking Egypt in Year 5 of *Merneptah's reign. The Egyptian wall-reliefs do not depict the Akawasha but the inscriptions indicate that they, together with some of the other *Sea-peoples, were circumcised; their hands, rather than their genitals, were amputated and piled up for presentation to the Egyptian king when the total of his dead enemies was enumerated.

One suggestion tentatively identifies the Akawasha with the Achaeans (the Mycenaean *Greeks), but if this is correct, then the evidence relating to the practice of circumcision amongst the Akawasha is puzzling since there are no other indications that the *Greeks were circumcised.

BIBL. CAH ii, ch xxviii; Huxley, G. L. *Achaeans and Hittites.* Oxford: 1960; Gurney, O. R. *The Hittites.* Harmondsworth: 1964, pp 46-58.

Akhenaten (Amenophis IV)   King   1379-1362 BC.

The son of *Amenophis III and *Tiye, Amenophis IV changed his name to Akhenaten (probably meaning 'Servant of the Aten') in Year 5 of his reign, thus indicating his allegiance to the Aten, the creator-god who was symbolised by the sun's disc.

*Tuthmosis IV had begun to elevate the Aten many years before and, under *Amenophis III, the god was given special honours. Akhenaten's unique contribution was to ensure that the Aten's cult approached a form of monotheism; the god was regarded as unique and omnipotent, a universal, supreme and loving deity who was symbolised by the life-giving sun. The king, as the god's sole earthly representative, became virtually interchangeable with the Aten and communed with him every day.

It is difficult to determine the extent to which these ideas were innovative and revolutionary; they were at least partly a restatement of an earlier belief in a supreme deity which had been represented by the gods Re or Amun. Also, in addition to personal religious motives, Akhenaten was probably prompted by political pressures to try to curb the over-reaching powers of the priests of Amen-Re, by advancing the cult of the Aten. His actions re-established the king's own role as the god's sole representative on earth.

Akhenaten's early reign was spent at Thebes. A period of co-regency with *Amenophis III may have occurred, but at Thebes, Akhenaten was already building special temples to the Aten where he and his chief wife, *Nefertiti, worshipped the god. This cult continued alongside the orthodox worship of the great Theban deity, Amen-Re. In Year 6, he made a clear break with tradition and moved the political and religious capital from Thebes to a new site in Middle Egypt, perhaps because the cult of the Aten could no longer exist alongside the other gods. Akhenaten closed their temples, disbanded their priesthoods and diverted their revenue to the Aten's cult. In addition, the names of all the other deities were officially erased and the Aten became the exclusive royal god.

The new capital was called Akhetaten, which meant the 'Horizon of the Aten'. Palaces, official and administrative quarters and temples to the Aten were built, in addition to villas and houses. The modern term of Tell el Amarna or Amarna is often used for the site. Partial excavation of the city and the neighbouring Royal Tomb and courtiers' tombs has revealed much information about this time, often referred to as the Amarna Period. The text of the Great Hymn to the Aten was found inscribed in some of the courtiers' tombs; this provides an outline of the tenets of Atenism and is regarded as a major influence on Biblical Psalm 104. Texts on boundary stelae ,which marked the perimeter of the new capital, describe the royal conditions laid down for the foundation of Akhetaten.

*Nefertiti (who took the additional name of Nefernefruaten) reared six daughters at Akhetaten. The royal family is frequently represented in the so-called 'Amarna Art' of the period. This type of art, with its distinctive characteristics, was inspired by religious innovations and is exemplified by reliefs and statuary discovered at Akhetaten. Instances also occur at other sites, such as the standing colossi of Akhenaten from the Aten temples at Thebes. The king imposed both the Aten doctrine and its associated art forms; the art emphasises creativity and the naturalistic representation of plants, birds and animals and extols the joy and beauty of life; it also appears to show the king with an abnormal physique. Certain bodily features are emphasised almost to the point of caricature and it has been suggested that such physical abnormalities may have been due to a glandular deficiency, although, since the king's body has never been found, the reasons behind this strange artistic convention must remain speculative. The abnormalities shown in the king's physique became the norm in Amarna art and all other human figures are represented with the same features. At Thebes, the tomb of the courtier *Ramose is decorated with wall-scenes that provide a striking example of both the orthodox and Amarna styles of art.

Akhenaten has been blamed for allowing Egypt's empire in Syria to disintegrate while he pursued his religious reforms. In the Amarna Letters (the diplomatic correspondence found at Akhetaten), vassal princes beg in vain for Egyptian aid against the predatory ambitions of other great powers. However, some of the decline in Egypt's interest and influence in this area may already have already begun in *Amenophis III's reign.

At home, the internal organisation had begun to crumble, and the counter-revolutionary methods of Akhenaten's successors, *Tutankhamun and *Horemheb, sought to restore the old order. Even his immediate heir, *Smenkhkare, who may have ruled briefly with him, perhaps attempted some restitution of the traditional gods.

Akhenaten was first buried in the royal tomb at Amarna; later generations regarded him as a heretic and a disastrous ruler and every effort was made to expunge his name from the records and to return to religious orthodoxy.

Modern scholarship has variously interpreted him as a fanatic, a political opportunist, a mystic and a visionary, a prophet before his time, and the first individual in history. It has also been suggested that he was the pharaoh of the Exodus, and Sigmund Freud proposed that he had been the inspiration of *Moses and of Jewish monotheism.

BIBL. Aldred, C. *Akhenaten, King of Egypt.* London: 1991. Davies, N. de G. *The Rock Tombs of El-Amarna.* (six vols) London: 1903-8; Mercer, S. A. B. *The Tell el Amarna Tablets.* (two vols) Toronto: 1939; Aldred, C. and Sandison, A. T. The Pharaoh Akhenaten a problem in Egyptology and pathology, *Bulletin of the History of Medicine* 36, pp 293-316; Peet, T. E., Woolley, C. L., Frankfort, H. and Pendlebury, J. D. S. *The City of Akhenaten.* Parts 1-3. London: 1923-51; Martin G. T. *The Royal Tomb at El-Amarna*: Vol. 1, The Objects; Vol. 2, *The Reliefs, Inscriptions and Architecture.* London 1974, 1989. Redford, D. B. *Akhenaten. The heretic king.* Princeton, N. J. 1984; Smith, R. W. and Redford, D. B. *The Akhenaten Temple Project.* Vol. 1: *The initial discoveries.* Warminster: 1977.

Alexander the Great   King of Macedon   Ruled Egypt 332-323 BC.

The son of Philip II, king of Macedon, Alexander was destined to conquer the known world and, after the provinces of the Persian empire fell before him, Tyre besieged and Gaza taken, he finally reached Egypt in the autumn of 332 BC. He met with little opposition from the Persian satrap in Egypt, and the native population, who disliked *Persian administration, welcomed him as a liberator. He spent scarcely six months in the country however, travelling as far south as the First Cataract, but in that time he established a Greek system of control over the military and finance of Egypt. He appointed a viceroy with the Persian title of satrap and made provision for the imposition and collection of taxes. The first satrap was Cleomenes of Naucratis and under his general Ptolemy, son of Lagos (later *Ptolemy I), Alexander established a small standing army.

Two important events are recorded during the conqueror's stay in Egypt, although it is difficult to determine the true facts surrounding these occasions. Near the ancient village of Rhakotis, opposite the island of Pharos, he traced the foundations of a new capital city for Egypt – Alexandria – on the Mediterranean coast. According to *Plutarch, who wrote a life of Alexander, the choice of this site for the city was confirmed for the king in a prophetic dream. Tradition places its foundation on April 7, 331 BC, and Alexandria became not only the Egyptian capital but also the most important port in the Mediterranean. It provided Egypt with access to the rest of Alexander's empire and enabled the country's wealth to be more readily exported, but it also became the great Hellenistic centre of learning and knowledge.

The other significant event during Alexander's time in Egypt was his visit to the famous oracle of Jupiter Amun at Siwa, Egypt's most westerly oasis in the Libyan desert. According to legend, the god recognised Alexander as his son and promised him dominion over the whole world. Although this was the usual formalised recognition that Egypt's great state-god gave to the pharaoh, Alexander appears to have interpreted this as a form of personal deification. He went on to conquer many other lands and, in Egypt, the oracle was interpreted as the divine recognition of Alexander and his successors as the legitimate rulers of Egypt, despite their foreign origin. Alexander was probably crowned in a traditional ceremony in the temple of Ptah in the ancient capital of Memphis, where he performed a sacrifice to the sacred Apis bull.

In 331 BC, he left Egypt to continue his conquests in the east. He eliminated the Persian empire and finally reached India, but on his return journey, he fell ill and died in Babylon in 323 BC. His body was reputedly brought back to Egypt and remained first in Memphis before being buried in Alexandria, although his tomb (to which the Emperor Caracalla paid the last recorded visit in AD 215) has never been discovered.

After his premature demise, Alexander's generals divided his empire between them. Ptolemy, who had charge of the troops in Egypt, now claimed the position of satrap and ultimately became an independent ruler in Egypt, as *Ptolemy I, the founder of the Macedonian Dynasty. He inaugurated a divine cult for Alexander at Alexandria and thus established the basis for an official state-cult of the rulers of this dynasty.

As pharaoh, Alexander evidently tolerated the worship of the native Egyptian gods and indeed emphasised his own role as the country's religious leader. During his reign, a sanctuary in the Temple of Luxor was rebuilt and decorated with wall-reliefs which showed him in the company of the Egyptian gods, and he also appears in new reliefs and inscriptions which were added to the walls of a room in the Temple of Amun at Karnak which *Tuthmosis III had originally built.

The Hellenistic sculpture of the early years of the Ptolemaic Dynasty preserves the powerful facial expression of Alexander, for the king's heavy brow, deep-set eyes and piercing gaze appear even on the statues of other people.

BIBL. Wilcken, C. *Alexander the Great*. London: 1932; Bell, H. I. *Egypt from Alexander the Great to the Arab conquest*. Oxford: 1956; Fraser, P. M. *Ptolemaic Alexandra*. Oxford: 1972; Green, P. *Alexander of Macedon, 356-323 BC*. Berkeley: 1991.

Amasis King 570-526 BC.
Amasis originally held the position of army general in Nubia under
*Psammetichus II, but he was placed on the throne following a nationalistic
uprising which attempted to rid Egypt of King *Apries.

According to *Herodotus, Amasis came from an ordinary background;
historical sources represent him as a popular, shrewd and sometimes drunken
ruler. The civil war in which the native Egyptians supported him against *Apries
and his *Greek mercenary forces came to a conclusion with Amasis' triumph at
the battle of Momemphis. At first, he treated *Apries well but ultimately the
populace decided the former ruler's fate.

When he became king, Amasis nevertheless found it necessary to make use of
the services of *Greek mercenaries as his predecessors had done, but he kept the
support of the native Egyptians who had given him the throne by balancing his
reliance on foreign help with an action to check the growth of Greek merchants in
Egypt. He limited their activities to Naucratis, an exclusively Greek city which
had been founded in the Delta in the reign of *Psammetichus I, and this became
the only centre in Egypt where they were permitted to trade freely.

He was succeeded by his son, *Psammetichus III; six months later, *Cambyses
invaded Egypt with the result that the country became a province of the Persian
empire.

BIBL. Herodotus, *The Histories,* Bk. ii, 1-2.

Amenardis I (Amonortais) Divine Wife of Amun (740-700 BC).
The daughter of King Kashta, the founder of the Twenty-fifth Dynasty, Amenardis
I was adopted as a 'daughter' by *Shepenopet I, the daughter of Osorkon III. Thus,
she became heiress to the title and position of the 'Divine Wife of Amun'. Earlier
in the New Kingdom, this title had been borne by the king's chief wife, who had
then enacted the role of consort to the god Amun in the religious state rituals. By
the Late Period, this title was transferred to the king's daughter who became a
priestess with great political and religious influence. Although the Divine Wife's
power was limited to Thebes, here she now held equal status to the king,
possessing her own house, land and officials and holding the authority to make
offerings to the gods. Thus, each king, through his daughter, secured ultimate
control over Thebes and ensured that no male rival seized power in the southern
capital. The Divine Wife was not allowed to marry, but adopted as her 'daughter'
and heiress the daughter of the next king. Thus, Amenardis I eventually adopted
the princess Shepenopet II, the daughter of King *Piankhy, as her successor.

Amenemope, Author of a Wisdom Text, Ramesside Period, c.1300 BC..
In the 'Instruction of Amenemope', the genre known today as the 'Wisdom
Literature' reaches the final stage of its development. This text is completely
preserved on a papyrus in the British Museum and also survives in other sources;

7

although these are all of a later date, the text was probably composed during the Ramesside Period (c.1300 BC). It differs from earlier examples of wisdom literature in that the 'ideal man' whom these texts sought to describe and promote is no longer one who enjoys status and worldly success; instead, he is a modest man, humble before his god and other men, who does not seek great wealth or acclaim. Individual success is now sought through rightful action and through living acccording to 'Ma'at' – the Egyptian principle of truth, order and correct balance. The text contrasts the 'heated man' with the 'silent man' and stresses the virtue of self-control. However, since the state of perfection is now reserved for the gods, even the 'ideal man' can no longer hope to attain this level. The text is particularly important because not only does it illustrate changed attitudes relating to ethics within Egypt, but it can also be compared with similar concepts found in the Book of Proverbs in the Bible.

BIBL . *AEL* ii.pp. 146-63; Blackman, A. M. *The Psalms in the light of Egyptian research* in Simpson, D. C. *The Psalmists*. London: 1926; Simpson, D. C. The Hebrew Book of Proverbs and the teaching of Amenophis. *JEA* 12 (1926) pp. 232-9; Williams, D. J. The alleged Semitic origins of the Wisdom of Amenemope. *JEA* 47 (1961) pp. 100-6.

Amenhotep, son of Hapu,   Sage,   reign of *Amenophis III,   c.1417-1379 BC.
Amenhotep, son of Hapu, was one of the most highly revered figures of the New Kingdom. Under *Amenophis III, he held the titles of 'King's Scribe', 'Scribe of Recruits', and 'Overseer of all the works of the King'. As royal architect, he was responsible for the construction of the Temple of Luxor and also for the erection of the Colossi of Memnon, the massive statues of Amenophis III which flanked the entrance to his funerary temple on the west bank at Thebes. He also supervised the great estates of Sitamun, the daughter of *Amenophis III and *Queen Tiye.

Amenhotep's birthplace was the town of Athribis, and he was related to the vizier *Ramose. After his death, Amenhotep was accorded the unprecedented honour of being given a mortuary temple in western Thebes which was endowed in perpetuity by a royal decree. Such temples were usually only built for kings, but Amenhotep's monument equalled those of the kings and here he received a cult as a god.

Later generations revered him as a great sage; he was worshipped as a god of healing and had a sanatorium in the temple at Deir el Bahri, where the sick came in search of a cure. Under Ramesses IV, his mortuary cult was maintained alongside those of the dead, deified kings and in the Ptolemaic Period, he was worshipped as a god. Scenes in the temple at Deir el Medina show him as a god in the company of *Imhotep, and in the unfinished temple of Thoth at Medinet Habu, he appears with Thoth (god of learning) and *Imhotep, receiving the cult from the king. Proverbs which were translated into Greek reputedly preserved his wisdom; he was also the possessor of a large stone statue which is now in the Cairo Museum.

BIBL. Robichon, C. and Varille, C. *Le temple du scribe royal Amenhotep, fils de Hapou 1.* Cairo: 1936.

Amenophis I King 1546 - 1526 BC.

The son and successor of *Amosis I, Amenophis I continued his father's military policy but his aim was not merely to restore Egypt's borders but to extend her boundaries by using the army which, by its expertise, had re-established the country's independence after the *Hyksos rule.

It is probable that Amenophis I campaigned in Syria, perhaps reaching as far as the River Euphrates, and also against the *Libyans to prevent an invasion of the Delta. His primary concern was to re-establish Egypt's supremacy in *Nubia, where he introduced the position of governor which eventually became the powerful role entitled 'King's Son of Kush'. The biographical inscriptions found in the tombs at El Kab of the two warriors – Ahmose, son of Ebana, and Ahmose Pennekheb – who fought with *Amosis I and *Amenhotep I, provide details of these campaigns. In addition to his military preoccupations, Amenophis I, like his father, devoted considerable energy to his domestic policy, rebuilding the temples and restoring the country's prosperity.

His funerary arrangements broke with the royal tradition of burial which had incorporated a pyramid and a funerary temple in one complex. His tomb, at Dira Abu'n Naga at Thebes, was cut into the rock high in the hills and was quite separate from the funerary temple which was situated down in the Theban plain. This arrangement was continued by all the later rulers buried at Thebes, and *Tuthmosis I (son of Amenophis I) was the first king to build a tomb in the place which was known later as the Valley of the Kings. Amenophis I's decision to build a rock-cut tomb rather than a pyramid may have been an attempt (although unsuccessful) to defeat the robbers who had ransacked the highly visible pyramids since the Old Kingdom.

Amenophis I shared his funerary temple with his mother, the powerful queen *Ahmose-Nefertari, who may also have been buried in his tomb. However, subsequent ransacking of the tomb resulted in the removal of their coffins and bodies and their reburial in the great cache near Deir el Bahri which was discovered in the 1881.

This king was responsible for founding the special community of craftsmen and necropolis workers who built and decorated the kings' tombs throughout the New Kingdom. *Tuthmosis I later built their village at Deir el Medina, but Amenophis I was worshipped as their patron and, with Ahmose-Nefertari, received a cult as the divine guardian of the royal necropolis. Several chapels were dedicated to him, and the royal necropolis workers and their families prayed to him for justice and help in times of trouble. As a god, his most popular form was as Amenophis, Lord of the Village, and the community celebrated several annual feasts in his honour, at which the royal workmen acted as priests.

In two papyri (Chester Beatty IX and Cairo-Turin), he is also mentioned as the king who performs an important ritual in certain temples, to ensure the continuation of the king as a god, as a royal ancestor and as a ruler in the afterlife.

BIBL. Cerny, J. Le culte d'Amenophis Ier chez les ouvriers de la Necropole thebaine. *BIFAO* 27 (1927) pp. 159-203; Winlock, H. E. A restoration of the reliefs from the mortuary temple of Amenhotep I. *JEA* 4 (1917) pp. 11-15; Nelson, H. H. Certain reliefs at Karnak and

Medinet Habu and the Ritual of Amenophis 1. *JNES* 8 (1949) pp. 201,310; Cerny, J. A. *A Community of workmen at Thebes in the Ramesside period.* Cairo: 1973.

Amenophis II   King   1450 - 1425 BC.

The son of the great warrior pharaoh *Tuthmosis III by his chief queen Hatshepsut-meryetre, Amenophis II was born at Memphis. Later, as a prince, he was in charge of the delivery of wood to the great naval dockyard at Peru-nefer, near Memphis – a fact preserved in a papyrus in the British Museum. His youthful prowess in sport is also recorded on a limestone stela which was set up near the Great Sphinx at Giza. The rulers of the Eighteenth Dynasty were trained as youths in various sports, not only as valuable military exercises to prepare them for leading campaigns but also as an enjoyable activity. They trained in target-shooting with bows and arrows and in driving teams of chariot horses, and they also became outstanding oarsmen.

Amenophis II was probably the greatest of the royal sportsmen and his muscular strength is extolled in the inscriptions. He was a great archer, oarsman and athlete, and his skill with horses was such that his father allowed him to train the finest animals in the royal stable. By his eighteenth birthday he had apparently mastered all the skills required for warfare.

When he came to the throne, Amenophis II attempted to emulate his father and to retain the empire which *Tuthmosis III had conquered. His skills as a sportsman were now channelled into warfare and he emerges as the most bloodthirsty of the pharaohs of this dynasty. All rebellions were severly crushed, and a series of three or four campaigns were launched against Syria, while, in the south, the border was fixed at Napata, near the Fourth Cataract on the Nile. A damaged stela from Karnak and one from Memphis, which partly duplicates it, provide a narrative of his first and second Syrian campaigns; they emphasise the king's personal bravery and prowess and include a list of captives, giving exaggerated numbers.

At home, Amenophis II enjoyed a long and prosperous reign; he continued his father's building programme, adding to the Temple of Karnak and the Temple of Amada in Lower Nubia and constructing temples in the Delta. During this reign, the tombs of officials – such as that of Kenamun, the Steward of the dockyard at Peru-nefer – were also particularly fine.

Amenophis II's own tomb in the Valley of the Kings was discovered in 1898 by V. Loret. There had been some interference, but Loret found the mummy of the king as well as those of other royal persons, in addition to some funerary furniture. Following the desecration of the royal tombs in antiquity, during the Twenty-first Dynasty, the High-priests of Amun undertook an inspection of the tombs and removed and, where possible, restored the royal mummies, before reburying them either in Amenophis II's rock-cut tomb or in another large tomb in the vicinity of Deir el Bahri. Both these caches were discovered in the nineteenth century and the royal and priestly mummies were removed to the Cairo Museum where they were subsequently studied. Although his tomb was so important in respect of this discovery, little remains of Amenophis II's funerary temple on the west bank at Thebes.

Amenophis II's chief wife was Tio who, as the Great Royal Daughter of

*Tuthmosis III and his chief wife, was probably Amenophis II's full sister. She was the mother of Amenophis II's son and successor, *Tuthmosis IV.

BIBL. Van de Walle, B. Les rois sportifs de l'ancienne Egypte. *Chron. d'Eg. 13* (1938) pp. 234-57; Smith, G. E. *The Royal Mummies*. Cairo: 1912; Maspero, G. *Les momies royales de Deir el-Bahari*. Cairo:1889.

Amenophis III   King   1417 - 1379 BC.

Amenophis III succeeded to the throne as a child, being the son of *Tuthmosis IV and his chief queen, *Mutemweya; his divine birth, as the son of the god Amun, was depicted in wall-scenes in the Temple of Luxor.

Amenophis III was the heir to vast domains and he ruled over the most opulent court in the ancient world. Military activity in his reign was probably limited to the repression of a *Nubian uprising in Year 5; the campaigns of previous kings had ensured that this ruler could enjoy the benfits of Egypt's empire at its zenith, and diplomatic and peaceful relations with the other great rulers of the Near East replaced the warfare of the earlier years. This situation is reflected in the letters from foreign kings and rulers (particularly of *Mitanni and Babylonia) which were found in the royal archive at the site of Tell el Amarna. However, during the long reign of Amenophis III, some of the vassal princes in Palestine had already begun to break their ties with Egypt, leading to the decline of Egypt's influence abroad during the reign of his son,*Akhenaten (Amenophis IV) and the growth of *Hittite expansion.

In Amenophis III's reign, a novel method of dispersing information and making royal announcements within Egypt and abroad was introduced. Events were proclaimed on a series of large commemorative royal scarabs which carried hieroglyphic inscriptions and in all of these, *Queen Tiye was associated with her husband as his Great Royal Wife. The scarabs announce the king's marriage to *Tiye, a commoner, and later, the arrival of *Ghilukhepa, the Mitannian bride of Amenophis III; the construction of a great irrigation lake for *Tiye; and the hunting exploits of the king, when he captured wild bulls and shot one hundred and two lions.

*Tiye bore the king the royal heir, Prince Thutmose (who died prematurely), and a younger son, Amenophis, who succeeded Amenophis III as king; among their other children were the daughters Sitamun, who married her father, and Baketaten. Amenophis III may also have been the father of *Smenkhkare and *Tutankhamun. There were also foreign princesses in the king's extensive harem, such as the *Mitannians *Ghilukhepa ,*Tadukhepa and a sister of the king of Babylonia. These women arrived in Egypt with their entourages and played their role in the international diplomacy of the period. Indeed, many foreigners now visited and resided in Egypt where cosmopolitan ideas and fashions flourished.

Amenophis III is remembered as a great builder and patron of the arts and these activities occupied the later years of his reign. He added the third pylon in the Temple of Karnak and increased the number of statues of lioness-headed Sekhmet in the nearby Temple of Mut. He rebuilt the Temple of Luxor, dedicated to Amun,

Mut and Khonsu, and decorated it with fine wall-reliefs and a magnificent court which featured columns with lotus-bud capitals. He built the large palace at Malkata on the west bank at Thebes, which incorporated several royal residences and the country's main administrative quarters. Constructed of wood and mudbrick, the walls were plastered and painted with scenes of plants and animals; the complex also included a festival hall where the king celebrated his jubilees in Years 30, 34 and 37 to renew his royal powers. There were also other royal palaces including the residence at Gurob in the Fayoum.

Little now remains of his mortuary temple on the west bank at Thebes. It was the largest ever built, but only the two great statues (the so-called Colossi of Memnon) which once stood at the main entrance, have survived; the rest of the building was used as a quarry and the stone was transported for the construction of Ramesside temples.

The king's tomb was prepared in the western branch of the Valley of the Kings. The opulence and high quality of the craftsmanship in this period are evident in the tombs of some of his courtiers, such as Kheruef, Queen *Tiye's High Steward, Khaemhet, the Overseer of the Granaries, and *Ramose, who was probably Vizier under Amenophis III and his son. Another royal official, *Amenophis, son of Hapu, was deified and honoured as a sage by later generations; he was responsible for the transportation and erection of the Colossi of Memnon.

Despite Amenophis III's patronage of the great state-god Amun, he sought to restrict the growth of his priesthood's power. He increased recognition of other cults, notably that of Ptah at Memphis and Re at Heliopolis, and at Court he promoted a special form of Re, the royal god since the Old Kingdom. This was the Aten or sun's disc, a deity whose worship *Akhenaten would later elevate to a form of monotheism. Amenophis III also emphasised the divinity of the king to an unprecedented degree, dedicating a temple to his own cult at Soleb and to Queen *Tiye at Sedeinga in Nubia. Colossal statues of the king also sought to promote his divinity to the people.

The existence of a co-regency between Amenophis III and his son, *Akhenaten (Amenophis IV), is controversial; it is also unclear if Amenophis III spent time at Akhetaten (Tell el Amarna) towards the end of his reign. His mummy, recovered from his ransacked tomb and reburied in the royal cache in the tomb of *Amenophis II, indicates that he suffered severe toothache and abcesses during his lifetime. He was also obese, and the embalmers attempted to give his mummy a lifelike and realistic appearance by introducing subcutaneous packing, thus preserving the fullness of his form. Further evidence of the king's ill-health is provided by the account of how the *Mitannian king, *Tushratta, sent him a statue of the goddess Ishtar of Nineveh, who was renowned for her healing powers, in the hope that she might alleviate his suffering.

BIBL. Aldred, C. The beginning of the el-Amarna Period. *JEA* 45 (1959) pp. 19-33; Blackenberg van Delden, C. *The Large Commemorative Scarabs of Amenhotep 111* Leiden:1969; Griffith, F. L. l. Stela in honour of Amenophis III and Taya from Tell el-Amarnah. *JEA* 12 (1926) pp. 1-2; ; Lansing, A. Excavations at the palace of Amenhotep III at Thebes. *Bull. MMA. 13* (1918) March supplement. pp. 8-14.

Ammenemes I King 1991 - 1962 BC.

Ammenemes (Amenemhet) I was regarded as the founder of the Twelfth Dynasty and of the Middle Kingdom; he assumed the additional title of 'Repeater of Births' which was adopted by those pharaohs who regarded themselves as inaugurators of a new era. He can almost certainly be identified as the vizier of *Mentuhotep IV of the Eleventh Dynasty, from whom he usurped the throne. During his reign, he re-established the unity of Egypt, re-organised the internal administration, and consolidated the power of the monarchy.

The capital was now moved from Thebes to the site of Lisht (known as It-towy, meaning 'Seizer of the Two Lands', in antiquity). Situated on the edge of the Fayoum, this city was a better centre from which to control the whole kingdom. The king also re-established the district boundaries which had been obliterated in the chaos of the First Intermediate Period. He had the support of the local governors of these districts who must have assisted him in his struggle to seize the throne, and he could apparently call on them for military aid. For example, when Khnumhotep I (a local governor buried in one of the rock-tombs at Beni Hasan) was asked for assistance, he accompanied Ammenemes I to Elephantine with a fleet of twenty ships, to remove the vestiges of opposition to the king's rule. Ammenemes I also re-allocated water supplies and fixed taxes, and in order to repel the *Asiatics (nomad tribes), he constructed a barrier in the Wadi Tumilat, known as the 'Wall of the Prince'.

During the troubled times of the First Intermediate Period, new people had appeared in Lower *Nubia; Egyptologists refer to them as the 'C-group'. During the period of his co-regency with his son, *Sesostris I, King Ammenemes I inaugurated a military campaign against these people. An inscription at Korosko, dated to Year 29, records the king's arrival there, and he also initiated the construction in Nubia of a series of border forts which probably reached as far as the Second Cataract and were intended to control the local population. In Sinai, the turquoise mines were re-opened, and at home, the king pursued an active building programme.

In Year 20 of his reign, Ammenemes I made his son Sesostris his co-regent, and they ruled together for ten years, when Sesostris led military campaigns abroad. The co-regency became an instrument of royal policy during the Twelfth Dynasty with the aim of ensuring a smooth succession in a line of kings who had no royal ancestry.

Ammenemes I was buried in a traditional pyramid at Lisht, surrounded by the tombs of his courtiers. He had revived the type of pyramid complex which had flourished in the Old Kingdom, thus reasserting the king's power and divinity. However, it was Amun (the local god of Thebes) who became the patron deity of these kings and who replaced Re, the supreme god of the Old Kingdom.

Literary sources suggest that Ammenemes I was assassinated, probably by palace conspirators, while Sesostris was away on a campaign in Libya. The king's death is mentioned in the 'Story of *Sinuhe' and also in the unique Wisdom Text, the 'Instruction of Ammenemes I for his son Sesostris', where the theme of regicide occurs. This text (preserved in Papyrus Millingen and other sources) was at first believed to be a genuine historical account in which the king addresses his son after he has escaped an assassination attempt. It is couched in terms of a prophecy in which he warns Sesostris, with great bitterness, of the deceit shown by those who tried to kill him. However, it now seems more probable that the text was composed after Ammenemes I's death, perhaps by a scribe at the Court of *Sesostris I, but that it was set out as a 'prophecy' to exalt the memory of Ammenemes I and to justify the claim of *Sesostris I to be the new king. It provides a unique example in Egyptian literature of the expression of a king's personal disillusionment.

The 'Prophecy of *Neferti' is another pseudo-prophecy which relates how Ammenemes I would save the land from destruction; it sets out to justify his reign, although it was almost certainly composed after his accession to the throne, with the aim of glorifying him and confirming his right to rule Egypt. As a man of non-royal descent, the son of a commoner named Sesostris and a woman of Ta-Sti (a district of Nubia), Ammenemes I obviously felt the need to establish his royal credentials. He was a great ruler and administrator who, despite his untimely end, left his heirs a united kingdom.

BIBL. *AEL* i .pp. 135-8, 139-44, 222-35; Gardiner, A. H. *Notes on the Story of Sinuhe.* Paris: 1916; Simpson, W. K. The Residence of It-towy. *JARCE* 2 (1963) pp. 53-64.

Ammenemes II King 1929 - 1895 BC.

By the time that Ammenemes II (son of *Sesostris I) had become king, the Twelfth Dynasty had overcome its initial insecurity and was well-established. Following the concept introduced by *Ammenemes I, *Sesostris I had associated Ammenemes II with him as co-regent; during this period the latter had pursued a non-military campaign to *Nubia.

There is not a great amount of evidence available about his reign, although it is known that he continued to make agricultural and economic improvements, to support mining and quarrying projects, and to trade with Punt (in Year 28 of his reign, a stela records an expedition to the land of the *Puntites). He also had important contacts with northern countries. A sphinx discovered at Katna (north of Homs in Syria) was inscribed with the name of one of his daughters and the statuette of another daughter was found at Ras Shamra in Syria. Treasure discovered in the Temple of Mont at Tod in Upper Egypt provides the most impressive evidence of his contact with Syria. This came to Egypt probably as a gift or as tribute from the ruler of Byblos or some other principality. Housed in four bronze caskets and inscribed with the name of Ammenemes II, the treasure included items of Mesopotamian and Aegean craftsmanship; in addition to ingots of gold and silver, there was among the silver vessels one of Aegean design, and there were also Babylonian cylinder seals and amulets from Mesopotamia.

Ammenemes II chose a new site for his pyramid – at Dahshur in northern Egypt; it followed the same pattern as his father's monument at Lisht.

BIBL. Vandier, J. A propos d'un depot de provenance asiatique trouvé à Tod. *Syria* 18 (1937) pp 174-82, pls 28-9.

Ammenemes III   King   1842 - 1797 BC.

The son of *Sesostris III, Ammenemes III's reign saw Egypt reach the pinnacale of prosperity in the Middle kingdom. The country was well-organised and administered and, with *Nubia returned to Egyptian cntrol and the rulers of northern princedoms giving allegiance to Egypt, the king had an opportunity to concentrate on major domestic projects.

The power of the provincial nobility had been reduced by *Sesostris III and no longer threatened royal supremacy, so with a period of internal and external peace it was possible to expand the economy by making improvements in irrigation and land reclamation. The most impressive scheme was in the Fayoum. Here, later Classical writers wrongly accredited Ammenemes III with inaugurating the excavation of the bed of Lake Moeris and naming it after himself. He did complete a scheme, perhaps started by his father, to reclaim 17,000 acres of arable land in the area of this lake (known today as the Birket Karun) and to enclose it within a semi-circular embankment. In this area, the Egyptologist W.M.Flinders Petrie discovered the bases of two colossal statues of the king; *Herodotus refers to two 'pyramids' which rose out of the 'Sea of Moeris', but this is probably a partly incorrect reference to these statues which, in *Herodotus' time, would have been surrounded by the waters of the lake.

An important building which came to be known as the 'Labyrinth' was situated at Hawara in the Fayoum. It was described as a major feature by both *Diodorus and *Strabo while *Herodotus claimed that it was more impressive than a pyramid. Its main function was as the funerary temple of Ammenemes III, who had two pyramids, one at Hawara and the other at Dahshur. The Labyrinth probably also incorporated a palace and administrative headquarters as well as perhaps dwellings for the royal builders, similar to the pyramid workmen's town of Kahun, which was built by *Sesostris II.

Ammenemes III's other building activities included additions to the temple of Sobek of Shedet (the crocodile god) and a temple to the cobra-goddess Renenutet at Medinet Maadi. He paid particular attention to the Fayoum and so great was his prestige in that area that he was deified and received a cult there which continued even two thousand years after his death.His pyramid complex at Dahshur was investigated (with that of *Sesostris III) by J. de Morgan and here, in shaft tombs belonging to the royal women, he found their magnificent jewellery, which is amongst the finest ever discovered in Egypt.

Quarrying expeditions and an expansion of turquoise mining in Sinai helped to supplement the country's new wealth and power; at Serabit in Sinai, the temple to Hathor, the Mistress of Turquoise, was enlarged. Numerous fine scupltured portraits of the king also indicate the high level of craftsmanship which had been attained in this reign.

The king's influence, extending from *Byblos in Syria to the Third Cataract on the Nile, was not destined to continue under his successors. Ammenemes IV, who probably acted as co-regent with his father for some time, had an insignificant reign and may have been ousted by his sister, Sebeknefru who, from association with her father, claimed the right, albeit briefly, to rule Egypt as a king.

BIBL. Herodotus, *The Histories*, Bk. ii, 149 ff; Gardiner, A. H. and Bell, H. I. The name of Lake Moeris. *JEA* 29 (1943) pp 37-50; de Morgan, J. *Fouilles à Dahchour*. (two vols) Vienna: 1895-1903.

Amosis I   King   1570 - 1546 BC.

Amosis I was the son of *Seqenenre Ta'o II and *Ahhotpe, who were both children of Ta'o I and Tetisheri. He succeeded his brother, *Kamose, as ruler and married *Ahmose-Nefertari, who was probably *Kamose's daughter.

He was later regarded as the founder of the Eighteenth Dynasty, a man who introduced a new era. In c.1567 BC he succeeded in expelling the *Hyksos, driving them back into southern Palestine and completing the task started by his immediate predecessors, *Seqenenre and *Kamose, the Theban princes of the Seventeenth Dynasty. Details of the campaigns are preserved in the biographical inscriptions in the tomb at El Kab of Ahmose, son of Ebana and of Ahmose Pennekheb. Both men fought for Amosis I and it is clear that he gained the respect of his soldiers.

After bringing about the fall of Avaris, the *Hyksos capital in the Delta, the king proceeded into southern Palestine; once the *Hyksos were subdued, he then dealt with the insurrection in Nubia and having secured Egypt, he returned to subdue Palestine and southern Phoenicia so that the *Hyksos could not renew their strength there and return to Egypt.

Although he is primarily regarded as a great military king, *Amosis I also concentrated on re-establishing an internal administration in Egypt that would effectively execute his commands. Little is known of how he achieved this; there are few remains of his temple building programme, although it is evident that he fostered the cult of the Theban god Amen-Re, and was worshipped after his death at Abydos, Egypt's great centre of pilgrimage. The royal queens were of great importance during his reign. His mother, *Ahhotpe, may have acted as his co-regent in the early years of his reign and Amosis provided her with fine jewellery in her funerary treasure. His wife, *Ahmose-Nefertari, was revered by later generations and exerted considerable power.

Amosis I was buried in a tomb at Dira Abu'n Naga at Thebes, near his ancestors of the Seventeenth Dynasty. His son, *Amenophis I, inherited a united and stable country and Amosis was remembered as the founder of the New Kingdom who had restored Egypt's freedom and greatness.

BIBL. *AEL* ii.pp 12-21; Vandersleyen, C. *Les Guerres d'Amosis, fondateur de la XVIIIe dynastie*. Brussels: 1971, pp. 17-87.

Ancestors,   Previous kings of Egypt.

The concept of the Royal Ancestors was probably as old as the monarchy. They were the body of legitimate rulers whom the ruling king worshipped collectively; at death, he became one of them. Each king, whether he was the direct heir or had usurped the throne, regarded the former kings as his ancestors and was able to rule Egypt only with their agreement. Thus, they were considered to be present at each important ceremony such as the coronation, to affirm the king's right to rule and to support his efforts. Indeed, the stability of the kingship over some three thousand years probably owed much to the cult of the Ancestors.

As the god's son, pharaoh was expected to perform certain rituals in the temples to sustain this unique relationship. As the Ancestors' heir, he also had obligations towards them and, by means of a mortuary cult, he supplied them with the necessary provisions for the afterlife. This took the form of a temple ritual in which the king, or the high-priest as his delegate, presented offerings of food and drink to the Ancestors. Even in his own lifetime, the king was represented in his temple as one of the Ancestors and he would have performed the ritual to include his own future, dead, deified self.

This ritual is preserved in various papyri in addition to being depicted on the walls of the special temples (mortuary temples) in which the rites were performed. In Papyrus Chester Beatty IX and the Cairo-Turin Papyrus (which both date to the time of *Ramesses II), *Amenophis I and *Ramesses II are represented as the officiants; thus, this is sometimes known as the 'Ritual of Amenophis I'. However, the 'Ritual of the Royal Ancestors' is a more accurate title since it will have been performed by all the kings. It is evident that, in certain temples, once the food had been offered up to the temple deity at the conclusion of the Daily Service, it was taken and presented to the Ancestors before being removed from the temple and divided up amongst the priests as their daily rations.

The Ancestors were given a presence in these temples in the form of the King Lists; these were tables of the names of all the pharaohs from the first king down to the current ruler, but they excluded those kings who were not considered to be legitimate rulers such as the *Hyksos and the Amarna pharaohs. The most famous are those carved on the interior walls of the temples of Abydos and of Karnak; another list – the Saqqara Table – was discovered in the tomb of Tjuneroy, an overseer of works. With *Manetho's history and the Turin Canon (a hieratic papyrus from the reign of *Ramesses III), these lists provide invaluable evidence for the chronology of Egypt although originally their purpose was to ensure the kings' presence at their temple ritual.

BIBL. Gardiner, A. H. *The Royal Canon of Turin*. Oxford: 1959; David, A. R. *A guide to religious ritual at Abydos*. Warminster: 1981; Fairman, H. W. Worship and festivals in an Egyptian temple. *BJRL* 37 (1954) pp. 165-202.

Ankhesenpaaten   Queen   1361 - 1352 BC.

Ankhesenpaaten was the third daughter of *Akhenaten (Amenophis IV) and Queen *Nefertiti. She grew up at Akhetaten (Tell el Amarna) and appears in scenes with her parents and sisters. While still a princess, she bore a daughter, Ankhesenpaaten-sherit; *Akhenaten was probably the father of this child as well as of the child of his eldest daughter, *Meritaten.

When *Tutankhamun became the royal heir, succeeding his brother *Smenkhkare, he married Ankhesenpaaten as the royal heiress and the couple may have spent their early years at the Northern Palace at Tell el Amarna. The marriage was intended to consolidate *Tutankhamun's claim to the throne. Furniture found in *Tutankhamun's tomb shows the couple in scenes of domestic intimacy, following the new tradition set by *Akhenaten and *Nefertiti. On the gilded coronation throne, *Tutankhamun is shown being anointed by his wife; they share a pair of sandals, each of them wearing only one sandal, and the rays of the Aten (sun's disc) descend and bestow bounty on them.

The length of time the couple remained at Tell el Amarna is uncertain; one opinion is that they continued to live and rule there for most of Tutankhamun's reign, making only a gradual return to the worship of the pantheon of traditional gods. At some point, however, they took up residence at Memphis and changed their names from Tutankhaten and Ankhesenpaaten to *Tutankhamun and Ankhesenamun, reflecting their restored allegiance to the god Amun.

With *Tutankhamun's untimely death, he was buried in the Valley of the Kings at Thebes; two female foetuses were also buried there, each in a set of miniature gold coffins, and it is probable that these were the offspring of the royal couple.There can have been no living sons or daughters, for a cuneiform text quotes a letter which was sent by a royal widow (almost certainly Ankhesenamun) to *Suppiluliumas, king of the *Hittites and Egypt's arch enemy. In this, she states that she has no son and begs *Suppiluliumas to send one of his sons to marry her, promising that he will become king of Egypt. The *Hittite king, understandably suspicious of this unexpected request (which would have conferred the rulership of Egypt on a foreigner), sent an official to investigate, but the queen protested her good faith and a *Hittite prince, Zennanza, was dispatched to Egypt. However, he was murdered en route, presumably by agents of the rival faction in Egypt, and ultimately this led to war between Egypt and the *Hittites.

The queen's reasons for sending the letter are obscure; she says that she does not wish to marry one of her subjects, but there is an alternative explanation. As the *Hittites had just overthrown the *Mitanni (whose royal family had provided wives for Egyptian kings), it was perhaps politically expedient for Egypt to seek a royal alliance with the *Hittites at this time. Nevertheless, Ankhesenamun seems to have been forced to subdue her scruples and marry a subject – the royal courtier *Ay, who then succeeded *Tutankhamun as king. Ankhesenamun's position as the royal heiress was probably vital in securing *Ay's claim to the throne. It was probably his influence which had encouraged *Tutankhamun to begin the restoration of the traditional gods and their monuments. According to one modern theory, *Ay may have been the father of *Queen Nefertiti and therefore, the grandfather of Ankhesenamun.

Nothing more is heard of Ankhesenamun; if she did marry *Ay and bestow the throne on him, he chose not to include her in the scenes in his own tomb, where he is shown with his first wife,Tey.

BIBL. Kitchen, A. *Suppiluliuma and the Amarna Pharaohs*. Liverpool: 1962; Harrison, R. G. et al. A mummified foetus from the Tomb of Tutankhamun. *Antiquity* 53, no. 207 (1979) p. 21.

Ankhmahor Court official. c.2300 BC.

Ankhmahor (surname Sesi) possessed an unique and interesting mastaba-tomb in the 'Street of Tombs', excavated by V. Loret in 1899; this lay north of *Teti's pyramid at Saqqara. It is sometimes known as the 'Tomb of the Physician' because of the subject matter of the wall-scenes. These represent the usual range of activities that appear in tombs, including farming, sacrificing animals and mourning the deceased, but in one room there is a unique set of reliefs which depict surgical operations.

There are two scenes which illustrate circumcision of an adult: in one, a man entitled 'circumcising priest' anaesthatises the patient with ointment while, in the other the operation is performed. According to *Herodotus, the Egyptians were the first people to practise circumcision, although it was probably not compulsory for everyone. It was obligatory for those of the royal and priestly classes and was probably carried out by the priests (as in these scenes) in the temples. The *Jews may have acquired the custom from the Egyptians.

Two other reliefs in this tomb show two men undergoing a treatment which has been variously interpreted as surgery, pedicure and manicure, or massage. These all cause problems of interpretation, for tomb scenes usually represented events or activities of a pleasurable nature in a person's life, or reflected his professional status and importance which he wanted to recreate by means of magic in his afterlife. Other explanations have to be considered when the scenes depict painful operations. One possibility is that circumcision had a particular religious significance for Ankhmahor; alternatively, he may have been a surgeon, but he bore no medical titles and appears to have held an important political position as a minister.

BIBL. Herodotus, *The Histories*. Bk. ii, 104; Ghalioungui, P. *Magic and medicine in ancient Egypt*. London: 1963 pp. 96-8.

Ankhsheshonqy Author of a Wisdom Text possibly c.50 BC.

One of Egypt's most enduring forms of literature was the Instruction in Wisdom or Wisdom Text. Even in later times new texts were composed and Papyrus British Museum 10508 has been dated by the handwriting of the text to the late Ptolemaic period, although it may have been composed earlier; a firm date has not yet been established for it. The papyrus was acquired by the British Museum in 1896. It is written in Demotic (the later, cursive script derived from Egyptian hieroglyphs) and both the content and the grammatical construction of the prose are very different from earlier examples of Wisdom Texts.

The text was probably composed by an anonymous scribe, but the maxims are set in the context of a story and are attributed to a priest of Re at Heliopolis, named Ankhsheshonqy. They are humorous and set out the pragmatic wisdom as part of a story.

A series of events occurs in Ankhsheshonqy's life: he visits Harsiese (an old friend who has become chief royal physician) at Memphis and he invites him to stay longer with him. Harsiese tells Ankhsheshonqy that he and some other

19

courtiers are plotting to kill the king; Ankhsheshonqy tries to dissuade him from this action, but a servant overhears their conversation and informs the king. Harsiese and his associates are put to death, and Ankhsheshonqy, although an innocent bystander, is implicated and sent to prison where, with time to ponder and to write, he composes and sets down the wisdom instructions for his son's benefit.

This idea of conveying personal wisdom to a younger person is therefore retained and developed in Egypt even thousands of years after the earliest examples–attributed to *Hardedef and *Imhotep–were composed.

BIBL. *AEL* iii. pp. 159-83; Glanville, S. R. K. *Catalogue of demotic papyri in the British Museum.Vol.2:The Instructions of 'Onchsheshonqy (British Museum Papyrus 10508).* London: 1955.

Antinous, Imperial courtier, reign of Hadrian, Roman Emperor 117 BC-AD 38.

Antinous, who was the lover and friend of Emperor *Hadrian, accompanied him on his tour of Egypt in AD 130. Tradition relates that he drowned himself in the Nile in order to fulfil a prophecy that predicted severe losses for *Hadrian, and to forestall even worse events.

*Hadrian founded a city (Antinoupolis or Antinoe) in memory of Antinous, at the place where he died. On occasion it was the custom in Egypt to deify persons who were drowned in the Nile, and *Hadrian followed this practise by establishing a cult for Antinous at this city. Very little remains of the site (opposite er-Roda in Middle Egypt), but it was apparently a fine and thriving place in antiquity.

Antony (Marcus Antonius), Roman Consul 44 and 34 BC and Triumvir 43-38 and 37-33 BC.

Mark Antony rose to power as the supporter of Julius *Caesar; he served under him in Gaul, and held the positions of Consul and Triumvir. In 40 BC he married Octavia, the sister of Octavian (later*Augustus), who eventually became his arch enemy.

The Hellenistic East came to hold a great attraction for him; at first, he probably hoped that he would gain power, prestige and wealth if he could control it, but eventually he identified himself with it and came to shun Roman traditions. This eastern attraction was ultimately symbolised by his alliance with *Cleopatra, queen of Egypt.

He summoned her to meet him in Cilicia, to answer for her conduct of military matters at Philippi, and he perhaps hoped to gain control of Egypt as a client-state of Rome.*Cleopatra arrived for the meeting in a spectacular gilded barge and charmed him with her wit and beauty. They spent time together in Alexandria, and Antony presented the queen with the contents of the library of the kings of Pergamum for the Alexandrian Library. Both probably also saw considerable political advantages in the alliance; the queen provided Antony with money and supplies but she also hoped, as a favoured client of Rome, to restore the fortunes of her dynasty and her country.

Octavian (*Augustus) was fearful of Mark Antony's ascendancy in the East, and began to wage a propoganda war against him; the Roman Senate and the people were persuaded that he spent his time in drunken revelry at Cleopatra's Court and were also outraged when, at the Donations of Alexandria, Cleopatra and her children were allocated certain provinces. This propoganda exercise preceded military action when Octavian declared war against Cleopatra and Antony and defeated their troops at the Battle of Actium in 31 BC. Finally, Octavian pursued them to Egypt and, rather than face the humiliation of submitting to him, Cleopatra and Antony committed suicide.

There has been much speculation over their personal and political relationship; as shrewd and ambitious rulers, they both undoubtedly hoped to gain from such an alliance.

BIBL. Plutarch. *Life of Antonius.*

Any   Author of a Wisdom Text   c.1400 BC.

The Instruction of Any is a Wisdom Text written as a late imitation of those that were produced in the Old and Middle Kingdoms. It is preserved on Papyrus Boulaq 4 in the Cairo Museum, which dates to the Twenty-first or Twenty-second Dynasty, and also in the form of school-boy copies in other sources; it was probably composed in the Eighteenth Dynasty.

This text differs in two main respects from earlier examples: it reflects a livelier literary style, and is couched in terms of the advice which Any, a minor official, gives to his son, in comparison with the royal or aristocratic background of most of the earlier texts. Thus it illustrates the expansion of the middle classes during the New Kingdom and indicates the advice and training they received. Secondly, a new element is introduced in the Epilogue where the son, instead of accepting his father's advice without question, now disputes it; this introduces a debate between father and son, although the validity of the teachings is eventually accepted.

BIBL. *AEL* ii.pp. 135-45; Suys, E. La sagesse d'Ani: Texte traduction et commentaire. *Analecta Orientalia* 11. Rome: 1935.

Apophis I   King   c.1570 BC.

The *Hyksos king, Auserre, adopted the Egyptian personal name of Apophis, and for the earlier part of his reign he ruled Egypt without facing evident hostility. He used the epithet 'son of Re' and gave his patronage to the learned professions.
He later faced opposition from the Theban princes of the Seventeenth Dynasty and fought *Seqenenre and his son *Kamose.

The *Hyksos first established their rulership in the Delta and then throughout Middle and Upper Egypt; their capital city, Avaris, was situated in the Delta. In the reign of Apophis I, the Thebans drove them first from southern Upper Egypt and then out of Middle Egypt, a feat which was recounted on two large stelae set up by *Kamose in the Temple of Amun at Karnak.

The start of the conflict is described in Papyrus Sallier I which recounts how, during Apophis' reign, the Theban prince *Seqenenre revived the ritual of harpooning hippopotami in a pool or canal at Thebes. Since this rite was believed to provide a magical safeguard for the native Egyptian kingship and since the hippopotamus was regarded as the embodiment of Seth, the chief *Hyksos deity, this was a provocative action and Apophis ordered *Seqenenre to stop the ritual. This in turn led to the outbreak of fighting between the *Hyksos ruler and the Thebans, and ultimately, the Theban *Amosis I drove the foreign rulers from Egypt and founded the New Kingdom.

BIBL.Winlock, H. E. *The rise and fall of the Middle Kingdom in Thebes*. New York: 1947; Save-Soderbergh, T. The Hyksos rule in Egypt. *JEA* 37 (1951) pp 53-71; Save-Soderbergh, T. On Egyptian representation of hippopotamus hunting as a religious motive. *Horae Soederblomianae* 3. Uppsala: 1953.

Apries   King   589 - 570 BC.

Apries, son and successor of *Psammetichus II, adopted a change of policy from that pursued by his predecessors. Instead of following a defensive and peaceful course, he became involved in the Judaean revolt against *Nebuchadrezzar II of Babylon in 588 BC, which ended with the sacking of Jerusalem in 587/6 BC. He appears in the Bible as the Pharaoh 'Hophra', although the extent of his support and involvement against *Nebuchadrezzar's forces is uncertain.

However, it was another expedition which brought about his own downfall. A large and prosperous colony of *Greeks had been established at Cyrene on the North African coast and this caused considerable resentment amongst the local *Libyan population. In 570 BC, a *Libyan chief, Adicran, asked for Apries' help and protection, and the king sent an army which was resoundingly defeated. His Egyptian subjects blamed Apries for this and, as a result of the ensuing civil war, Apries was deposed and replaced by *Amasis, an army general whom the people chose as pharaoh.

*Amasis took Apries alive and at first treated him well, establishing him at the capital city of Sais, but later he was thrown to the populace. Nevertheless, he was apparently accorded the final honour of being buried as a king.

BIBL. Herodotus, *The Histories* Bk. ii, 161-3,169.

Arsames   Persian satrap   c.425 - 400 BC.

When Egypt was under Persian domination during the last quarter of the fifth century BC, Arsames was the satrap left in charge of the country. His letters to his subordinates, written in Aramaic on leather and probably sent out from Memphis, have provided information about this sparsely recorded period of history.

BIBL. Kienitz, F. K. *Die politische*; Driver, G. R. *Aramaic documents of the Fifth Century BC*. Oxford: 1957.

Ashurbanipal King of Assyria. 669 - 627 BC.

*Esarhaddon, king of *Assyria (681-669 BC), pursued the policy of his father *Sennacherib, expanding and subjugating peoples even more vigorously. When *Esarhaddon became ill and died at Harran, his successor Ashurbanipal inherited the Egyptian problem.

The Egyptian king *Taharka had regained possession of his northern centre, the city of Memphis, but was once again expelled, this time by Ashurbanipal in his first campaign (667 BC). Ashurbanipal also replaced petty princes and governors in Egyptian towns since those whom *Esarhaddon had installed had now fled, and he left them to exert influence on his behalf while he was absent.

*Taharka's successor Tanuatamun, (another king in the Ethiopian line of the Twenty-fifth Dynasty), now re-occupied Memphis, but Ashurbanipal, returning from Nineveh and re-entering Egypt, drove Tanuatamun from Thebes back to Napata, where he eventually died. Ashurbanipal recorded that he conquered Thebes, ransacking the Temple of Amun at Karnak and carrying away to Nineveh a massive amount of booty. According to an account written in cuneiform on the Rassam cylinder, Ashurbanipal enjoyed a complete victory but the Egyptian version, inscribed on the Dream Stela at Gebel Barkal, records that Tanuatamun was successful.

Assyria's days as a great power were numbered; with a Scythian invasion and the growth of the new empire of the Medes in north-western Iran, Assyria faced constant threats. In 626 BC (a year after Ashurbanipal's death), the *Assyrian power was finally crushed by the Babylonians under their ruler, *Nabopolassar.

BIBL. Winton Thomas, D. (Ed.) *Documents from Old Testament times*. London: 1958; Von Zeissl, H. *Athiopen und Assyrer in Agypten*. Gluckstadt: 1944.

Asiatics ('Aamu).

The Egyptians gave the term 'Aamu (Asiatic) to a range of foreign peoples whom they encountered to the north and north-east of Egypt. The name was applied to the desert tribesmen who made constant incursions into the Delta from southern Palestine and to the more northerly inhabitants of Syria and the lands beyond.

Sometimes, it is used to refer to slaves who resided in Egypt, who were brought back from the great military campaigns in Syria and Palestine which were waged in particular by the kings of the New Kingdom. The term was also used for the *Hyksos – the foreign dynasts who established their rule in Egypt during the Second Intermediate Period.

In records found at Kahun (a pyramid workmen's town of the Twelfth Dynasty), the 'Asiatics' are distinguished in the work lists; this not only shows the range of activities they undertook in the community, including domestic and temple duties and work on the building sites, but also indicates that they formed a substantial element of the town's population.

Some Asiatics, particularly in the Ramesside period, reached the highest levels: Bay (who was probably a Syrian), became Chancellor and exercised great influence on the kingship, and another Asiatic, Ben-Azen, held the position of Cup-bearer to King *Merneptah.

BIBL. Griffith, F. Ll. *Hieratic papyri from Kahun and Gurob.* (three vols) London:1897-8.

Assyrians   Conquerors of Egypt   c.680 - c.663 BC.

Assyria's recovery as a great power in the reign of Adad-nirari II (912-891 BC) heralded the beginning of an empire which was destined to sweep away the old *Hittite supremacy and to encompass the Nile valley.

Great Assyrian rulers such as *Tiglath-pileser III and *Sennacherib came into conflict with Egypt over the small states in Syria/Palestine. Finally, *Esarhaddon took the fight into Egypt and drove the Ethiopian ruler *Taharka (whose dynasty now ruled Egypt) back to the south; although he returned briefly to Egypt, a later Assyrian king, *Ashurbanipal, again forced him back to his southern kingdom.

Under *Ashurbanipal, the Assyrian empire was at its height, and he was able to establish his supremacy in Egypt, sacking Thebes in 664 BC and carrying booty back to Nineveh.Troubles at home forced him to return to Assyria and he left *Necho, a prince of the city of Sais, in charge of Egypt. One of *Necho's successors, *Psammetichus I, was able to consolidate the position of the Saite princes as kings of the Twenty-sixth Dynasty, by using foreign mercenaries to establish his supremacy over the other native princes.

The Assyrians never returned to Egypt, but the new and dangerous alliance of the Babylonians and the Medes persuaded the Egyptians to ally with Assyria in 616 BC. However, the Babylonians sacked Nineveh, capital of Assyria, in 612 BC, and became the new threat for Egypt.

In the ninth century BC, the Assyrian kings had succeeded in establishing the greatest empire the world had yet seen; it was based on a constitution as a nation rather than incoporating a collection of client city-states (as earlier empires had been) and it was supported by an advanced army which possessed sophisticated weapons and which relied on compulsory military service.

BIBL. Von Zeissl, H. *Athiopen und Assyrer in Agypten.* Gluckstadt: 1944; Pritchard, J. B. (Ed.) *ANET.* Princeton, 1969.

Augustus (Octavian)   Roman Emperor   27 BC - AD 14 .

Gaius Julius Caesar Octavianus took the title of Augustus when he became the sole ruler of the Roman empire in 27 BC; he was its first emperor and, as the political and legal heir of Julius *Caesar, his achievements were outstanding.Augustus probably feared the power enjoyed by Mark *Antony in the East, centred on Egypt, and he focused considerable attention on a propoganda war against *Antony and Queen *Cleopatra VII, accusing Antony of debauchery and treachery to Rome. This hostile verbal attack was followed by military action when he declared war on *Cleopatra and *Antony; he defeated them at the Battle of Actium in 31 BC and pursued them to Alexandria, where they committed suicide rather than submit to defeat and the humiliation to which he would have subjected them. Octavian ordered that Ptolemy Caesarion (*Cleopatra's son by Julius *Caesar) should be killed, but he allowed the children of Mark *Antony and the queen to survive and to rule Egypt nominally for eighteen days before he took over on August 31, 30 BC. Egypt then became a *Roman province and lost all independence. Unlike other major Roman provinces, which were governed by the Roman Senate, Octavian created a special status for Egypt so that it became subject only to the Emperor who nominated a Prefect to govern it; the first of these was Cornelius Gallus (30-29 BC).Augustus visited Egypt only on the occasion of conquest in 30 BC, but he introduced wide-ranging reforms there. Egypt now became a Roman possession and the pattern of government which Augustus established continued in operation for some three hundred years. Many of the *Ptolemaic administrative measures were retained but there were also important new measures such as the imposition of Roman law.

Augustus had enhanced the city of Rome and he spared Alexandria from destruction, apparently because he admired its size and beauty and greatly respected its founder, *Alexander the Great. Indeed, under Augustus, the city was enlarged and the suburb of Nicopolis, which had an amphitheatre and a racecourse, was added. The Caesareum (a great temple begun by *Cleopatra to honour Mark *Antony) was also completed, although its use was changed to a place where the divine cult of the Caesars was performed.

As pharaoh, Augustus preserved the fiction of his role as Egypt's religious leader, the divine offspring of the gods. He is represented making offerings to the sacred Apis-bull, and he made additions to a number of Egyptian temples including the Birth-House and the Temple of Isis at Denderah, and temple wall-scenes at Philae which show him offering to the gods. His power as the god-king was also emphasised in Nubia with the foundation of a temple at Kalabsha dedicated to the local god Mandulis, and of a temple at Dendur. The first Prefect, Cornelius Gallus, marched south to pacify the district around Thebes, and the Roman policy was to establish their presence and emphasise their influence as far south as possible. Augustus inaugurated Roman rule in Egypt and left a well-established province there. Although his policies provided stability and economic growth, they removed from Egypt the last vestiges of its independence as a kingdom and reduced the country to the status of Rome's granary.

BIBL. Syme, R. *The Roman Revolution*. Oxford: 1939, 1952.

Ay   King   1352 - 1348 BC.

Although the theory is only supported by circumstantial evidence, it has been suggested that Ay may have been the son of *Yuya and *Thuya and therefore the brother of Queen *Tiye. Both *Yuya and Ay bore the title 'Father of the god' and both were 'Superintendents of the King's Horses'; they also had family associations with the town of Akhmim (where Ay built a rock-chapel to the god Min) and the names of their wives (*Thuya and Tey) were similar. Indeed, Ay held most of the titles during the reign of *Akhenaten that *Yuya had held under *Amenophis III, and these may have been transferred from father to son.

One interpretation of the title 'Father of the god' is that it was bestowed on a king's father-in-law. At Tell el Amarna, only Ay held this title, and one theory proposes that he was Queen *Nefertiti's father. It is known that her nurse or tutor was Ay's wife, Tey, who cannot therefore have been her mother; it is possible that another unknown wife of Ay may have been *Neferiti's mother and may have died in childbirth, leaving Tey as her step-mother. The same theoretical reconstruction suggests that another woman known by the name of Mudnodjme may have been either a full-sister or half-sister of *Nefertiti.

At Amarna, Ay was a close adviser and personal secretary of *Akhenaten and he must have exerted considerable influence on the king's policy and religious experiments. *Akhenaten allowed Ay to start work on an imposing tomb at Amarna; the largest of the nobles' tombs there; it was never finished or occupied, but the most complete version of the famous Hymn to the Aten was discovered near the doorway in 1884. This preserved the basic tenets of Atenism and is the fullest account of these religious concepts that we possess.

When *Akhenaten died and *Tutankhamun came to the throne as a child of nine or ten years, Ay became the vizier. He was probably responsible for the removal of the Court from Amarna to the old capital and for the parallel return to religious orthodoxy. When *Tutankhamun died, Ay succeeded him as king as there were no direct royal heirs; he probably consolidated his claim by marrying the royal widow, *Ankhesenpaaten, once her impassioned requests to the *Hittite king to send his son to become her husband had failed.

Ay reigned briefly. He appears in ritual wall-scenes in *Tutankhamun's tomb as the heir presumptive, performing the burial rites for the dead king, including the Ceremony of Opening the Mouth which was believed to restore life to the king's body and representations in statuary and wall-reliefs. When he returned from Amarna, Ay commenced work on a new tomb for himself at Thebes; this may have been the relatively small tomb in which *Tutankhamun was ultimately buried, Ay having subsequently taken over the larger tomb which was being prepared for *Tutankhamun in the western region of the Valley of the Kings.

In the larger tomb, Ay is represented with Tey, his first wife; there is no reference to *Ankhesenpaaten. Ay and Tey are shown in a scene depicting fowling in the marshes, an activity which was customarily depicted in noble but not royal tombs. It is possible that a certain Nakht-Min (the general of the army and Royal Fan-bearer in the reign of *Tutankhamun) was the son of Ay and Tey. Ay's Theban mortuary temple was taken over by his successor, *Horemheb. This man had been an army general and probably became Ay's co-regent because there was no direct living heir to take over the throne. The reliefs in Ay's unfinished Theban tomb were eventually desecrated and the excavators found no convincing evidence that he had ever been buried there. His role in the Amarna revolution and counter-revolution is unclear; as a supporter of *Akhenaten's reforms and even perhaps inspiring some of the king's ideas, Ay seems to have changed course later, perhaps realising the dangers inherent in the situation. He appears to have provided continuity and some stability throughout this troubled period.

BIBL. Aldred, C. *Akhenaten, Pharaoh of Egypt.* London: 1968; Seele, K. C. King Ay and the close of the Amarna age. *JNES* 14 (1955) pp. 168 ff; Newberry, P. E. King Ay, the successor of Tutankhamun *JEA* 18 (1932) pp 50-2.

'Aha King c.3070 BC.

It is probable that 'Aha ('The Fighter') was the second king of the First Dynasty and the immediate successor of *Narmer, the founder of dynastic Egypt, who almost certainly can be identified with the name of Menes. Nevertheless, there has been considerable controversy over the correct identification of these three names: an ivory tablet, discovered in a tomb at Nagada by the archaeologist de Morgan in 1897 (and now in the Cairo Museum), is inscribed with both the hieroglyphic signs reading 'Mn' ('Menes') and the name of 'Aha. This led to one conclusion that Menes and 'Aha were the same person, but subsequently it was shown that this actually represented an occasion on which 'Aha was visiting a place connected with his predecessor, Menes, when he was perhaps taking part in the erection of a temporary structure to be used in Menes' funeral.

Other evidence provided by jar-sealings from Abydos shows that the names of 'Mn' and '*Narmer' occur together, and although this does not perhaps confirm conclusively that *Narmer is to be identified with Menes, most scholars now agree that, on balance, the facts indicate that *Narmer and Menes were the same person and that 'Aha was his immediate successor.

BIBL. Emery, W. *Archaic Egypt.* Harmondsworth: 1961; Emery, W. B. *Hor-Aha. Service des Antiquités de l'Egypte: excavation at Saqqara,* 1937-8, 1. Cairo:1939.

'Apiru

The term 'Apiru has been the subject of wide discussion and speculation. It occurs in both Syria and Mesopotamia as a general term applied to soldiers, mercenaries, raiders, captives and slaves; there is also general acceptance that it can be identified with the Habiru (Hapiru who are mentioned in the Amarna Letters) as a general term for 'bandits' or 'outcasts', but with no reference to a specific ethnic group.

In a stela which dates to the reign of *Ramesses II, there is a reference to the building of a city bearing the king's name in which the 'Apiru are employed as labourers; at one time, it was speculated that these people should be identified with the Hebrews of the Old Testament who were engaged in building works immediately before the Exodus. The identification of the 'Apiru with the Hebrews is not now widely accepted, and in the Egyptian texts, the term is probably used as a general reference to the *Asiatic prisoners who were employed in the state building and quarrying projects. The word may be derived from the Egyptian verb 'hpr' which meant 'to bind' or 'to make captive'.

BIBL. Wilson, J. A. The 'Eperu of the Egyptian inscriptions. *AJSL* 49 (1932-3) pp 275 ff.; Bottero, J. (Ed.) *Le Probleme des Habiru.* Paris: 1954; Greenberg, M. *The Hab/piru.* New Haven: 1955.

B

Beduin (Shoshu).

From the earliest times, the Egyptians came into conflict with the Beduin (whom they called 'Shoshu'), who were the desert tribes that wandered along and lived on the borderlands of Egypt. They formed part of that desert environment which, with its teeming wild animals and as the location of most of the cemeteries, represented a place of death and hostility to the Egyptians.The Beduin lived in tents and pursued a largely nomadic existence but, to feed their families, they traded goods such as galena (used as eye-paint) with the Egyptians. Nevertheless, the Egyptians always regarded them as savages. Attracted by the pleasant and easy life of the Nile valley, the Beduin constantly harrassed Egypt from earliest times. When the system of centralised government collapsed, the Beduin incursions were successful; as part of the government's continuous policy to protect Egypt's boundaries, every attempt was made to keep this menace at bay and, in times of internal stability, strings of military fortresses were built and corps of police patrolled the desert with dogs.

The Beduin are mentioned in the famous literary piece, the 'Story of *Sinuhe', in which the Egyptian Sinuhe flees from Egypt and joins the Beduin in their wandering existence, eventually becoming the chief of a tribe.

The persecution of the *Jews which foreshadowed the Exodus from Egypt was part of a general campaign in Ramesside times against foreigners and, in the reign of *Sethos I, a great slaughter of the Beduin is recorded.

BIBL. Faulkner, R. O. The wars of Sethos I. *JEA* 33 (1947) pp. 34 ff.

Byblites, Inhabitants of Byblos.

One of the main commodities which Egypt lacked was an ample supply of good quality timber for use in the construction of tombs, coffins, ships, doors and other requirements. Therefore, from the earliest times, they traded with the people of Byblos, the major port on the Syrian coast, in order to obtain supplies of cedarwood from the hinterland. Byblos retained its independence from Egypt, but excavations undertaken there by the archaeologists, Montet and Dunand, have provided evidence that Egypt had direct contact with Byblos from very early times and that the Byblites were much influenced by Egyptian styles and customs.

The Thinite rulers of the Second Dynasty were already importing cedar through Byblos. The first Egyptian object at Byblos which can be dated with accuracy is a fragment of a stone polished vase which bears the name of King *Kha'sekhemui, but there was increased activity by the Old Kingdom and reliefs in *Sahure's pyramid complex show ships returning from Syria, perhaps from an expedition to obtain wood. Bearded foreigners appear on the ships; they are obviously envoys or visitors, not bound captives, and they raise up their arms in praise of the king. Excavations at Byblos have also revealed stone vessels which bear the names of Old Kingdom kings such as *Teti and *Unas. These and other pieces were probably brought as offerings by Egyptian traders to the local goddess, the Mistress of Byblos, who was identified both with the native Semitic deity, Astarte, and with the Egyptian goddess, Hathor, who was also widely worshipped in Sinai and *Punt.

Byblos was never an Egyptian colony but Egyptian traders were welcomed regularly in times of peace and prosperity. When Egypt suffered troubles (as in the First and Second Intermediate Periods), this trade slackened or disappeared and ships no longer travelled to Byblos. During the First Intermediate Period, trade was renewed under the Heracleopolitan kings and the subsequent rulers of the Eleventh Dynasty; in the Middle Kingdom, very close contacts were restored with Byblos, to the extent that the native rulers of the city used an Egyptian title which meant 'hereditary prince' or 'governor' and they even wrote their names in hieroglyphs. The Byblites used goods and wore jewellery which were either of Egyptian origin or were locally produced in imitation of Egyptian styles.

In the New Kingdom, cedarwood was one of the few commodities which Egypt imported as an essential raw material that they were unable to produce at home. This wood and other commodities passed through the port of Byblos and most of Egypt's Mediterranean trade was conveyed along the Syrian coast. During *Tuthmosis III's campaigns to Syria, his troops were provisioned through the coastal harbours, and men and equipment were probably moved there by sea, in ships built in Egypt, at the Peru-nefer dockyard near Memphis. Indeed, in the Egyptian navy, there was a type of vessel called a 'Byblos ship', which was named after the port; this was a large, sea-going ship which was used to sail along the Syrian coast and elsewhere in the Red Sea.

By the Twentieth Dynasty, the situation had changed, and in the narrative known as the 'Story of *Wenamun', the Theban official Wenamun is sent to Syria to buy cedarwood for the second barque of the god Amen-Re, but the ruler of Byblos refuses to provide him with the timber until he is paid in cash. In another literary source which recounts the famous *Osiris myth, Byblos is mentioned again, this time as the place where Isis discovered her husband's body.

BIBL. Montet, P. *Byblos et l'Egypte*. Paris: 1928; Dunand, M. *Fouilles de Byblos, 1926-1932*. Vol. 1. Paris: 1937, 1939, 1933-38. Vol. 2. Paris: 1950, 1954.

C

Caesar   Roman Dictator   49 - 44 BC.

Gaius Julius Caesar, the most famous of all Roman rulers, was Dictator until 44 BC when he met his fateful end. He was a man of military and administrative genius; his most outstanding achievements included the conquest of Gaul, and from 49 BC he enjoyed considerable prestige at Rome, acquiring both royal and divine powers. From 48 to 45 BC, his campaigns took him to Pontus, Africa, Spain and Egypt, where he pursued Pompey who had become embroiled in the dynastic struggles at the Egyptian Court. Egypt was still an independent kingdom, ruled by the *Ptolemies, but it came increasingly under the influence of Rome.

Egypt's queen, *Cleopatra VII, had been ousted from the joint rulership of her country in favour of her brother, and she appealed to Caesar to restore her as the rightful ruler; she regained her throne and her brother was drowned in the Nile. Caesar remained in Egypt long enough to accompany *Cleopatra on a voyage along the Nile in 47 BC; their son, Ptolemy Caesarion, was eventually adopted as *Cleopatra's co-regent in 36 BC, and he is depicted with his mother in the reliefs on the south exterior wall of the temple at Denderah, where they stand before the divine triad of Hathor, her husband Horus of Edfu, and their son Ihy.

BIBL. Plutarch, *Life of Caesar.*

Cambyses   King of Persia   525 - 522 BC.

Cyrus II, the Achaemenid ruler who established the *Persian empire, sent his son Cambyses to overthrow Egypt's Twenty-sixth Dynasty and to annex the country as part of his empire. Cambyses first dealt with *Phoenicia and acquired their fleet and then went on to attack Egypt, routing the Egyptians at the Battle of Pelusium in 525 BC after a considerable conflict. Fleeing to Memphis, the Egyptians finally surrendered after a siege, and the kingdom passed from *Psammetichus III (*Amasis' son, who had only ruled the country for a few months) to the Persians. Thus, the Twenty-seventh Dynasty ushered in the first period of Persian domination which lasted until 401 BC when independence was briefly regained for some sixty years (Twenty-eighth to Thirtieth Dynasties), before Artaxerxes III reconquered Egypt in 343-2 BC and the brief second period of *Persian domination (the Thirty-first Dynasty), followed.

Following his conquest of Egypt, Cambyses' reign lasted only another three years. He experienced failure in various endeavours, including the disappearance, as the result of a sandstorm, of a complete army that he had sent out to the Siwa Oasis. According to *Herodotus, Cambyses' fury at his misfortune may have upset the balance of his mind. Herodotus describes Cambyses as an evil and cruel ruler who neglected the gods and even killed one of the sacred Apis-bulls whose cult was pursued at Saqqara. This story may be fictional, for in the Serapeum at Saqqara, where the mummified bulls were eventually buried, there is a sarcophagus of one of these animals which bears an inscription recalling that it was dedicated by Cambyses. Although other documentary evidence indicates that he may have destroyed some of the temples of the gods, in at least one account it is claimed that he honoured Egypt's deities.

In 522 BC, Cambyses returned to Persia to deal with a pretender to his throne; he may have died en route, and Egypt was briefly left in charge of a satrap named Aryandes.

BIBL. Herodotus, *The Histories,* Bk. iii, 1 ff.

Carians   Allies of Egypt   c.660 BC.

King *Psammetichus I of Egypt recruited a number of peoples to fight as mercenaries on his behalf and to consolidate his victories against the *Assyrians and Ethiopians. These included the *Greeks, *Phoenicians and the Carians, a people who lived in Asia Minor. They continued to play an important role in Egypt's policy throughout the Twenty-sixth Dynasty, a situation which was not readily accepted by the native Egyptian population.

BIBL. Herodotus, *The Histories,* Bk.ii, 153 ff.

Cheops   King   c.2589 - 2566 BC.

Khufu, and his successors Khafre and Menkaure, are more generally known by the Graecised forms of their names which are Cheops, *Chephren and *Mycerinus.In the fifth century BC, *Herodotus preserves a tradition that the Egyptians who lived during the reigns of Cheops and his son *Chephren, hated and despised their rulers; Cheops closed the temples and tyrannically forced his subjects to build his massive tomb, known today as the Great Pyramid at Giza. He used the proceeds from his daughter's prostitution to help towards the cost of this enormous edifice.

Although this is probably largely a fanciful story told to *Herodotus when he visited Egypt, Cheops is also represented in Egyptian sources as an autocrat. In the Westcar Papyrus, it recounted how the king was entertained by the magician Djedi and ultimately learnt of the fate of his dynastic line; he is contrasted here with his predecessor, *Sneferu, whose genial nature is emphasised. Cheops was obviously a devoted and pious son, for he completed the burial of his mother *Hetepheres, apparently causing her mortal remains to be interred in a new tomb near his own pyramid, after her original tomb had been ransacked.

In contrast with his reputation as a tyrant, Cheops was also accredited with great sacred wisdom and knowledge and was stated to be the author of a hermetic book. In fact, few verifiable details have survived regarding his character or his reign, and he can now only be judged as the builder of his great funerary monument, the Great Pyramid, which was one of the Seven Wonders of the ancient world. He abandoned the traditional royal burial place at Saqqara and selected a new site at Giza for his pyramid. Giza had several sound advantages: the plateau provided a dominating and spectacular setting for his pyramid and the subsidiary buildings. It was near the capital city of Memphis and there was ready access to a major source of building material in the limestone quarries at Tura. The grandiose scheme included the pyramid and a necropolis for the burial of his family and members of the court. Three small neighbouring pyramids may have housed the burials of favourite queens, although this is by no means certain.

The Great Pyramid rose to a height of 481 feet and its bulk is greater than that of any building known to have been constructed by man. There were two complete changes of plan relating to the construction of the internal chambers and corridors. Originally, the complex would also have incorporated a funerary or mortuary temple (for the service of offerings), a covered causeway, and a Valley Temple located at the place where the desert met the cultivation. There were pits cut into the subterranean rock around the pyramid to house five wooden boats – three on the east side and two on the south. Two boat pits were discovered in 1954; one was opened, and the boat it contained was removed and reconstructed by archaeological and restoration experts. This vessel of cedarwood which measures over 130 feet in length, can now be viewed in a special museum built at Giza. The exact purpose of such boats remains uncertain: they may have been intended for the king to use in his next life when he sailed across the sky with his father Re, the sun-god, or they may actually have taken part in the funerary ceremonies, conveying the king's body and his burial goods to the pyramid.

From the size and scope of his funerary complex, it is evident that Cheops was an absolute ruler with control of a unified country that was untroubled by any major external threat or military action. Irrigation of the land, use and administration of Egypt's resources, and the availability of sufficient manpower provided the king with unprecedented wealth and the power to achieve his great ambitions.

BIBL. Reisner, G. A. *A History of the Giza necropolis*. Vol. 1. Cambridge, Mass.:1942; Edwards, I. E. S. *The Pyramids of Egypt*. Harmondsworth: 1985, pp. 116-68.

Chephren King 2558 - 2533 BC.

*Herodotus names the fourth ruler of the Fourth Dynasty as Chephren, which was the Graecised form of the Egyptian 'Khafre'; he was probably the son of *Cheops whose example he followed by building a magnificent pyramid complex at Giza. There is little difference in the measurements of the area or the height of their two pyramids, and the component parts of Chephren's complex – pyramid, funerary temple, causeway and valley building – are better preserved than those of his father. Part of the limestone outer casing is still visible on Chephren's pyramid and in the burial-chamber, the polished granite sarcophagus has survived.

The funerary temple is remarkable for the size of the limestone blocks which have been used in its construction and which are unsurpassed in any other Egyptian buildings. In the valley building, the severe architectural forms and the use of red granite are particularly impressive and it was here that the fine diorite statues of the king (including the famous example in the Cairo Museum) were discovered. It is evident that, during this reign, the art of the Old Kingdom reached one of its highest levels of achievement. In general, Chephren's pyramid complex is the best preserved sample of this type of religious architecture and it formed the basis and pattern for most future pyramid developments. Unlike *Cheops' complex, there was no provision for the burial of the king's family and courtiers in rows of mastaba-tombs at the base of the pyramid, but Chephren's queens and royal children were interred in rock-cut tombs in the ground near the pyramid, while the Court officials either used unfinished tombs left over from *Cheops' reign or built new tombs near *Cheops' city of the dead.

A unique feature of Chephren's complex is the Great Sphinx which lies to the north-east of his pyramid. Carved from an outcrop of rock at the side of the causeway which leads up to the pyramid temple, the Sphinx represents a human-headed, crouching lion and may have portrayed Chephren's facial features. Later, it became known to the Egyptians of the New Kingdom as the god 'Horus-in-the-Horizon' who was the guardian of this area. It became a notable feature and was visited by kings; in the famous Dream Stela, *Tuthmosis IV recounts how, when he was a prince out hunting, he fell asleep at the foot of the Sphinx and dreamt that the Sphinx appeared to him and complained of the sand which threatened to engulf it. When he became king, *Tuthmosis IV ordered the sand to be cleared away from the Sphinx, and the story is preserved on a stela which he caused to be set up between the paws of the Sphinx.

The Giza Sphinx is the largest and one of the oldest examples of these hybrid creatures to be found in Egypt; throughout the succeeding ages, it retained a popular mythology as a symbol of mystery and hidden truths.

As an individual, Chephren, like his father, remains a shadowy figure; *Herodotus provides the only account of him, stating that he was tyrannical and impious and was hated by his subjects, whom he forced to build his pyramid.

BIBL. Edwards, I. E. S. *The Pyramids of Egypt.* Harmondsworth: 1985, pp 116-69; Holscher, U. *Das Grabdenkmal des Konigs Chephren.* Leipzig: 1912.

Cleopatra VII   Queen   51 - 30 BC.

The last of the Macedonian rulers of Egypt, Cleopatra VII has been preserved in legend as a woman of formidable intellect and ambition who used her beauty and charm to advance Egypt's fortunes. In 51 BC, she became joint ruler with her father Ptolemy XII Auletes (who died in 51 BC) and then with her brother and husband, Ptolemy XIII. When he died in 47 BC, her younger brother (also her husband) Ptolemy XIV succeeded him.

Rome, attracted by Egypt's wealth, had influenced Ptolemaic policy for some time; Pompey, an important figure in the East, involved himself in the internal and financial affairs of Ptolemy XII Auletes and when Auletes died, Pompey was appointed by the Roman Senate to act as the legal guardian of Cleopatra VII and her brother. Pompey's ambitions brought him into conflict with Julius *Caesar and, after defeat at the Battle of Pharsalia (47 BC), Pompey fled to Egypt where he was assassinated by Egyptian courtiers.

When *Caesar came to Alexandria, (48-47 BC) Cleopatra persuaded him to support her cause, hoping to strengthen her position and to regain her throne. Their son, Ptolemy XV Caesarion, ruled jointly with Cleopatra from 36 BC.

The queen's subsequent liaison with Mark *Antony was of longer duration; again, she hoped that he would help her to restore Egypt to its past glory by using Rome's powers to enhance the fortunes of her allies and clients. She hoped that her marriage to Mark *Antony would provide her with the opportunity to divide the eastern possessions between themselves.

There were children from her associations with both *Caesar and *Antony. In 34 BC, Cleopatra and *Antony staged the great ceremony known as the Donations of Alexandria, at which some of the eastern provinces and anticipated conquests were assigned to Cleopatra and her children. Thus Cleopatra obtained Egypt, Cyprus, Libya and Coele Syria, while Alexander Helios received Armenia, Media and Parthia. Ptolemy was given Phoenicia, Syria and Cilicia, and Cleopatra Selene gained Cyrene. Mark *Antony had to justify to the Roman Senate this disposal of property. He did this by claiming that he was merely presenting Roman territory to Rome's clients.

Mark *Antony was an astute man, and from 37 BC onwards his close association with Cleopatra brought him both money and supplies. *Augustus (Octavian) regarded *Antony (who had married his sister) and his Egyptian power-base as an eastern threat to Roman ascendancy. He waged a successful propoganda campaign against Mark *Antony and the Egyptian queen and persuaded the Roman Senate that *Antony had spent years in debauchery and drunkenness at Alexandria. Antony was denounced as an enemy of Rome and military action soon followed: *Augustus defeated him at the Battle of Actium in western Greece in the September of 31 BC. For some unknown reason, Cleopatra withdrew her squadron when the battle was raging and, followed by Mark *Antony, fled to Alexandria. Here they awaited *Augustus, who arrived ten months later. Alexandria was captured and *Antony and Cleopatra committed suicide, the queen preferring death to the inevitable humiliation that submission to Rome would have brought. According to legend, she used a snake's bite to end her life on August 12, 30 BC. *Augustus could not allow her son Caesarion to live, but her children by Mark *Antony apparently survived and ruled Egypt nominally for eighteen days before *Augustus became pharaoh on August 31, 30 BC.

Cleopatra was a remarkable woman and a formidable queen. She was reputedly the only *Ptolemaic ruler to learn to speak Egyptian (which endeared her to her native subjects) and was also fluent in several other languages. The coins which depict her likeness do not support the legend of her great beauty, but a marble bust in Berlin shows something of her character and physical charm.

BIBL. Bell, H. I. *Egypt from Alexander the Great to the Arab Conquest*. Oxford: 1956; Austin, M. M. *The Hellenistic world from Alexander to the Roman conquest*. Cambridge: 1981.

Constantine I ('The Great') Roman Emperor AD 306 - 337.

Flavius Valerius Constantinus, the son of Saint Helena, was proclaimed Roman Emperor at York in AD 306. He was the first Emperor to support the Christians and during his time of stable government, not only did the persecutions cease but he actively supported the growth of Christianity. In AD 311, the Edict of Toleration ended the persecutions started under Emperor *Diocletian and in AD 313, the Edict of Milan restored the property of the churches. Constantine not only ensured that churches and monasteries could now legally hold property but he also provided for grants to be made available for churches and supported church building and restoration programmes from public funds. The Caesareum at Alexandria (where the cult of the Roman Emperors had been celebrated) was now dedicated as a church to St. Michael, and it later became the official seat of the Patriarch of Alexandria. Constantine held a series of Councils to attempt to unite the various factions in the Church, the most notable being the Council of Nicaea.

In Egypt, the government was reorganised, the country was made into a diocese and divided into six provinces. Constantine founded Constantinople in AD 324-30, and it was inaugurated as a city in AD 330. It was the first Christian city and, as an imperial capital, was intended to act as an eastern counterbalance to Rome; its significance to Egypt was that it lessened Alexandria's influence in the East and also became the recipient, instead of Rome, of much of Egypt's grain surplus.

Christianity developed and spread in Egypt both during and after Constantine's reign; in the Temple of Luxor, originally dedicated to the Egyptian gods Amun, Mut and Khonsu, there remains an altar dedicated to Constantine.

BIBL. Jones, A. H. M. *Constantine and the conversion of Europe*. London: 1972; Baynes, N. H. *Constantine the Great and the Christian Church*. London: 1972.

Copts.

The word 'Copt' is derived from the Greek 'Aigyptios' (which became 'Qibt' after the Arab invasion in the seventh century AD); it was first used in the sixteenth century AD in Europe to distinguish the Christian inhabitants of Egypt.

The Egyptians readily adopted Christianity which developed several concepts which were already familiar to them. Their particular contribution was the concept of physical retreat from the material world, at first as hermits in desert caves and later in purpose-built monasteries. At the Council of Ephesus in AD 451, the doctrine that Christ combined a human and a divine nature was sanctioned, but the Egyptian Christians rejected this and adopted the monophysite heresy as the foundation of their beliefs, forming a sect which broke away from the rest of Christendom. By the sixth century AD, the Coptic Church had extended southwards into Nubia, but following the Arab conquest of Egypt in AD 640, many Egyptians were converted to Islam and the new faith reached Nubia in the thirteenth century AD. Strong pockets of Christianity survived in Egypt particularly in the south around Thebes; today, the Copts form an important minority group there, and the Coptic Patriarch also has nominal authority over the Ethiopian Church.

Both native and Hellenistic styles influenced the culture of Coptic Egypt. At first, pagan themes predominated but by the fourth and fifth centuries AD, Coptic art increasingly expressed itself through Christian motifs, eventually becoming the distinctive art of Christian Egypt. Traces of its influence can also be seen in Islamic art. Some of the monasteries can still be visited and in these, as in the churches and houses, the artists have used decorative and ornamental frescoes.

Coptic is the final stage of the ancient Egyptian language and was initially developed as a medium for the translation of Biblical texts. In Coptic, the Egyptian language, previously written in hieroglyphs, Hieratic and Demotic, now used the Greek alphabet with the addition of seven signs from Demotic for those Egyptian sounds which were unknown to the *Greeks. The oldest Coptic manuscripts date from the third century AD when Christianity began to spread through Egypt, but earlier attempts with this script had been made in previous centuries. Translations of the books of the Old Testament were followed by those of the Gospels and other writings, and the works of St. Antony (AD 251-356) were of particular importance. Coptic has a relatively small vocabulary and many Greek words were therefore included, but an important development was the introduction of written vowels which the earlier Egyptian scripts had omitted.

Ultimately, Coptic was used to help with the decipherment of Egyptian hieroglyphs and provided some information about the pronunciation of the ancient language. Coptic manuscripts were imported into Europe from the beginning of the seventeenth century AD, and some of these were acquired by a Jesuit, Athanasius Kircher, who, in his work *Lingua Aegyptiaca restituta* (1643), began a serious study of Coptic (which was understood) and Egyptian. He made the important discovery that Egyptian hieroglyphs and Coptic were related and later, when Champollion began to decipher hieroglyphs, his knowledge of Coptic advanced his studies and helped him to reach important conclusions.

Gradually, Arabic replaced Coptic as Egypt's main language; Coptic was last spoken in Christian villages in the seventeenth century AD but it survives today as the liturgical language and script of the Coptic Church.

Textiles were another major feature of early Coptic culture. Made of wool and linen, many still survive in the form of vestments, wrappings, tunics and domestic furnishings and provide a valuable insight into a lively and distinctive folk-art.

BIBL. Walters, C. C. *Monastic Archaeology in Egypt.* Warminster: 1974.

Cyaxares King of the Medes c.600 - 560 BC.

With his father Phraortes, Cyaxares built a new and important empire in north-west Iran and led the Medes to power against their enemies. His reign coincided with those of *Nebuchadrezzar of Bablyon and *Necho II and *Psammetichus II of Egypt. In 590 BC and five years later, he fought against neighbouring Lydia. This ended in a diplomatic marriage between the families of the two rulers; this conflict prevented him from participating in the disputes between the Babylonians and the Egyptians.

BIBL. Wiseman, D. J. *Chronicles of Chaldaean kings.* London: 1956.

D

Darius I   King of Persia   521 - 486 BC.

The conflict over the succession and *Cambyses' death brought Darius I to the Achaemenid throne; during his long reign, he devoted much time and energy to the organisation of his great empire.

He appears to have taken a considerable interest in Egypt's ancient civilisation and, unlike other *Persian rulers, he actively tried to promote Egypt's own interests. One of his first acts was to send a satrap (governor) to Egypt to bring together the wisest amongst the soldiers, priests and scribes so that they could write down and preserve the country's laws down to Year 44 of the reign of *Amasis. This information is inscribed on the back of a much later papyrus known as the 'Demotic Chronicle', and there are comments on the role of Darius as a great law-giver in another source – the writings of the Classical author *Diodorus Siculus (i:95).

Darius I also made additions to the Egyptian gods' temples and encouraged their worship; he tried to act as a proper king and personally supervised the government of the country rather than delegating these duties entirely to satraps. By this period, soldiers and officials from many parts of the Persian empire would have visited Egypt and, in turn, Egyptian doctors and officials were received at the Persian Court; the royal Achaemenid palaces were decorated by artists and craftsmen from Egypt and other areas of the empire.

Darius I undertook a major practical scheme in Egypt when, in 518 BC, a canal was completed to link the Nile and the Red Sea – this project had been started under *Necho II who had been forced to abandon it. Darius' achievement is recorded in both hieroglyphic and cuneiform texts on a series of stelae which were set up along the banks of the canal, and it is also mentioned by *Herodotus. On completion of the canal, a fleet stocked with tribute sailed down its length and around Arabia to Persia, thus demonstrating how the communications between the Persian homeland and Egypt had been improved.

Events outside Egypt – the revolt of the Ionian cities in 499 BC and the defeat of Darius' nephew at Marathon in 490 BC – set the scene for the Egyptian uprisings of 486 BC. Also in that year, Darius I was succeeded by his son, *Xerxes, who in his second year subdued the Egyptian revolt.

BIBL. Posener G. *La premiere domination Perse en Egypte.* Cairo: 1936; Herodotus, *The Histories,* Bk ii, 158; Bk iv, 39.

Decius   Roman Emperor   (AD 249 - 251 .

In AD 249-50, Decius initiated the first severe persecutions of the Christians which occurred in Alexandria in AD 250; after this, the pressure lessened because of the new preoccupation with the Gothic war. Decius (honoured by the Roman Senate with the name Traianus) is shown as Pharaoh of Egypt in a wall-scene in the Temple of Khnum at Esna; his inscription here is the latest in the temple and is amongst the last hieroglyphic texts to have been discovered in Egypt. His name appears at Esna carved in a cartouche on the wall – the last time an Emperor is mentioned in an Egyptian temple inscription.

Den King c.2985 - 2930 BC.

The fifth king of the First Dynasty, Den succeeded Djet on the throne, and it is possible that his mother may have been the mysterious but powerful queen Mer(it)neith who acted for him as a regent while he was still a minor. He was a dynamic and enterprising ruler and pursued an active foreign policy which is illustrated by a small ivory tablet , now in the British Museum; this shows the king slaying an *Asiatic in a desert region (probably Sinai) and is accompanied by an inscription which reads: 'First time of slaying the Easterners.'

Den had large burial monuments at both Abydos and Saqqara, although it remains uncertain which of these was his actual tomb. The Abydos monument had architectural innovations including an entrance stairway, and its granite pavement is evidence of the advances which had been made in artistic and stone-working skills.

Later generations accredited Den with prescriptions in the Ebers and Berlin medical papyri, and in his reign, it appears that two major features connected with the kingship were introduced – the Double Crown and the royal *nsw-bit* name. Both these concepts emphasised the king's role as the ruler of both the northern and southern regions of Egypt.

BIBL. Emery, W. B. *Archaic Egypt*. Harmondsworth: 1961; Emery, W. B. *Great Tombs of the First Dynasty*.(three vols) Cairo and London 1949-58; Petrie, W. M. F. *The Royal Tombs of the First Dynasty*. London:1900.

Diocletian Roman Emperor AD 284 - 305.

Gaius Aurelius Valerius Diocletianus was commander of the Imperial Guard and became emperor when Numerian (AD 283-4) was assassinated. He was the last reigning Roman emperor to visit Egypt: he was present at the fall of Alexandria after a siege of eight months, and then journeyed south. He withdrew the southern Egyptian border from Nubia and re-established it near Philae in c.AD 298; the Roman Town Gate at the north-east end of the island of Philae probably dates from this time. On his return northwards, he and his entourage stayed at Panopolis and in AD 302, he was in Alexandria shortly before the persecution of the Christians occurred. They hated him for his role in inaugurating this suffering which continued for at least another ten years. He chose Jupiter as his own patron god and, throughout his long and stable reign, he sought to re-introduce traditional beliefs and ideas.

In Egypt, the reign of Diocletian is regarded as the watershed between the Roman and Byzantine periods. He made several important economic changes relating to the Egyptian taxation and monetary systems: in AD 296, the coinage was officially revalued and it was no longer permitted to remain separate from the coinage in the rest of the Roman Empire, while an attempt was also made to fix a maximum price for all goods and services.

BIBL. Jones, A. H. M. *The Later Roman Empire 284-602*. Oxford: 1964.

Diodorus Siculus   Historian   late first century BC.

The Greek author Diodorus Siculus made a brief visit to Egypt in c.59 BC, and he devoted Book I of his History to aspects of ancient Egypt. Although his first-hand experience of the country enabled him utilise and quote from his personal impressions, he did this only occasionally and preferred to derive his account from earlier writers, relying heavily on Hecataeus of Abdera, Agatharchides of Cnidus, and *Herodotus.

Diodorus covers many of the same subjects as *Herodotus and, although his book is longer, his style of writing is far less entertaining; also, although both authors deal with the same material in many cases, each introduces details which are not found in the other account – their treatment of the subject of mummification is a good example of this.

Diodorus gives an account of the *Osiris Myth which is covered much more fully by the later writer *Plutarch; he also describes animal worship, the cult and burial of the dead, the Egyptian systems of administration, law, education and medicine, and the flora and fauna to be found in the country. He also speculates on the causes of the inundation of the Nile and provides some interesting comments on the practise of cannibalism which he maintained occurred during times of great famine, although the sacred animals were spared. Another subject he considers is the forced labour camps which were introduced to deal with criminals. He comments that these were a good example of the Egyptians' attitude towards the rehabilitation of the criminal.

His chronological account of the history contains many inaccuracies and a modern assessment of his work would be that it is a compilation of information from other sources rather than a serious historical record. Nevertheless, his writings form an important although unverifiable source for those periods (such as the fifth and fourth centuries BC) for which other evidence is scarce.

BIBL. Diodorus of Sicily, *General History* (twelve vols) Book I, 12-27, London: 1933; Waddell, W. G. An account of Egypt by Diodorus the Sicilian, being the First Book of his Universal History translated into English. *The University of Egypt:Bulletin of the Faculty of Arts I,Part 1* (May 1933), pp 1-47; Part 2 (December 1933), pp. 161-218; Africa, T. W. Herodotus and Diodorus on Egypt. *JNES* 22 (1963) pp. 254 ff.

Djer (Iti)   King   c.3042 - 2995 BC.

The third king of the First Dynasty, the name of Iti (Horus-name Djer) occurs in the Abydos King-list. He was apparently a ruler with an active foreign policy: a reference in the large Cairo fragment of the Palermo Stone mentions the 'Smiting of the Setje' (probably in Sinai) and his name also occurs in a rock-carving at Wadi Halfa, where it accompanies a battle scene and thus indicates that his military campaigns reached as far south as the Second Cataract.

His funerary monument at Abydos may have been his actual tomb or a cenotaph, if he and the other rulers of this dynasty were buried at Saqqara. At Abydos there is evidence that the practise of human sacrifice reached its peak during his reign, for at his two funerary complexes the subsidiary burials of some six hundred attendants were found. In later times, his Abydos 'tomb' was regarded as the burial-place of the god *Osiris and a huge sarcophagus representing the god was placed there.

It is probable that his wife was Queen Herneith, whose mudbrick tomb at Saqqara dates to his reign. In the north wall of his Abydos 'tomb', a macabre discovery was made: four bracelets made of gold, turquoise and lapis lazuli were discovered, still encircling the detached arm of a woman (probably a queen); this ancient booty had probably been hidden there by tomb-robbers who were disturbed in the course of their actions.

BIBL. Emery, W. B. *Archaic Egypt.* Harmondsworth: 1972; Emery, W. B. *Great Tombs of the First Dynasty.* (Three vols) Cairo and London: 1949-58; Petrie, W. M. F. *The Royal Tombs of the First Dynasty.* London: 1900.

Djoser   King   c.2667 - 2648 BC.

Djoser was probably the first king of the Third Dynasty which introduced the period currently known as the Old Kingdom; as such, he was recognised and remembered as the founder of a new epoch.

Until this time, there had been no marked distinction between the burial place of the king and of the nobility, but Djoser (probably inspired by his vizier and architect, *Imhotep) introduced the custom of burying the king in a pyramid while the nobility continued to be interred in mastaba-tombs.

Djoser's Step Pyramid at Saqqara represents the evolution of a new architectural form and also a major development in the technique of building in stone. This first pyramid was stepped, unlike the later examples which were geometrically true pyramids with plain, sloping sides. The Step Pyramid was originally conceived as a mastaba tomb and only achieved its final form through a series of changes in plan. Successive enlargements imposed a stepped pyramid on a basic, flat-topped, square mastaba, so that ultimately it consisted of six enormous steps which rose to a hitherto unattained height of approximately two hundred feet. The burial chambers of the king and eleven members of his family were situated underneath the pyramid in the subterranean rock, as they would have been in a mastaba tomb; in later pyramids, the burial chamber was eventually moved into the pyramid structure itself.

The Step Pyramid was only the central and major element in a rectangular complex which was surrounded by a enclosure wall; the area between the pyramid and the wall was occupied by open courtyards, temple chambers used for ceremonials and the daily offerings made on behalf of the king, and shrines for the celebration of his jubilee (sed-festival) Some of these buildings were dummies, solidly built in stone, with no provision for internal chambers.

The Step Pyramid complex provides evidence of some interesting architectural developments. For the first time, the builders attempted to reproduce in stone those forms and structures which had hitherto only been designed in brick, wood and light materials. Thus, small blocks of limestone were used in the construction of this pyramid – these reflected the size of the mudbricks used in earlier buildings; stone doors are carved as though they were half-open on their sockets, imitating the wooden doors previously in use; and the architects have simulated in stone the papyrus, reed and other plant materials employed in primitive structures. For the first time fluted or ribbed stone columns appear; these represent the bundles of stems or the single stems of plants while the flowers of the plants form the capitals of the stone columns.The use of such columns was still experimental and the builders obviously considered it prudent to keep them attached to adjacent walls rather than to allow them to be free-standing supports. The encircling wall of the complex was panelled and bastioned, reflecting the recessed and panelled mudbrick walls which formed part of the mastaba tomb.

At the Step Pyramid site there was also a serdab (a cell-like chamber), which housed a limestone seated statue of the king (now in the Cairo Museum); there were slits in one wall of the serdab, which permitted the statue to 'look out' and partake of the food offerings presented outside the serdab.

Djoser's reputation as a great king survived for centuries. An inscription of Ptolemaic date on the island of Sehel at the First Cataract relates how the king, saddened by a seven year famine that afflicted Egypt, sought help and advice from his famous vizier *Imhotep and from the god Khnum, who was responsible for the Nile inundation.

BIBL. *CAH* i, ch xiv; Edwards, I. E. S. *The Pyramids of Egypt*. Harmondsworth: 1985, pp 53-89; Drioton, E. and Lauer, J-P. *Sakkarah. The Monuments of Zoser*. Cairo: 1939; Frith, C. M., Quibell, J. E. and Lauer, J-P. *The Step Pyramid*. (two vols) Cairo: 1935-6.

'Dynastic Race' c.3400 - 3100 BC.

There is a marked change in predynastic Egypt when the existing advanced neolithic culture with its complex tribal character was replaced by two kingdoms, one in the north and the other in the south. Three major developments also suddenly emerged, with no apparent background within Egypt – the concept of writing, monumental brick architecture, and significant advances in the arts and crafts.

There are two possible explanations for these changes: either they developed naturally from the indigenous culture in Egypt, or they came about because of the advent of a new people in the Nile Valley – the hypothetical 'Dynastic Race' who, although some evidence exists to support their occurence, are nevertheless discounted by many scholars. Excavations have indeed revealed human remains which display two distinctive and differently shaped types of skull and it has been suggested that one of these groups may be representative of an incoming people. The original homeland of such a 'race' is also speculative; some evidence suggests a strong association with Mesopotamia, or it has been proposed that these people may have come from an as yet undiscovered region, from which immigration occurred to both Egypt and Mesopotamia.

The similarities between the cultures of Egypt and Mesopotamia reach their height during the years prior to Egypt's First Dynasty and the Babylonian Jemdet Nasr period. Evidence of hieroglyphic writing first appears in Egypt in the First Dynasty, and at an earlier date in Mesopotamia. Although the languages have some affinities, it was probably only the concept and some general underlying principles that were transmitted, and Egypt soon developed its own characteristic language and script.

The great Egyptian mudbrick tombs, their facades decorated with recessed brick panelling, date from the First to the Third Dynasties and are typified by the mastaba tombs at Nagada. It has been suggested that a much earlier prototype exists for these in the form of the Mesopotamian temples.

With regard to design the Egyptian maceheads are reminiscent of Mesopotamian art; the earliest cylinder seals in Egypt are indistinguishable from the Mesopotamian examples of the Jamdat Nasr period, and these seals were also in use in Elam, Anatolia and north Syria. On the knife handles and stone palettes in Egypt, the artistic designs show composite animals which are typically Mesopotamian. One example – the Gebel el Arak knife, now in the Louvre Museum, depicts two scenes on its ivory handle: one is a hunting scene which shows a bearded man in Sumerian costume holding apart two lions, while the other represents a sea-battle against invaders, in which native Egyptian ships are apparently ranged against craft, *belims*, of the early Mesopotamian type.

However these facts are interpreted, it is most unlikely that any newcomers arrived in Egypt as a horde invasion; neither is indirect trade between Egypt and Mesopotamia a convincing argument to explain these features found in Egypt, since the influence seems to be one way and no evidence has been found of Egyptian transmission to early Mesopotamian culture. It is possible that the newcomers infiltrated Egypt over many years and perhaps came by different routes: some may have arrived via the Red Sea and perhaps the Wadi Hammamat and Koptos, whereas others entered through Syria and the Isthmus of Suez into the Delta. The Gebel el Arak knife indicates that at least some of the invaders came by sea and used military force.

These people may have settled in the Nile Valley and adopted native customs, and the lack of any permanent foreign influence on Egyptian culture would suggest that any infiltrations had ceased by the beginning of the First Dynasty. However, it cannot totally be ruled out that a hypothetical people may have provided an impetus for the development of Egypt's civilisation and that their descendants became the ruling class whose burial customs in particular were distinct from those of the indigenous population in the earliest dynasties. Nevertheless, even if there is some truth in this theory, it is clear that the two races had fused in the early historical period and had become indistinguishable in the general population.

BIBL. Kantor, H. J. Further evidence for the early Mesopotamian relations with Egypt. *JNES* 11 (1952) pp. 239-50; Derry, D.E. The Dynastic Race in Egypt. *JEA* 42 (1956) pp. 80-5; Engelbach, R. An essay on the advent of the Dynastic Race in Egypt and its consequences. *Ann. Serv.* pp. 193-221.

E

Esarhaddon   King of Assyria   681-669 BC.

Esarhaddon was the son of King *Sennacherib and he came into conflict with *Taharka, King of Egypt; details of his campaign against Egypt (which followed his subjugation of Syria) are preserved in cuneiform texts on stelae and tablets.

It is reported that he besieged Memphis and destroyed it, driving *Taharka back to the south. Booty and people were carried away from Egypt, and Esarhaddon introduced the policy of appointing new rulers, governors and officials to replace those whom he mistrusted. The newly appointed included *Necho of Sais who later became a king of the Twenty-sixth Dynasty.*Taharka was able briefly to repossess Memphis when Esarhaddon died as he set out on a new campaign, but the next *Assyrian ruler, *Ashurbanipal, regained the city in 662 BC and brought in new governors and officials to replace Esarhaddon's men who had fled from Memphis.

BIBL. Borger, R. Die Inschriften Asarhaddons Konigs von Assyrien. Osnabruck:1967; Pritchard, J. B. (Ed.) ANET 1969, Babylonian Chronicle, 292-4, 302-3.

Eusebius   Historian   c.AD 320.

Eusebius was one of the sources in whose writings *Manetho's Aegyptiaca was preserved (the others were *Josephus, *Africanus and *Syncellus). However, these present *Manetho in an abridged and sometimes contradictory form, and Eusebius' facts sometimes disagree with those of *Africanus.

Eusebius was a Christian chronographer and his writings in particular represent Egypt to later generations as a land where superstition and religious fanaticism prevailed; to some extent at least, he held a biased and ill-informed view of this ancient civilisation.

BIBL. Manetho (transl. by Waddell,W. G.) London 1940.

G

Ghilukhepa   Princess of Mitanni, wife of *Amenophis III c.1407 - 1379 BC.
Diplomacy between Egypt and her northern neighbours was occasionally
cemented by royal marriage. By the middle of the Eighteenth Dynasty, Egypt and
*Mitanni (the great northern Mesopotamian state, referred to as 'Nahrin' in the
ancient texts) had become major diplomatic partners, and the letters sent by the
*Mitannian king *Tushratta to the Egyptian royal family are preserved in the
archive at Tell el Amarna. From this source and from a commemorative scarab
issued in Year 10 of the reign of *Amenophis III, it is evident that Ghilukhepa
(Kirgipa), the daughter of King *Shuttarna and sister of his successor, *Tushratta,
came to Egypt to marry *Amenophis III, bringing with her a large entourage
including three hundred and seventeen women. The marriage consolidated
Egyptian-*Mitannian relations and was undoubtedly marked by the exchange of
substantial gifts.

Nothing more is heard of the *Mitannian princess, although *Tushratta sent his
greetings in his correspondence with the Egyptian royal family, and later, his niece
*Tadukhepa also entered the harem of *Amenophis III. Neither princess managed
to dislodge the Great Royal Wife *Tiye, from her supreme position at Court.

BIBL. Engelbach, R. A'Kirgipa' commemorative scarab of Amenophis III presented by His
Majesty King Farouk I to the Cairo Museum. *Ann. Serv.* 40 (1941) pp. 659-61.

Greeks   c. 664-30BC

The Greeks began to arrive in Egypt in substantial numbers during the Saite
Period, particularly in the reigns of *Psammetichus I and *Necho II. They came
first as mercenaries and enabled the Saite rulers to gain freedom from *Persian
domination, but later influxes included traders and tourists. Their first great
commercial city in Egypt was Naucratis, which was founded under
*Psammetichus I, and later *Necho II was obliged to confine Greek commercial
activity to Naucratis because of the strength of native protest against the Greek
merchants. Greek and *Phoenician mercenaries continued to support the Egyptian
kings of later periods, introducing new fighting techniques and modernising the
Egyptian army.

When *Alexander the Great conquered Egypt in 332 BC and was succeeded by
*Ptolemy I, the country came to be ruled by a dynasty of Macedonian Greeks. A
new fiscal and economic structure was introduced, and Greek cities such as

Alexandria and Ptolemais were established and Greek colonists also settled in the country districts. Alexandria became the great commercial centre, overshadowing Naucratis, and, with its famous Museum and Library, it was also recognised as a great intellectual centre, drawing scholars from all parts of the Mediterranean world.

The *Ptolemies adopted the role of Pharaoh and restored or built Egyptian temples throughout the country, including those at Edfu, Denderah, Philae, Esna and Kom Ombo. The conquerors introduced the Greek language and Greek customs, but the native population largely continued with their age-old practises. In some areas of the culture, hybrid forms developed: art in the tomb of *Petosiris is a good example of this. Generally it was in the new cities with their Greek theatres, gymnasia and chapels, that the Hellenistic culture predominated, while in the countryside, the Greek settlers were more inclined to absorb the existing Egyptian customs. Despite the kingdom's wealth, the native population enjoyed few benefits, and there was unrest which on occasions erupted into rebellions such as those in 208-186 BC and 88-86 BC which were centred around Thebes.

For the last century of Ptolemaic rule, Egypt became a client state of Rome, but in 30 BC, events brought *Augustus (Octavian) to Egypt as conqueror and emperor.

BIBL. Bevan, E. A. *History of Egypt under the Ptolemaic Dynasty.* London: 1927; Kienitz, F. K. *Die politische.*

Gyges   King of Lydia   c.660 BC.

A contemporary of the Egyptian ruler *Psammetichus I, an alliance was made between these two kings in c.655 or 654 BC, and it is probable that Gyges' action in sending troops to help Egypt enabled *Psammetichus I to overthrow the *Assyrian domination and establish a renewal of national power. This action also encouraged the kings of the Twenty-sixth Dynasty to pursue a policy of reliance on foreign and mercenary military support.

BIBL. Luckenbill,D. D. *Ancient Records of Assyria and Babylonia.* (two vols) Chicago: 1926-7 (1968), 2: para. 785.

H

Hadrian   Roman Emperor   AD 117 - 138.

The ward and eventually the successor of the emperor *Trajan, Hadrian was a conscientious emperor whose reign allowed the consolidation and development of the Roman Empire.

He travelled more extensively than any previous emperor and in AD 130, he spent several months in the Roman province of Egypt. There he participated in a great lion-hunt in the desert region west of the Delta, and held discussions with the scholars at the Museum in Alexandria. Accompanied by his wife Sabina and a large retinue, he also spent several days at the famed Colossi of Memnon at Thebes, to hear the 'singing statue'. Greek verses inscribed on the legs of the northern statue, composed by the Court-poetess Balbilla, tell how the statue sang in greeting for Hadrian on the second day of his visit.While he was in Egypt, Hadrian also suffered a personal tragedy when *Antinous, his friend and lover, was drowned in the Nile. The Emperor preserved the memory of *Antinous by founding a city,Antinoupolis,at the place where the young man died.

Various sacred buildings commemorate Hadrian's reign as Pharaoh of Egypt. With his predecessor *Trajan, he added reliefs to the Birth-House built by the Emperor *Augustus at the Temple of Hathor at Denderah; a temple was erected in his honour on the road to Armant from Medinet Habu; in the Temple of Isis on the island of Philae, Hadrian's Gateway was built; and in the Temple of Khnum at Esna there are important texts on the walls of the hypostyle hall.

BIBL. Von Groningen, B. A. *Preparatives to Hadrian's visit to Egypt. Studi in onore de A.Calderini, E R Paribeni.* Milan: 1957. II: 253-6.

Hardedef, Prince,   Reign of *Cheops,   c.2589 - 2566 BC.

Prince Hardedef, son of *Cheops who built the Great Pyramid at Giza, was revered by later generations as a sage. The Instruction in Wisdom which is accredited to him is the earliest extant example of this genre of literature, and, unlike some of the later texts, he may indeed have been the actual author of the piece. Addressed to his son, Au-ib-re, the text advises the boy to build wisely for the future, and is preserved on later records including a wooden tablet and ostraca. It was also claimed that Hardedef discovered certain spells from the Book of the Dead written in letters of lapis lazuli in the Temple of Thoth at Hermopolis. He also occurrs in the Westcar Papyrus as one of the princes who provided diversions to entertain King *Cheops, in his case introducing the famous magician Djedi to the Court.

Hardedef probably received a personal cult and was certainly esteemed by later generations; in the Middle Kingdom hymn, which was reputed to come from the tomb of King *Intef, the harpist sings that he has '...heard the sayings of *Imhotep and Hardedef with whose words men speak so often,' but he concludes that it is writings and books which endure far more successfully than the funerary monuments of even these wise and learned men.

Hardedef's tomb has been discovered: at Giza, to the east of the tomb of Crown Prince Kawab (another son of *Cheops) and of the pyramid of *Cheops himself. The decorations in Hardedef's tomb-chapel show evidence of malicious damage and his name and inscriptions are barely legible. This destruction may have resulted from dissension in the royal family relating to the succession after *Cheops' death.

BIBL.*AEL* i.pp 58-9. Brunner-Traut,E. Eine Kalksteinscherbe mit dem Text einer Niluberschwemmung zur Zeit Ramses III. *ZAS* 76 (1940) pp 3-9, pl. I.

Hatshepsut Ruler of Egypt 1503 - 1482 BC.

Hatshepsut was the daughter of *Tuthmosis I and Queen Ahmose, who was probably the younger sister of *Amenophis I. *Tuthmosis I's heir, his son *Tuthmosis II by a secondary queen Mutnefer, was married to Hatshepsut to strengthen his claim to the throne. *Tuthmosis II ruled Egypt for some eight years, dying prematurely in 1504 BC. His heir (whom he may have associated with him as co-regent) was his child by a concubine Isis, and perhaps to consolidate the boy's claim, he was married to Neferure, the daughter and apparently the only child of *Tuthmosis II and his chief wife Hatshepsut.

Because this boy, *Tuthmosis III, was very young on his accession, his stepmother Hatshepsut acted as his regent and at first she claimed only the titles she had used as *Tuthmosis II's principal queen – 'King's Daughter, King's Sister, God's Wife and King's Great Wife' – but in Year 2 of *Tuthmosis III's reign (1503 BC), she became joint pharaoh and was crowned as a king with full powers, titles and regalia. She was able to exercise power for almost twenty years, and although *Tuthmosis III was retained as her co-ruler, she was the senior pharaoh and held complete control. She was able to do this partly because of her stepson's youth, partly because she had the support of powerful officials including the priests of the god Amen-Re, and partly because of her own royal lineage which was greater than that of either her husband or her stepson.

Her claim to rule as the legitimate pharaoh was supported by fictitious scenes on the walls of her funerary temple at Deir el Bahri, where her divine birth is shown, as the offspring of the god Amen-Re (identified with her human father, *Tuthmosis I) and Queen Ahmose. Another ruler of this dynasty – *Amenophis III – had his divine birth similarly depicted on wall-scenes in the Temple of Luxor. Hatshepsut also preserved another fiction – that she was crowned while her father was still alive; these scenes again attempt to justify her reign as *Tuthmosis I's chosen heir. As pharaoh, particularly in Amen-Re's temple at Karnak, she was frequently shown in the pose and dress of a male ruler and the masculine forms of pronouns were often used in inscriptions which referred to her.

During the Queen's reign, the military policy of her forebears was suspended, and there is a reference only to one insignificant raid in Nubia. Instead, Hatshepsut concentrated on domestic policy and trading ventures, sending expeditions to *Byblos for timber, to Sinai for turquoise and to *Punt for incense. She also pursued an active building programme: an inscription in her small temple, the Speos Artemidos, states that she restored the sanctuaries of Middle Egypt which had been neglected since the *Hyksos period, while at Thebes, she honoured her patron god, Amen-Re.

Hatshepsut's chief courtier, *Senenmut, was the architect responsible for her Theban buildings and especially for the planning of the magnificent terraced funerary temple at Deir el Bahri. Here, as well as the scenes of the Queen's divine birth and coronation, the famous expedition to *Punt was recorded and also the transportation of the two obelisks by river from Elephantine to Karnak.

*Senenmut had entered the royal employ in the reign of *Tuthmosis II and he became the Queen's favourite courtier and the tutor to her daughter. His ambition and support were undoubtedly important factors in Hatshepsut's own political ascent. Eventually, *Tuthmosis III was fully grown and no longer willing to accept a subordinate role; he overthrew Hatshepsut's power and from 1457 BC he became sole ruler. The Queen may have died from natural causes, having outlived both *Senenmut (who died in or before Year 19) and her daughter Neferure (who died before Year 11). When she was merely principal queen, she had prepared a tomb in the cliff area near Deir el Bahri, but as a pharaoh, she had become eligible for a tomb in the Valley of the Kings, and this was excavated by Howard Carter in 1903. It was found to contain two sarcophagi, one of which was intended for her own burial while the other had been altered to receive the body of her father *Tuthmosis I, which she planned to transfer from its own original tomb. It is unlikely however, that she was ever buried in this tomb.

*Tuthmosis III, as sole ruler, now set out to reconquer possessions in Syria which had drifted from Egypt's influence during Hatshepsut's reign, and he also tried to obliterate all trace of his hated stepmother. Her statues were destroyed, walls were built around her obelisks at Karnak to conceal them, and her name was systematically erased from monuments. Later king-lists continue this denial of her reign by omitting her name from the records.

BIBL. Edgerton, W. F. *The Thutmosid Succession*. Chicago: 1933; Naville, E. *The Temple of Deir el Bahari*. (seven vols) London: 1894-1908; Sethe, K. *Das Hatschepsut-Problem noch einmal untersucht*.(Abh. Berlin, 1932, Nr. 4).Berlin:1932.

Herihor   High-priest of Amun   1100 - 1094 BC.

Herihor inaugurated the line of seven High-priests of Amun at Thebes who were to claim great power in the south during the late Twentieth and the Twenty-first Dynasties. Nothing is known of his background and early career, he probably came from quite humble origins and may have pursued an army career before becoming the First Prophet of Amun at Karnak, since he held the title of 'Commander of the Army', which he passed on to his son Piankh.

It was perhaps control of the army which initially enabled him to gain power, but he may also have consolidated his position as High-priest by marrying

Nodjme, probably the daughter of Amenhotep, the previous High-priest of Amun. It is likely that Herihor became High-priest shortly before Year 12 of the reign of *Ramesses XI. Soon after Year 17 he acquired further influence by taking on the titles and offices of *Pinehas, who was the 'King's Son of Kush' and 'Overseer of the Southern Countries'.

Scenes in the Temple of Khonsu at Karnak (started under *Ramesses III) are of particular interest with reagard to the extent of Herihor's powers. Here, building additions were made and decorated with scenes which showed Herihor and his pharaoh *Ramesses XI; in some of these Herihor appears to be the same size as the king when he performs ritual acts before the gods and his names and titles are enclosed in cartouches – a custom normally reserved for royal names. In scenes in the temple forecourt, he is shown wearing the royal uraeus and the Double Crown and also using the royal titulary for himself, with no reference to the king.

At one time, scholars considered that Herihor had taken over the throne on the death of *Ramesses XI or had even deposed him, but the evidence now indicates that, although Herihor had considerable influence at Thebes and ruled Upper Egypt from his residence there, this was always under the king's supreme jurisdiction, however nominal this may have been. Outside the Theban region the king undoubtedly still held sway, and the 'kingship' of Herihor was restricted to those scenes and inscriptions which occurred in the Khonsu temple at Karnak, which Herihor himself had ordered to be extended.

In Year 19 of Ramesses XI's reign, some event occurred which apparently ushered in a new and favourable era; this was marked by a device used in some other reigns – the so-called 'Repetition-of-Births' – to indicate a fresh and auspicious beginning, and henceforth the years of this reign were counted from Year 1 of this renaissance.These are still the regnal years of *Ramesses XI and do not indicate a different set of regnal years for Herihor.

Other information about this period is provided by the semi-fictitious story of *Wenamun, an envoy sent by Herihor to obtain timber from Syria. In this tale, Herihor is in control at Thebes while another couple – Nesbenebded and Tentamun – rule at Tanis in the Delta; the implication is that the god Amun has divided the kingdom between Herihor and Nesbenebded, while *Ramesses XI, the rightful king, probably still ruled nominally and resided at Memphis.

When *Ramesses XI died, Nesbenebded became the first king of the Twenty-first Dynasty and ruled from Tanis; from other sources he is known by the name of Smendes. Herihor's descendants continued, as High-priests of Amun, to rule the south from Thebes, and inherited the considerable powers of state that Herihor had acquired.

BIBL. Lefebvre, G. *Histoire des grands prêtres d'Amon de Karnak jusqu'a la XXIe dynastie*. Paris: 1929, pp 205 ff., 272 ff ; Kitchen, K. A. *3rd Int.* pp. 248 ff.

Herodotus Historian c.484 - 430 BC.

Herodotus is regarded as the 'Father of History'. The writings of Herodotus were the first attempt to separate fantasy from firsthand observation and factual evidence made available to the author.

Born at Halicarnassus between 490 and 480 BC, Herodotus travelled extensively and visited Egypt in c.450 BC, when the country was under *Persian domination. He eventually retired to Thurii, in Italy, where he expanded his *Histories* which provided an account of the events which led to the conflict between Greece and Persia. Book Two, called 'Euterpe', is a digression in which he concentrates on Egypt and includes much information from his own experience there as a tourist with a lively and enquiring mind. His travels in Egypt probably took him as far as the First Cataract, although his emphasis on the Delta region and the absence of any detailed account of the Theban monuments have led to speculation that his travels may not have been as widespread as he claimed. Also, although he was a clever reporter and wrote in a lively and informative manner, he obtained some of his facts from conversations with less than accurate informants, whom he met en route. Nevertheless, this provides the first comprehensive account of Egypt composed by a foreigner which has survived intact, and his example was followed, less successfully, by later writers such as *Diodorus Siculus and *Strabo.

Although some of the popular traditions that he quotes were not accurate and other statements cannot be checked against confirmed evidence, modern investigations have supported other claims that he makes and, for the later period of Egypt's history, he remains one of the major and most important sources.

The book is primarily a historical and geographical treatise; it deals with the geographical formations and the features of the landscape, including the source and inundation of the Nile, and the plants and animals, dealing particularly with the strange characteristics of the hippopotamus, ibis, phoenix and crocodile. The latter were adorned with gold earrings and bracelets and were fed with human victims; after death they were mummified.

Herodotus' account of the history of Egypt is based on information given to him by the priests, and it contains many inaccuracies, although he correctly named Menes as the first king who built the first town. The characters and actions of *Cheops, *Chephren and *Mycerinus are also described, and he includes personal details such as *Amasis' frequent drunkenness. Herodotus also comments on the hieroglyphic system as well as the monuments he visited; these included the pyramids (which he correctly identified as royal burial-places), the Labyrinth and Lake Moeris in the Fayoum, temples at Sais and Bubastis, and the great city of Memphis.

He was the first foreign observer to describe the Egyptian religious beliefs and customs: festivals, magical rites, interpretation of dreams, and animal cults. He claimed that the Egyptians were the most religious of people and he tried to identify the forerunners of the Greek gods amongst the Egyptian pantheon. His description of the process of mummification remains one of the basic sources of knowledge of these techniques, and modern scientific investigations have shown that his account is mainly accurate. However, the reason he gives for the development of this custom – to preserve the body so that the soul (having passed through various animal incarnations) could return to it on a future occasion – was not correct, because the Egyptians did not believe in the transmigration of souls.

Despite its shortcomings, Herodotus' account of Egypt nevertheless provides a stimulating and entertaining view seen through the eyes of an early traveller.

BIBL. Herodotus, *The Histories* Book II. London: 1939; Africa, T. W. Herodotus and Diodorus on Egypt. *JNES* 22 (1963) pp. 254 ff.; Engelbach, R.and Derry, D. E. Introduction:Herodotus with notes on his Text. *Ann.Serv.* 41 (1942) pp. 235-69; Herodotus. *The Histories*.Harmondsworth: 1972.

Hetepheres Queen c.2613 - 2589 BC.

The wife of *Sneferu and mother of *Cheops, Hetepheres outlived her husband and was probably originally buried by her son in a tomb at Dahshur. In 1925 G. A. Reisner and the Harvard expedition were excavating the area to the front of the east side of the Great Pyramid at Giza when they uncovered the concealed entrance to a tomb-shaft which led to a second and secret tomb belonging to this queen.

In about the fifteenth year of his reign, *Cheops, learning that his mother's original tomb had been plundered, ordered the removal of her surviving burial goods to a new tomb near his own pyramid. This was carried out with the utmost secrecy to avoid any further desecration, and the alabaster coffin, chipped by the thieves who had tried to remove the lid, was taken to the new tomb. The archaeologists found this to be empty, but the viscera from the queen's body remained, contained within a separate alabaster canopic chest which had been hidden in a niche in the wall. These viscera are of considerable importance because they indicate that mummification (in which the viscera were removed from the body through an abdominal incision) was already in practice for the royal family in the early Fourth Dynasty.

Silver bracelets inlaid with stones representing butterflies, have survived from the queen's jewellery. She was also supplied with a carrying-chair, a gold-cased and inlaid bed and canopy, an armchair, pottery, linen and gold toilet objects. The furniture had collapsed but it has been carefully and skilfully restored and can now be seen in the Cairo Museum. Hetepheres' funerary goods are important because they provide an insight into the quality of design and the materials which were in use at that period.

BIBL. Reisner, G. A. and Smith, W. S. A. *History of the Giza Necropolis, Vol.2: The Tomb of Hetepheres, the mother of Cheops.* Cambridge, Mass. 1955.

Hittites c.1740 - 1190 BC.

In the second millennium BC, the 'Land of Hatti' emerged first as a state and then as an empire, created by kings who ruled from a mountainous homeland in the north of Asia Minor (Anatolia). The name 'Hittite' has been applied to these people by modern scholarship; they established their power over a wide area, coming into contact and conflict with other great states of the area, particularly Egypt and *Assyria. Although they are mentioned in the Old Testament, the extent of their influence is most clearly expressed in the *Assyrian cuneiform inscriptions, and in such Egyptian records as the historical inscriptions which recount the battles and campaigns, and the royal archive at Tell el Amarna.

Excavation of the capital city of the Hittites – Boghazkoy – and the discovery there of the state archive of cuneiform tablets has increased knowledge of their civilisation, so that it is evident that they excelled in military matters, in political and legal organisation, and in the administration of justice.

During the reign of *Akhenaten, because the Egyptians then paid less attention to their northern empire and vassal states, the Hittites were able to push forward their own conquests in Syria, but the Ramesside kings, *Sethos I and *Ramesses II, renewed Egypt's military ambitions in Syria/Palestine and thus came into direct conflict with the Hittites. Eventually, their hostilities were brought to an end by the Egypto-Hittite Treaty, and thereafter the two royal families entered into cordial relations, exchanging letters and gifts. *Ramesses II's marriage to a Hittite princess further strengthened this alliance.

The revitalisation of *Assyria heralded a new conflict, and the Hittite lands were ultimately subdued and became provinces of the *Assyrian Empire.

BIBL. Gurney, O. R. *The Hittites*. Harmondsworth: 1964; Mercer, S. A. B. *The Tell el-Amarna Tablets*. Toronto:1939.

Horemheb   King   1348 - 1320 BC.

Horemheb came of unknown parentage from the town of Hnes and rose to become king of Egypt. During *Akhenaten's reign, he was the 'Great Commander of the Army', and it is possible that his wife Mudnodjme (who appears with him in the Turin statue-group) was *Nefertiti's sister and that this marriage was destined to raise him from obscurity and ultimately to provide some justification for his claim to the throne.

Under *Tutankhamun, he became King's Deputy and undertook extensive administrative duties. It was during these years, before he became aware that he would become king, that he prepared a magnificent tomb at Saqqara which has been excavated and studied: the wall-reliefs, many of which are now scattered throughout museums around the world, demonstrate the superb quality of the art and reflect the earlier military stages of his career.

When *Ay died, Horemheb became king, probably because there was no living royal heir. It is probable that he was already *Ay's co-regent, and the Coronation Statue in Turin implies that there was a smooth transition from *Ay to Horemheb, although it has been speculated that the two men were rivals and that *Ay had pre-empted Horemheb by seizing the kingship when *Tutankhamun died.

On his accession Horemheb obviously had the support of the army and of the orthodox priesthood of Amun at Karnak. His reign was devoted to the restoration of unity and stability and, in his inscriptions, he dated his reign as if it succeeded immediately after that of *Amenophis III, thus disregarding as illegitimate those rulers who were associated with *Akhenaten and the Amarna Period.

Horemheb probably established his capital at Memphis and set out to re-organise the country. According to his Edict, badly preserved on a stela at Karnak, he took firm measures to restore law and order: the army was now divided and placed under two (northern and southern) commanders; abuses which had flourished in central and local government in Akhenaten's reign were now eliminated, thus easing the oppression of the poor; and the king instituted law-courts in all the major cities, appointing priests from the temples and mayors from the towns as judges who were directly responsible to him. Distrust of the old nobility led him to appoint to the re-established temples priests who were drawn from the army. To improve the people's morale and to enable them to worship again in a traditional manner, he repaired and refurbished the temples that had been neglected during the Amarna interlude; he endowed them with estates and appointed new priests and officials. Gradually, Horemheb sought to obliterate the worst excesses of corruption in the judiciary and the tax collection system, and to restore and renew old beliefs and values.

His major building programme included preliminary work on the Great Hypostyle Hall at Karnak. He usurped his predecessors' monuments including *Tutankhamun's wall-reliefs at the Temple of Luxor and *Ay's Theban funerary temple. The extent of his action against the heretic *Akhenaten remains unclear. He may have been responsible for razing Akhetaten (Amarna) to the ground, desecrating the Royal Tomb, and dismantling the Aten temples at Thebes and using the material from these as infill for the pylons in the Temple of Karnak. It is possible that it was the subsequent Ramesside rulers rather than Horemheb who were most active in destroying traces of the Amarna kings.

Horemheb prepared a large tomb for himself in the Valley of the Kings at Thebes, equipped with a fine red granite sarcophagus. The tomb was discovered by Theodore M. Davis in 1908, but it had been heavily plundered and there was no trace of a body.

At his death, Horemheb left a strong, unified country to his successor, Ramesses I, who was also a man of humble origins who had pursued an army career; his brief reign introduced the Ramesside Period and his descendants made every attempt to restore Egypt's glory.

BIBL. Hari, R. *Horemheb et la Reine Moutnedjemet*. Geneva: 1965; Hornung, E. *Das Grab des Haremhab in Tal der Konige*. Berne: 1971; Pfluger, K. The Edict of King Haremhab. *JNES* 5 (1946) pp. 260-8; Martin, G. E. Excavation reports on the Tomb of Horemheb at Saqqara. *JEA* 62 (1976) pp. 5 ff, 63 (1977) pp. 13 ff, 64 (1978) pp. 5 ff, 65 (1979) pp. 13 ff.

Huni King 2637 - 2613 BC.

Huni is named in the Turin Canon and the Saqqara List as the last ruler of the Third Dynasty, and he appears in the Papyrus Prisse as the immediate predecessor of *Sneferu; he was the father of Queen *Hetepheres, who represented the direct line of the royal family, and also probably of *Sneferu, who was born to Meresankh, one of Huni's minor queens. *Sneferu was married to *Hetepheres, the divine heiress and probably his sister, to ensure his claim to the throne. This was typical of royal marriages in the early Old Kingdom, when brothers frequently married their sisters to establish their dynastic rights.

A conical piece of red granite discovered on the Island of Elephantine and inscribed with Huni's name records the founding of a building which may have been a fortress on the island, forming part of the old border between Egypt and

Nubia. It is possible that the stepped pyramid at Medum may have been started in Huni's reign and finished by *Sneferu, who was probably responsible for the change in its design when the steps were filled in and the monument was converted into a true pyramid.

BIBL. Rowe, A. Excavations of the Eckley B. Coxe, Jr, Expedition at Meydum, Egypt, 1929-30. *Museum Journal*, Pennsylvania, March 1931; Borchadt, L. Konig Huni (?). *ZAS* 49 (1909) pp. 12-13.

Huye   Viceroy of Nubia   reign of *Tutankhamun   1361 - 1352 BC.

Huye held the post of Nubian Viceroy under *Tutankhamun. His rock-cut tomb, situated in the hill of Qurnet Murai at Thebes, dates to the end of the Eighteenth Dynasty and is the most important tomb in this area. Indeed, it provides one of the most important monuments of *Tutankhamun's brief reign, for the wall-scenes provide much information regarding the governor's administration during this period of the province from El Kab to Napata.

This area produced most of Egypt's gold and this is evident in the tomb scenes. One series shows his investiture as Viceroy and he is also seen receiving the tribute of his province. The exotic landscape of Nubia is represented, with huts, palm-trees and giraffes, and the tribute illustrates the variety and wealth of goods produced by this district. It includes gold rings, gold-dust in sacks, jewels and ebony items. The *Nubian chiefs are also shown, accompanying Huye from Nubia and being presented to him and his brother, Amenhotep.

Huye may also have been responsible for the construction of *Tutankhamun's great temple to Amen-Re at Gebel Barkal in Nubia.

BIBL. Reisner, G. A. The Viceroys of Ethiopia. *JEA* 6 (1920) pp. 28-55, 73-88; Davies, N. de G. and Gardiner, A. H. *The Tomb of Huy, Viceroy of Nubia in the reign of Tutankhamun.* London: 1926.

Hyksos   Kings   Dynasty 15: 1674-1567 BC; Dynasty 16: c.1684-1567 BC.

During the Second Intermediate Period, Egypt was ruled by a line of kings known as the Hyksos. According to the historian *Manetho (as preserved in *Africanus), there were six Hyksos kings in the Fifteenth Dynasty, thirty-two in the Sixteenth Dynasty, and during the Seventeenth Dynasty the Hyksos and the princes of Thebes ruled concurrently. *Josephus, quoting *Manetho, claimed that the Hyksos were a people of obscure racial origin who invaded Egypt from the east and subdued the country without a blow. They overpowered the Egyptian ruler, burnt the cities and temples of the gods and appointed a Hyksos leader, Salitis, as king. He exacted tribute from the Egyptians and lived at Memphis; a city known as Avaris (situated somewhere in the eastern Delta) became the Hyksos capital. *Josephus interpreted the name 'Hyksos' to mean 'Shepherd Kings' or 'captive shepherds', which lent support to his theory that the period of Hyksos rule was reflected in the Biblical story of the Israelite sojourn in Egypt. More recent theories have speculated on the origin of the Hyksos – whether they formed a mass invasion of new people and whether they included large numbers of Hurrians, an Indo-European group from Mesopotamia. The evidence indicates that the Hyksos should probably not be regarded as an entire race but rather as a group of Palestinian leaders who, perhaps because of the pressure of new migrations in the north in c.1700 BC, were pushed down into Egypt. The term 'Hyksos' is in fact derived from the Egyptian title which meant 'rulers of foreign countries'; this had been in use for centuries as a term of reference for the tribesmen who lived along and regularly harrassed Egypt's north-eastern borders.

During the Thirteenth Dynasty, the country had become fragmented under a line of weak rulers and consequently, the Hyksos (who were probably of predominantly Semitic origin) were able to penetrate Egypt's borders, first taking the eastern Delta and finally controlling the whole country. They were apparently successful in dominating Lower and Middle Egypt but by 1600 BC, the southern princes of Thebes and local rulers in Nubia exhibited a marked degree of independence and autonomy. Under their princes *Seqenenre Tao II, *Kamose, and *Amosis I, the Thebans ultimately drove the Hyksos from Egypt and established the New Kingdom with the Eighteenth Dynasty.

The Hyksos invaders were not a new ethnic force but consisted of the leaders of those same tribes who has always harrassed Egypt. In effect, they provided a change of rulership, but they took over the existing Egyptian administration and officials and they appear to have respected and encouraged Egyptian civilisation, introducing no distinctive new culture of their own. The later native traditions gave a biased account of them as cruel and impious, but this would seem to have been exaggerated; indeed, their rule and imposition of tribute was probably very similar to the pattern established by earlier native kings.

The city of Avaris was situated in the eastern Delta, although its exact location remains uncertain – it may have stood where Tanis was later built or at the site of Qantir, several miles further south. The Hyksos adopted Seth as their royal patron god, but their form of the deity seems to have had more in common with the Asiatic god Baal than with the evil divinity found in Egyptian mythology. The anarchy and destruction that later records attribute to the Hyksos were almost certainly propogandist, attempting to glorify the Theban princes who had 'saved' Egypt. Nevertheless, the Hyksos interlude changed some basic Egyptian attitudes: the pharaohs of the Eighteenth Dynasty pursued an aggressive rather than a defensive foreign policy, establishing a political and military buffer for Egypt by bringing the petty states of Syria-Palestine under their control and influence. The Hyksos period was also the time when various technical and military developments were introduced into Egypt, including forts, metalworking advances, new weapons, the use of horses and chariots, the vertical loom, and the lute and the lyre.

BIBL. Save-Soderbergh, T. The Hyksos rule in Egypt. *JEA* 37 (1951) pp. 53-71; Van Seters, J. *The Hyksos*. New Haven: 1966; Labib, P. *Die Herrschaft der Hyksos in Agypten und ihr Sturz*. Gluckstadt:1937.

I

Imhotep   Vizier   reign of *Djoser 2667 - 2648 BC.
Imhotep (the Greek version of his name is Imouthes) was a man of obscure origins and was the son neither of a king nor of a vizier. He became the architect and vizier of king *Djoser of the Third Dynasty and he held the titles of 'Hereditary Prince', 'King's Sealer' and 'Royal Carpenter and Mason'.

Today he is best known for the unique funerary complex which he designed and built for King *Djoser at Saqqara; this is the earliest known building in the world which was constructed of stone and indeed, *Manetho accredits Imhotep with the invention of building in stone. The central feature is a Step Pyramid; this was designed to mark the king's burial place and was probably a development of the earlier mastaba-type tomb. Many architectural innovations were used in this complex and new building techniques and materials were introduced. The extensive complex, with its courts and chapels, was never repeated although the pyramid form was retained for royal burials for several hundred years.

Few facts of Imhotep's life and work are known, but the oldest Wisdom Texts (which unfortunately have not survived) were attributed to him, and he apparently acted as adviser to the king on many matters. A rock inscription of Ptolemaic date on the island of Sehel at the First Cataract recalls that *Djoser sought help and counsel from Imhotep following a seven year period of famine, and that this brought about successful results.

It was as a physician that Imhotep was most revered, and he was deified and worshipped as a god of medicine and healing in the Late Period. Deification of kings or men was rare in Egypt and only a few rulers and wise men received such cults. Later, the *Greeks in Egypt identified him with their own god of medicine, Asklepios, and his chapel at Saqqara (known as the Asklepieion) became a centre to which cripples came from all parts of Egypt, in search of healing. He enjoyed widespread popularity, and buildings within various temple complexes were dedicated to him, including those at Karnak, Deir el Bahri and Deir el Medina. On the island of Philae, *Ptolemy V built a chapel in honour of Imhotep.

He enjoyed great renown amongst both Egyptians and *Greeks, and statues of the later periods show him as a priest: his head is shaven and he holds a papyrus roll, the symbol of learning and wisdom. Although Saqqara was his chief cult-centre and presumably his burial place, all attempts to discover his tomb there have failed.

BIBL. Sethe, K. *Imhotep der Asklepios der Agypten.*(Unters. 2, iv). Leipzig: 1902; Hurry, J. B. *Imhotep*. Oxford: 1926.

Ipuwer   Literary 'sage'   c.1786 - 1633 BC (?).

The text known as the *Admonitions of a Prophet* (preserved in a Nineteenth Dynasty papyrus in Leyden) descibes a time of chaos and devastation in Egypt, when law and order broke down, the fortunes of the rich and poor were reversed, and groups of foreigners (the '*Asiatics') entered Egypt. The aged king, protected from the true horrors of the situation by his courtiers, remained at his palace and was unaware of the social and political upheaval that was tearing his realm apart. However, a sage arrived at the palace; this was Ipuwer, who proceeded to relate these events to the king and urged that the only way to return to peace was through personal piety and a renewed reverence for the gods. There are no other facts which relate to Ipuwer's status or background although, from details in the text, it has been suggested that he was a treasury official who had come to the Court to report on the depletion of the treasury in the Delta.

This text is of great literary and historical interest and has much in common with other pieces (such as the 'Prophecy of *Neferti') in the genre known as the Pessimistic Literature. It has long been surmised that this text describes events which occurred at the end of the Old Kingdom, when centralised government based at Memphis collapsed and chaos ensued – a situation exacerbated by the declining power of the king, *Pepy II, who ruled for over ninety years. There are other interpretations, however, which claim that it reflects conditions at a different period – the Thirteenth Dynasty, when the Middle Kingdom was collapsing prior to the *Hyksos invasion of Egypt. Another explanation is that it does not relate to any specific period but that it is a literary form which sets out to explore, through poetry, the themes of national disaster and of order versus chaos. This provided the opportunity to emphasise that, in order to ensure stability and good government, a strong and vigorous king was essential to the Egyptian political system.

BIBL. *AEL* i. pp. 149-162; Gardiner, A. H. *The Admonitions of an Egyptian Sage from a Hieratic papyrus in Leiden* (*Pap. Leiden* 344 recto). Leipzig: 1909; Faulkner, R. O. Notes on 'The Admonitions of an Egyptian sage'. *JEA* 50 (1964) pp. 24-36. Notes on the Admonitions of an Egyptian sage. *JEA* 51 (1965) pp. 53-62.

Ipuy   Engraver   reign of *Ramesses II   1304-1237 BC.

The scenes in the tombs, belonging to craftsmen who lived at the royal workmen's town of Deir el Medina at Thebes, have preserved a vivid and colourful account of their activities and aspirations.

Ipuy was an engraver during the reign of *Ramesses II and the scenes in his tomb at Deir el Medina illustrate a range of subjects, including the manufacture and preparation of his funerary furniture and his funeral procession. There are also agricultural activities such as wine-pressing, and a famous scene shows Ipuy working a shaduf (ancient water device) to bring water from the river to nurture the plants in his garden, while his pet dog looks on.

Intef (Inyotef), Rulers of the Eleventh Dynasty   2133 - 1991 BC.

Intef or Inyotef was the family name of those Theban nobles who established the Eleventh Dynasty and restored some order after the troubled events and civil wars of the First Intermediate Period; they laid the foundations for the establishment of the Middle Kingdom which was introduced by the Twelfth Dynasty.

Although there is some confusion about the exact identity and order of the succession of some of these rulers, it appears that the founder of the Intef line was a local governor, later known as Intef the Great, who bore the title of 'Hereditary Prince'.

The Intefs fought against the rulers of the Tenth Dynasty who were based at Heracleopolis, and overthrew them, thus laying the foundation for unity and order to return to Egypt. They were buried at Thebes in a series of unusual 'saff' or 'row' tombs which have been excavated in the necropolis below the slopes of Dira Abu'n Naga.

The greatest rulers of this line were *Mentuhotep II (Nebhepetre) and *Mentuhotep III (S'ankhkare) who were powerful and effective kings.

BIBL. Winlock, H. E. *The rise and fall of the Middle Kingdom in Thebes*. New York: 1947; Newberry, P. E. On the parentage of the Intef kings of the Eleventh Dynasty. ZÄS 72 (1936) pp. 118-20.

J

Jews.

According to Biblical tradition, *Joseph, sold into slavery and sent down to Egypt, eventually gained status and wealth and brought his family (the tribe of Israel) to his new homeland. Centuries later, their descendants became part of the workforce persecuted by the Ramesside pharaohs and they were ultimately led out of Egypt by *Moses and established themselves in the Land of Israel.

Although there is no mention of these events in any Egyptian inscriptions which have as yet come to light, there is information which relates to the lives of Jews resident in Egypt at a later period. The discovery of a large collection of Aramaic papyri at Elephantine has shown that a sizeable Jewish community was present there during the *Persian period. At this time, Elephantine had become a large garrison colony and the Jews were part of the influx of foreigners who had now settled in Egypt. On this island they lived in proximity to the priests of the Egyptian ram-headed god Khnum and, from the papyri, it is evident that the temple to Yahweh which the Jews had been allowed to build at Elephantine, was burnt to the ground. They then petitioned the Persian governor of Judah to allow the temple to be rebuilt, and eventually, after considerable delay, it was restored.

Relations between the Egyptians and the Jews in later times are chronicled in the Bible. Sometimes there were conflicts, as when the Egyptian king 'Shishak' (probably a Twenty-second Dynasty pharaoh) attacked Jerusalem and removed the treasure, but on other occasions, the Pharaohs responded to appeals and protected the Jewish rulers against new and expansionist powers in the Near East, such as *Nebuchadrezzar II of Babylon.

BIBL. Redford, D. B. *A study of the Biblical story of Joseph Genesis 37-50*. Leiden: 1970; Kitchen, K. A. *Ancient Orient and Old Testament*. London: 1966, pp. 57 ff. 156 ff; Gordon, C. E. The religion of the Jews of Elephantine in the light of the Hermopolis papyri. *JNES* 28 (1969) pp. 116 ff; Kraeling, E. G. *The Brooklyn Museum Aramaic Papyri*. New Haven: 1953.

Joseph   Biblical person.

The story of Joseph is preserved in the Biblical Book of Genesis (Ch.37-50): the son of Jacob, he was sold into slavery by his jealous half-brothers and was sent down to Egypt where he entered the household of a wealthy Egyptian, Potiphar. His master came to respect him and made him overseer of the household, but the lies of Potiphar's wife finally brought Joseph to prison. He was subsequently released to interpret Pharaoh's dream and eventually he acquired great power, prestige and wealth, becoming vizier of the country.

61

His family – the tribe of Israel – were brought to Egypt to share in his good fortune, and his descendants remained there for some four hundred and thirty years, until a later king (probably one of the Ramesside rulers) forced them to work on building sites. Finally, *Moses led these people out of Egypt and they settled in a new homeland. When he died, it is said that Joseph was embalmed and buried in a coffin in Egypt, according to the traditions of the land.

There is no existing reference in the Egyptian records to either the sojourn in Egypt or to the Exodus, and therefore no conclusive dates can be established for these events. According to the historian *Josephus, the arrival of the *Hyksos in Egypt and their subsequent expulsion by the princes of Thebes could be identified with the arrival of the tribe of Israel and their Exodus. This theory has a major discrepancy for the *Hyksos were driven out whereas the Children of Israel made every effort to escape from the country and from pharaoh.

It has been suggested that Joseph may have entered Egypt at some time between the Old Kingdom (c.2340 BC) and the *Hyksos period (c.1650 BC), when it is known that groups of Semitic people were arriving and settling there, in the eastern Delta and in Upper Egypt. There has also been an intriguing attempt to identify Joseph with *Yuya, the father-in-law of *Amenophis III.

BIBL. Redford, D. B. *A study of the Biblical story of Joseph (Genesis 37-50)*. Leiden: 1970; Vergote, J. *Joseph en Egypte, Genese, 37-50, A la lumière des études égyptologiques recentes*. Louvain: 1950; Rowley, H. H. *From Joseph to Joshua*. London: 1950; *The Bible, Book of Genesis*, chs. 37, 39-50.

Josephus Historian c.AD 70.

Flavius Josephus was a Jewish historian whose writings were much used by Renaissance scholars as a basic source for ancient Egypt; they preserve, in heavily edited extracts, the chronological list of the kings of Egypt originally compiled by *Manetho. Although incomplete, this list forms one of the main sources for the modern reconstruction of Egypt's history. Josephus' account also contains comments on such religious matters as the possible relationship between the *Hyksos, *Joseph, *Moses and the Exodus, and it reproduces other tales accredited to *Manetho, such as the wars of *Sethos I and of *Ramesses II. Josephus claims that he quotes the exact words of *Manetho when he discusses the actions of the *Hyksos, although there is no other evidence the substantiate this. Since source material for the *Hyksos interlude is relatively scanty, his comments must be taken into account.

He states that the *Hyksos were an obscure race who came from the east and invaded Egypt in the reign of an unidentified Tutimaios, seizing the country without striking a blow. Their subsequent actions were ruthless: they burnt cities and razed temples to the ground, and they massacred or enslaved the native population. A *Hyksos leader, Salitis, was appointed king and he ruled at Memphis and built a new capital at Avaris in the Delta. Josephus also provides the names of Salitis' *Hyksos successors.

He believed that this account of the *Hyksos invasion represented the events that occur in the Biblical story of the sojourn in Egypt and he interpreted the name

'*Hyksos' as meaning 'Shepherd Kings' or 'captive shepherds', which lent support to this theory. His interpretation of the name '*Hyksos' was inaccurate and subsequently it has been shown that the name was derived from the Egyptian term which meant 'chieftains of foreign lands.'

BIBL. Josephus, *The Works of Flavius Josephus*.(trans.by William Whiston). New York:1887.

K

Kagemni Vizier c.2345 - 2181 BC .

Kagemni was a vizier and judge during the reigns of three kings during the Sixth Dynasty. His tomb, which lies to the right of that of *Mereruka at Saqqara, was excavated in 1893 and contains ten chambers. The wall-scenes in this tomb reflect the customary range of ceremonies and activities found in Old Kingdom mastaba-tombs: there are various agricultural pursuits and Kagemni is shown hunting in the marshes and inspecting fisheries as well as receiving gifts from his attendants. Generally, the tomb-scenes of this period reflect the everyday activities of the people employed on the great estates and provide a valuable insight into the lives of the great nobles their families and of their estate workers.

Kagemni's name is also known from a papyrus of the Middle Kingdom (c.1900 BC), which is now in Paris. In this text (often known as the 'Instruction for Kagemni') part of which is lost, it is clear that King *Huni (who ruled at the end of the Third Dynasty) had instructed his vizier to write down his own wisdom and experience to act as a guide for his children, among whom is the future vizier, Kagemni. The vizier, Kagemni, who possessed the tomb at Saqqara would have been alive several hundred years later, but the Middle Kingdom author of this text probably recalled Kagemni as the name of a famous Old Kingdom vizier and therefore included him in the text.

This genre of literature is sometimes referred to as 'Instructions' or 'Wisdom Literature'; these texts are believed to have originated during the Old Kingdom, and they are customarily couched in terms of advice given by an older man to his young charges.They offer counsel on how to pursue a successful course in life, and generally embody the Egyptian concepts of ethical and moral behaviour.

BIBL. Gardiner, A. H. The Instruction addressed to Kagemni and his brethren. *JEA* 32 (1946) pp. 71-4; *AEL* i.pp. 59-60; Gunn, B. *The Instruction of Ptah-hotep and the Instruction of Ke' gemni.* London: 1918.

Kamose, Prince of Thebes, Ruler of the Seventeenth Dynasty, c.1570(?) - 1567 BC.

The elder son of the Theban ruler *Seqenenre Ta'o II, Kamose continued the attempt to oust the *Hyksos kings from Egypt and, he is the first person for whom there still exists a historical account of the military actions that he took against these foreigners.

Two stelae set up in the Temple of Karnak record his campaign; one survives in fragments only but the beginning of the account is preserved on the Carnarvon

Tablet. This was discovered in Lord Carnarvon's excavations and was a scribe's copy, in hieratic, of the stela inscription. The second (known as the Kamose Stela) continues the narrative of the first stela. The narrative relates that in Year 3 of his reign (c.1575 BC), Prince Kamose discussed with his courtiers the plan to attack the *Hyksos king Auserre *Apophis. Egypt was relatively stable and peaceful (perhaps because *Apophis and *Seqenenre Ta'o II had concluded an uneasy truce) and the courtiers advised Kamose not to fight, but his pride and his desire to restore native rule throughout the whole country urged him on. In his own words, he stated 'My desire is to deliver Egypt and to smite the *Asiatics'.

In a surprise attack, Kamose took the initiative against *Apophis, who was driven from Middle Egypt. It is possible that Kamose briefly penetrated northwards as far as the *Hyksos capital of Avaris and he seems to have recovered most of Egypt south of Memphis. He recalled how he razed the towns and burnt the places of the Egyptians, as punishment for their co-operation with the *Hyksos kings. Finally, he returned to Thebes as a triumphant victor and received a great welcome, but an early death prevented him from launching another campaign in the Delta.

His mummy and coffin were discovered by Mariette's workmen in 1857, reburied in the rubble near his tomb; the reburial had probably been carried out by priests in order to prevent desecration of the body by tomb-robbers. The coffin was ungilded and the mummy was so poorly preserved that it immediately disintegrated; there were some items of jewellery and personal possessions, including a fine dagger. One item of jewellery bore the name of *Amosis I, who was Kamose's younger brother and successor; he married Kamose's daughter, *Ahmose-Nefertari, and continued the campaign to rid Egypt of the *Hyksos.

The evidence provided by Kamose's campaign indicates that the *Hyksos probably never occupied the whole country and that their power was concentrated mainly in the Delta and Middle Egypt. Although the Theban princes were probably forced to pay them tribute for a period of time, it is unlikely that the Thebans ever lost autonomy in their own territory.

BIBL. Habachi, L. *The Second Stela of Kamose.* Gluckstadt: 1972; Gardiner, A. H. The defeat of the Hyksos by Kamose: the Carnarvon Tablet, No.1. *JEA* 3 (1916) pp. 95-110; Gunn, B. and Gardiner, A. H. New Renderings of Egyptian texts: II. *JEA* 5 (1918) pp. 36-56; Winlock, H. E. The tombs of the kings of the Seventeenth Dynasty. *JEA* 10 (1924) pp. 217-77.

Keftians c.1567 - 1320 BC.

Some courtiers' tombs of the Eighteenth Dynasty contain wall-scenes which depict foreign peoples bringing tribute to Egypt. Amongst these are a group described as 'Men of Keftiu' and of the 'Islands in the midst of the Sea'. They carry gold and silver, precious stones, copper, bronze, ivory and distinctive metal vases of various shapes. In the tomb of Menkheperresoneb (High Priest of Amun under *Tuthmosis III), the leader of the Keftians is shown with the princes of the *Hittites, of Tunip in Syria, and of Kadesh, kneeling and offering tribute, but the Keftians were not subjects of Egypt and this scene overstates their submission.

They came to Egypt rather as envoys and ambassadors, bringing objects for the treasury and gifts for the Court, but also receiving other goods in exchange. They probably remained in Egypt for several months and then returned home.

The location of Keftiu and the origin of its people remain uncertain. It has been suggested that it could be equated with the Biblical Caphtor, and there is still speculation as to whether Keftiu was Crete or some part of Asia Minor, although many scholars accept that the Keftians were envoys sent to Egypt from Minoan Crete and that the 'People of the Islands in the midst of the Sea' were representatives of other Aegean islands then under Crete's control. The 'Minoan' influence on Egyptian art during the Eighteenth Dynasty is particularly noticeable in certain vase shapes and decorative motifs and also in the naturalistic composition of some hunting and battle scenes. It may also have influenced the wall decoration of the royal palaces at Malkata and Amarna, and in the tombs, Minoan and Mycenaean pottery was placed as treasured possessions.

The Keftians are first mentioned in New Kingdom scenes and inscriptions, but Egypt had already established contact with Crete during the Middle Kingdom when it is obvious that a cross-fertilisation of ideas occurred. Although fewer Egyptian objects have been found in Minoan contexts, quantities of the polychrome decorated ware of Cretan manufacture have been revealed at a number of Twelfth Dynasty sites in the Fayoum and elsewhere. These occur in larger numbers than in the New Kingdom and come mainly from domestic rather than tomb contexts. Such pottery may have entered Egypt through an intermediary or through trading routes. Although no reference to the Keftians in Egypt occurs as early as the Middle Kingdom, it is at least possible that they were already bringing their wares into the country.

BIBL. Vercoutter, J. *L'Egypte et le Monde Egéen Prehellenique.* Cairo: 1956; Wainwright, G. A. Keftiu. *JEA* 17 (1931) pp. 26 ff. and The Keftiu People of the Egyptian Monuments. *Ann. Arch. Anthr.*6 (1913) pp 24 ff. and, Keftiu: Crete or Cilicia? *JHS* 57 (1931) pp. 1 ff.

Kha'sekhem King c.2724 - 2703 BC.

Kha'sekhem may have been the immediate predecessor of the Second Dynasty king *Kha'sekhemui, or both names may refer to the same person. At Hieraconpolis, there are two distinct sets of monuments bearing these two names which seems to indicate that they were two separate rulers.

Items attributed to Kha'sekhem include two large stone bowls, two seated statues of slate and limestone (the latter is now in Oxford), and a fragmentary stela on which he is shown in conflict with the *Libyans.

BIBL. Quibell, J. E. *Hierakonpolis.* London: 1900-2; Newberry, P. E. The Set Rebellion of the Second Dynasty. *Ancient Egypt* (1922) pp 40-6; Emery, W. B. *Archaic Egypt.* Harmondsworth: 1972.

Kha'sekhemui King c.2703 - 2686 BC.
The similarity of the names Kha'sekhemui and *Kha'sekhem and their close association in the King Lists has led to the suggestion that they may have represented the same person and that *Kha'sekhem, having united the followers of the rival gods Horus and Seth, took the new name of Kha'sekhemui. However, it is more probable that Kha'sekhemui succeeded Kha'sekhem as a ruler of the Second Dynasty.

During his reign, there were apparently great advances made in technology and references occur both to a copper statue of the king and to a temple carved of stone. His reign undoubtedly laid the foundations for the innovations of the Third Dynasty when *Djoser (who may have been either the son or grandson of Kha'sekhemui) built the first stone pyramid. *Djoser's mother, Nymaathap, was either the queen or daughter of Kha'sekhemui.

BIBL. Petrie, W. M. F. *The Royal Tombs of the Earliest Dynasties,* 1901, Part 2. London: 1901; Quibell, J. E. *Hierakonpolis.* London: 1900-2; Emery, W. B. *Archaic Egypt.* Harmondsworth: 1972; Newberry, P. E. The Set Rebellion of the Second Dynasty. *Ancient Egypt.* (1922) pp. 40-6; Griffith, J. G. *The Conflict of Horus and Seth.* Liverpool: 1960.

Khattusilis III King of the *Hittites 1275 - 1250 BC.
The brother of *Muwatallis, Khattusilis III held great authority over the north-eastern provinces of the kingdom. Urhi-Teshub, (*Muwatallis' son and successor), sought to curtail this power, but after seven years Khattusilis III seized the Hittite throne from Urhi-Teshub and justified this action in an extensive document which is sometimes known as his 'Autobiography'.

His reign was marked by peace and prosperity and he is remembered for the famous treaty which he concluded with *Ramesses II, in Year 21 of the latter's reign (1269 BC). This treaty is the only one which has been discovered to date, although others were enacted between various Near Eastern rulers; it guaranteed peace and security for Egypt, the *Hittites and their vassal states in the Syria-Palestine region. It has survived in two versions: the Egyptian one is inscribed on a stela in the Temple of Karnak, while the *Hittite copy was discovered, in a less complete form, on two clay tablets in the archive at Boghazkoy, the *Hittite capital.

In such treaties the participants were equals and sought 'brotherhood' with each other; it was both a defensive and an offensive alliance and reaffirmed an earlier agreement made in the reign of *Suppiluliumas. It removed the possibility of war, with both parties agreeing not to encroach on each other's territory and to aid each other in the event of attack by a third power; it also provided for the equal extradition of refugees but insisted that they should be well-treated. In the Egyptian version, the gods of both lands were invoked as witnesses.

This treaty led to cordial relations and the exchange of correspondence between the two kings and their respective queens; thirteen years later the alliance was cemented by a marriage between *Ramesses II and a daughter of Khattusilis and his queen, Pudukhepa. Inscriptions on the walls of various Egyptian temples

67

related the story of the *Hittite princess' arrival in Egypt; she was subsequently renamed Manefrure and found sufficient favour with *Ramesses II to become his Great Royal Wife.

BIBL. Langdon, S. and Gardiner, A. H. The Treaty of Alliance between Hattusili, king of the Hittites, and the Pharaoh Ramesses II of Egypt. *JEA* 6 (1920) pp. 179 ff; Gurney, O. R. *The Hittites*. Harmondsworth: 1964.

Khentkaues   Queen   c.2494 - 2487 BC.

According to the legend in the Westcar Papyrus, the first three kings of the Fifth Dynasty were triplets fathered by the sun-god Re and born to a commoner, the wife of a priest of Re at the town of Sakhebu. This folk-tale preserves the historical fact that the Heliopolitan priests of Re exerted an unprecedented influence on the rulers of this dynasty, although in fact these kings were probably descended from a secondary line of *Cheops' family. *Userkaf, the founder of the Fifth Dynasty, probably married Khentkaues to strengthen his claim to the throne, for she was not only a descendant of the main branch of the royal family but also probably the daughter of King *Mycerinus.

She appears to have provided an important link between the Fourth and Fifth Dynasties, and her divine cult was maintained throughout the Fifth Dynasty. From her titles it can be inferred that she was the mother of two kings, *Sahure and *Neferirkare, and since she was the wife of *Userkaf, it is evident that these three early rulers of the Fifth Dynasty were father and sons and not in fact triplets as claimed in the Westcar Papyrus.

Khentkaues had a distinctive tomb at Giza, which is sometimes called the Unfinished or Fourth Pyramid, although it was actually a sarcophagus-shaped construction which imitated the tomb (Mastabat Fara'un) of *Shepseskaf. This monument was constructed on a base of natural rock faced with limestone, and was probably completed in the reign of the queen's son, *Neferirkare.

BIBL. Jequier, G. *Le Mastabat Faraoun*. Cairo: 1928; Hassan, S. *Excavations at Giza*. (eight vols) Oxford and Cairo: 1932-53; *AEL* i. pp. 215-22.

Khety (Dua-khety)   Author of a Wisdom Text   c.2100 BC.

A unique Wisdom Text, often referred to as the 'Satire of the Trades', is couched in terms of instructions or advice which a humble man, Duauf son of Khety (or Dua-Khety in some texts), gives to his son Pepy. The text is preserved in sources which date to the New Kingdom (mainly schoolboy exercises of the Nineteenth Dynasty), but it appears to have originated in the First Intermediate Period. The most complete versions, written by the same scribe, are to be found in Papyrus Sallier II and Papyrus Anastasi VII in the British Museum.

Duauf counsels his son and, unlike other authors of early Wisdom Texts, he is not a powerful and mighty individual (a king or a vizier), who is well-placed to advise his young charge; this is simply the wisdom of an ordinary man placed before his son. The teaching is set between a prologue and an epilogue; it is explained in the preliminaries that Duauf, although he is of humble origin, is taking his child to the Residence (the royal palace) to place him amongst the children of the magistrates. On the river voyage Duauf has the opportunity to emphasise to Pepy the considerable advantages of the scribal profession (which he will be able to enter if he makes good progress in his studies), and the father contrasts it vividly with the tribulations and hardships endured by other trades and professions, of which eighteen are described in some detail. He urges Pepy to make the most of his chance to learn and encourages him to apply himself to his work. Emphasis is placed on the excellence of schools which undoubtedly made this text a most popular choice to be copied by generations of schoolboys.

BIBL. *AEL* i. pp 184-92.

L

Libyans (Libu) c.1304 - 1116 BC.

The *Greeks used the term 'Libyans' for the occupants of the Mediterranean coast of Africa who had white skin, red or blonde hair and blue eyes.The name 'Libu' occurs before that, in the Ramesside period and is used to identify a particular tribe. Together with the *Tjemhu, *Tjehnyu and *Meshwesh (who were other Libyan tribes), the Libu were driven through hunger to attempt to invade and settle in the Delta; on occasions they united with the *Sea-peoples in their conflict against Egypt. *Ramesses II successfully drove them off and built a line of forts along the western coast in an attempt to hold them back. In Year 5 of his on,*Merneptah's reign, they united with the *Sea-peoples to attack Egypt, but were again repulsed; this was followed, in Years 5, 8 and 11 of *Ramesses III's reign, by further unsuccessful onslaughts.

Unlike some of the *Sea-peoples, the Libu were uncircumcised; this is known because there are wall-scenes in Egyptian temples which show how, in the battle against *Merneptah, the genitals of the slain enemies were piled up for presentation to the Egyptian king.

BIBL. *CAH* ii, ch xxviii; Holscher, W. *Libyer und Agypter*. Gluckstadt: 1937; Wainwright, G. A . The Meshwesh. *JEA* 48 (1962) pp. 89 ff.

M

Maketaten   Daughter of King *Akhenaten   c.1379 - 1367 BC.
Maketaten was the second daughter of *Akhenaten and Queen *Nefertiti. She
apparently died soon after Year 12 of *Akhenaten's reign. She was probably
buried in the Royal Tomb at Amarna in a subsidiary suite of chambers, where the
wall-scenes show the king and queen grieving as they stand at the side of her bier
while, outside the death chamber a female figure (probably a nursemaid) holds a
baby. These representations have caused much speculation, and it has been
suggested that Maketaten may have died in childbirth and that *Akhenaten may
have been the father of her child.

BIBL. Martin, G. T. *The Royal Tomb at El-Amarna.* London:1974; Aldred, C. *Akhenaten,
King of Egypt.* London: 1988.

Manetho   Historian   305 - 285 BC.
Manetho was an Egyptian priest who lived at the Temple of Sebennytos in the
Delta. Very little is known of his life; he may have had some association with
Mendes and the temple at Heliopolis. He lived during the reigns of *Ptolemy I and
*Ptolemy II. He knew both Egyptian hieroglyphs and Greek and had personal
knowledge of Egyptian religious beliefs and customs. He is credited with the
authorship of eight works which dealt with a range of subjects, including religious
doctrines, rituals and festivals.

  His most important work was the *Aegyptiaca* (History of Egypt), which was
based on registers which were compiled by the Egyptian priests and to which he
obviously had access. Although the *Aegyptiaca* was written in the reign of
*Ptolemy II, unfortunately no intact version has been discovered to date and it is
preserved only in edited extracts in the writings of *Josephus, and in an abridged
form in the works of Sextus *Africanus (early third century AD), *Eusebius (early
fourth century AD), and George called *Syncellus (AD c.800) in his *History of the
world from Creation to Diocletian.*

  Manetho's History is essentially a chronicle of Egyptian kings, written in
Greek, and if a complete version were available it would provide the best
chronological source for ancient Egypt. After the rule of the gods and demi-gods,
the kings from *Narmer (Menes) (c.3100 BC) down to the conquest by
*Alexander the Great in 332 BC, are divided into thirty dynasties. Estimates are
given of the lengths of the reigns and these often differ in the accounts of
*Eusebius and *Africanus. Manetho also provides anecdotes about various rulers,
and it is evident that he made use of popular stories and legends as well as official
records.

As they have come down to us, the records of Manetho are therefore often unreliable and inaccurate. The sources of *Eusebius and *Africanus often give divergent accounts, and both the chronology of the kings' reigns and the total years of each reign are unreliable. In particular, the chronology for the Old Kingdom and the Middle Kingdom is too high in almost every instance. Kings' names are sometimes distorted and in some dynasties only the overall number of the rulers is given – for example, in the Seventh Dynasty Manetho states that there were 'Seventy kings who reigned for seventy days'.

Nevertheless Egyptologists have accepted Manetho's division of the reigns into dynasties and this continues to be used as the basis for Egyptian chronology. Today, the dynasties are further divided into groups and placed within particular historical periods such as the Old Kingdom (the Third to the Sixth Dynasty), or the Second Intermediate Period (the Thirteenth to the Seventeenth Dynasty). More accurate dates for some reigns and dynasties can now be obtained from comparative information from excavated sites and material, and from treaties and other historical texts found in Egypt and neighbouring countries. Manetho's anecdotal details, for which there is often no alternative source, are treated with extreme caution.

Despite its shortcomings, it was Manetho's chronology that assisted Champollion in 1828 when he discovered the cartouches of various kings on the monuments and deciphered their names. By using Manetho's lists, he was able to determine their positions within the sequence of rulers and confirm his identifications.

BIBL. *Manetho,* (transl. by Waddell,W. G.) London: 1942.

Medjay.

The Medjay are mentioned in the Egyptian records as early as the Old Kingdom, when the term is used to denote a group of desert tribesmen in *Nubia who became scouts and light-armed auxiliaries in the Egyptian army. By the First Intermediate Period it is evident that they are still in the military service, since an inscription at the Hatnub quarry mentions them among the followers of the prince of the Hermopolitan nome.

By the Eighteenth Dynasty, this term simply comes to mean a 'policeman'. The Medjay were men who patrolled and guarded the desert frontiers, protected the cemeteries and undertook general duties to maintain order throughout Egypt. They even acted as law enforcement officers and protected the royal necropolis workers' village at Deir el Medina. The senior police officer in charge of the force was called 'Chief of the Medjay', and in each large town there was a police force under the control of a 'Captain of the Medjay.' By the New Kingdom, the term 'Medjay' no longer implied a person of *Nubian origin and many of them were now undoubtedly of native Egyptian stock.

BIBL. Davies, N. de G. *The Tombs of Two Officials of Tuthmosis the Fourth. EES.* London: 1923.

Menna   Official   reign of *Tuthmosis IV   c.1420 BC.

Menna was Scribe of the cadastral survey and Estate Inspector during the reign of *Tuthmosis IV (1425-1417 BC). His tomb is situated at Sheikh Abd el Qurna, Thebes, and is decorated with wall-scenes that illustrate agricultural activities and duties during this period.

Menna is shown overseeing the workforce in the fields as he did during his lifetime: the peasants carry and measure the corn, and winnow, thresh and transport it, and one scene illustrates the use of the surveying cord. Other traditional scenes show Menna and his wife being presented with gifts, and their relatives bring them food and flowers; there is also a funerary banquet and prayers are offered to *Osiris, the god of the dead.

The scenes also depict the ceremonies that surrounded the death of the tomb-owner, including the rituals performed on the mummy, and the journey of the deceased to Abydos, the burial place of Osiris, in order to enhance his chances of a blessed eternity. There is also a representation of the Day of Judgement scene in which the deeds of the deceased during his lifetime are judged by the assessor gods. Here, Menna's heart is shown in the balance where it is weighed against the symbolic Feather of Truth.

Mentuhotep II (Nebhepetre)   King   2060 - 2010 BC.

Nebhepetre Mentuhotep II had a successful and impressive reign and later came to be regarded as the pharaoh who had reunited Egypt after the troubles and dissension of the First Intermediate Period.

The rulers of Heracleopolis and their supporters who, by trying to recover the city of This, had reopened the conflict with the Thebans, fell to Mentuhotep II (the Theban leader) in c.2040 BC. A chapel relief from Gebelein records this action of destroying the Heracleopolitan supporters and consequently gaining the submission or support of the local governors (nomarchs) of Lower and Middle Egypt. It is evident that Mentuhotep II did not obliterate the entrenched nomarchs of Middle Egypt, but probably imposed only limited restrictions on them so that, as at Hermopolis and Assiut, they could continue to prosper.He appointed his own men to all the key positions of authority and consolidated his power at Thebes, thus gaining a firm control of the country.

This was a time of military activity since it was necessary to consolidate Egypt's neglected borders and to re-open the trading routes, mines and quarries. Punitive expeditions were sent out to quell the disturbances caused by the *Libyans of the western desert and the *Beduin who wandered in Sinai and the eastern desert. The necessary commodities of timber and gold were once again acquired from *Byblos and *Nubia, and routes across the desert from Koptos to the Red Sea were restored to provide access to the incense-land of *Punt.

*Nubia required special attention and the king himself sailed south to deal with the problem. Probably since the late Old Kingdom, when Egypt was itself in turmoil, an independent dynasty of rulers had established itself in Nubia; in fact, this may have been inaugurated by an Egyptian official. Mentuhotep II wished to regain control of Nubia and to restore the power that the kings of the Sixth

Dynasty had enjoyed, which had enabled them to easily acquire both commodities and manpower from there. He was successful in restoring Egyptian supremacy in the region of Lower Nubia as far as the Second Cataract and in renewing the tribute levy, but the Egyptians did not as yet have a permanent military presence there.

The famous Chancellor, Achthoes, concentrated on exploiting Lower Nubia, and evidently *Nubians came to fight as auxiliaries in the Egyptian army. A tomb at Deir el Bahri was found to contain the bodies of sixty Egyptian soldiers who had been killed while attacking a fortress or town which was perhaps in Nubia, but there were also Nubian servants in the Theban royal household. From tombs of this dynasty (the Eleventh), there are elaborate funerary models of Nubian as well as Egyptian soldiers who were designed to fight on behalf of their deceased Egyptian owner in his afterlife. (e.g. Mesehti, now in the Cairo Museum.)

Mentuhotep II built extensively throughout Upper Egypt, at Elephantine, El Kab, Gebelein, Tod, Abydos and Denderah, but his most impressive monument was his unique burial complex at Deir el Bahri, which was later overshadowed by Queen *Hatshepsut's own funerary temple. Mentuhotep II's building incorporated a pyramid and a temple, which were combined in an innovative way, and the complex also housed the burials of the royal women, including the king's mother and sister. The complex was approached by an avenue lined with sandstone statues of the king wearing his jubilee-festival garments, and both the setting and architectural features would have made this a most impressive monument to a great king.

The renewal of great building projects emphasised the strength and confidence of this reign, and the selection of Montu, god of war, as the patron deity of this dynasty expressed the attitude of Mentuhotep II as the founder of the line.

BIBL. Winlock, H. E. *Excavations at Deir el Bahri, 1911-31*. New York: 1942; Winlock, H. E. *The rise and fall of the Middle Kingdom in Thebes*. New York: 1947; Winlock, H. E. *The slain soldiers of Neb-hepet-Re Mentu-hotpe*. New York: 1945; Naville, E. *The XIth Dynasty Temple at Deir el Bahari*. London: 1907-13.

Mentuhotep III (S'ankhkare) King 2009 - 1998 BC.

S'ankhkare Mentuhotep III succeeded his great father, Nebhepetre *Mentuhotep II, as the last recorded king of the Eleventh Dynasty, although he was probably briefly succeeded by Nebtowyre *Mentuhotep IV.

In his twelve year reign, he apparently built on a large scale throughout many towns in Upper Egypt, where inscribed blocks testify to the existence of temples or chapels of this period. Also, during his reign, there was activity in the stone quarries at Wadi Hammamat, where an inscription dated to Year 8 recalls how a steward was sent there with the task of quarrying stone for the production of statues that were to be placed in temples and tombs. The king's burial place may have been situated at a location in a circular bay to the south of Deir el Bahri, similar to the place which his father selected for his own great complex.

BIBL. Winlock, H. E. *Excavations at Deir el Bahri, 1911-1931*. New York: 1942; Winlock, H. E. *The rise and fall of the Middle Kingdom in Thebes*. New York: 1947.

Mentuhotep IV (Nebtowyre)   King   1997-1991 BC.

Nebtowyre Mentuhotep IV does not appear in the Turin Canon (which enters no ruler for the seven years after the death of *Mentuhotep III), but his name is known from inscriptions in quarries to which he sent expeditions. He probably succeeded Mentuhotep III as the last king of the Eleventh Dynasty. An inscription which dates to Year 2 of his reign is particularly interesting, since it mentions his vizier, Amenemhe, whom he sent on an expedition to Wadi Hammamat to obtain his stone sarcophagus. It is this vizier who was almost certainly the man who ultimately usurped the throne to become *Amenemmes I, the founder of the Twelfth Dynasty.In the Prophecy of *Neferti, conditions of dissolution and chaos are described throughout Egypt; these were brought to an end only through the advent of a powerful king – *Amenemmes I – and it has been suggested that *Beduin incursions may have occurred during the reign of such a relatively weak king as Mentuhotep IV, thus producing further social and economic problems during this difficult time.

BIBL. Winlock, H. E. *The rise and fall of the Middle Kingdom in Thebes*. New York: 1947.

Mereruka   Vizier   reign of Teti   c.2340 BC.

Near to the pyramid of *Teti (2345-2333 BC), there is a substantial and well-preserved mastaba-tomb which belonged to Mereruka, who was the son-in-law and vizier of King *Teti. This tomb dates to the beginning of the Sixth Dynasty and is similar to that of *Ti; it was excavated in 1893.

Mereruka's tomb has thirty-one chambers and passages and was designed to accommodate his own burial and those of his wife, the princess Hert-watet-khet, and their son, Meri-Teti. Indeed, his wife's importance is emphasised in the wall-scenes, for she appears with her husband in these throughout the tomb.

The scenes are generally typical of those that occur on the walls of nobles' tombs in the Old Kingdom, but they are of outstanding quality and are very well-preserved. Mereruka is shown in a papyrus-boat hunting and fishing in the marshes; he also hunts in the desert, and inspects various craftsmen including jewellers, goldsmiths, carpenters and masons manufacturing vases; his attendants bring him gifts,and the formal events of his own funeral are depicted.

BIBL. Duell, P. et al. *The Mastaba of Mereruka*. Chicago: 1938.

Merikare   King   c.2100 BC.

This king is known from the Wisdom Text, 'The Instruction for King Merikare', which conveys the advice which was given to Merikare by his royal father; this is the earliest treatise on kingship which has survived, although it was apparently not the first to have been written. Although it provides an accurate reflection of historical events and conditions, it has been suggested that it may have been written by one of Merikare's own scribes rather than by his father, and was therefore perhaps an announcement of his own royal policy. The text has survived in three major sources (on papyri in Leningrad, Moscow and Carlsberg), which all date to the Eighteenth Dynasty; but the original composition refers to the First Intermediate Period and Merikare and his father were probably rulers at Heracleopolis in the Tenth Dynasty.

This is one of the most important compositions of that troubled period. As an instruction on royal behaviour it advises Merikare on how to deal with nobles and commoners, how to act towards rebels, and counsels on how he should try to be a benevolent ruler – 'Calm the weeper, oppress no widow, expel no man from his father's possessions...'. He is also instructed in good speech.

The pragmatism of the earlier Wisdom Instructions is tempered here with the addition of religious concepts such as personal piety and reverence for the gods and former rulers. As a literary work the text also marks an advance and foreshadows the increasing sophistication of Middle Kingdom compositions.

BIBL. *AEL* i.pp. 97-109; von Beckerath, J. Die Dynastie der Herakleopoliten (9./10.Dynastie). *ZAS* 93 (1966) pp. 13-20;Volten, A. *Zwei altagyptische politische Schriften: Die Lehre fur Konig Merikare (Pap.Carlsberg VI) Und die Lehre fur Konigs Amenemhet (An.Aeg.4)*. Copenhagen: 1945.

Meritaten   Queen   reigns of *Akhenaten and *Smenkhkare c.1370 - 1360 BC.
Meritaten was the eldest daughter of Queen *Nefertiti; her father was almost certainly *Akhenaten (Amenophis IV), and the princess appears with her parents in a number of sculptured reliefs.

When the death of *Maketaten (Meritaten's younger sister) occurred, probably soon after Year 12 of *Akhenaten's reign, *Nefertiti also seems to disappear from the record. It has been suggested that the queen may have fallen into disgrace and banished to live at the Northern Palace at Amarna, or she may simply have died. In either case, her place as the senior queen was apparently taken over by Meritaten who now replaces her mother in scenes and inscriptions in *Nefertiti's own palace – the Maruaten – at Amarna. There is evidence earlier in this reign to indicate that Meritaten bore a daughter, Merit-Aten-ta-sherit,who was the daughter of a king; the king in question was probably Meritaten's own father, *Akhenaten.

Meritaten is also mentioned in the Amarna Letters (the correspondence between the Egyptian royal family and various kings and princes of neighbouring countries). Her pet-name of Mayati is used in letters from both Abimilki, the ruler of Tyre, and Burnaburiash, the king of Babylon.*Akhenaten's successor was *Smenkhkare, a prince of the royal family whose parentage is uncertain and, as the royal heiress, Meritaten became his wife to consolidate his claim to the throne. In one of the courtiers' tombs at Amarna, there are wall-scenes showing *Akhenaten and *Nefertiti rewarding the tomb-owner with gold; in the accompanying inscription their royal names within the cartouches have been replaced with those of the new royal couple, *Smenkhkare and Meritaten.

*Smenkhkare's reign was brief, but Meritaten probably died before him, since, on the Boundary Stelae, *Akhenaten (with whom *Smenkhkare probably reigned as co-ruler) provided details of the burial arrangements to be carried out for himself, *Nefertiti, and Meritaten, with instructions that they were to be interred in the Royal Tomb in the eastern mountain at Amarna.

Meritaten was probably eventually buried at Thebes, although her tomb has never been found. In Tomb 55 in the Valley of the Kings at Thebes, the body which has been tentatively identified as that of *Smenkhkare was buried in a coffin which was originally made for Meritaten. The canopic jars in the tomb had also been prepared for Meritaten, but the names on these were altered and they were ultimately used to contain the mummified viscera of *Smenkhkare. One explanation for this is that *Smenkhkare died unexpectedly and that his wife's mortal remains were hurriedly removed to another place so that her coffin and canopic jars could be used for the king. Another more feasible theory is that this equipment was prepared for Meritaten when she was a princess, before her marriage to *Smenkhkare, but that it was never used for her burial, and with *Smenkhkare's untimely death, the coffin and jars were brought out of storage and the necessary alterations were made.

BIBL. Aldred, C. *Akhenaten; King of Egypt.* London: 1988; Mercer, S. A. B. *The Tell el Amarna Tablets.* (two vols.) Toronto: 1939; Gardiner, A. H. The so-called tomb of Queen Tiye. *JEA* 43 (1957) pp. 10-25.

Merneptah King 1236 - 1223 BC.

Merneptah, the thirteenth son of *Ramesses II by Istnofret, one of his principal wives, had little hope of becoming king but, because of his father's long reign, previous heirs predeceased *Ramesses II. After the death of the Heir Apparent in Year 55 of the old king's reign, Merneptah became the next successor. Already a man in his sixties, Merneptah had helped to manage state affairs for his father in the city of Pi-Ramesse and in the Delta and he now took on new responsibilites, ruling as prince regent for the elderly king throughout the last twelve years of his reign.

The later years of *Ramesses II had seen a decline in the vigilance exercised by frontier patrols, and when Merneptah finally became king he had to face several crises almost immediately. Between Years 2 and 5, it was necessary to send expeditions to Canaan and southern Syria to reassert Egypt's influence there, but in Year 5 Merneptah faced a much greater threat. Famine had driven the *Libyans to raid the western Delta and they now formed a coalition with the migrants who arrived in search of a new home. These were the so-called *Sea-peoples, who approached Egypt from the eastern Mediterranean and the Aegean islands. Under a *Libyan prince, a coalition of the *Libu, *Meshwesh and Kehek together with some of the *Sea-peoples, advanced on the Delta. They intended to settle in the fertile land of Egypt and brought with them their wives and children, their cattle and their personal possessions.

Merneptah, mobilised his army and dealt the coalition a grievous blow, emerging from the conflict as the conclusive victor. It was stated that over six thousand had been killed and many prisoners and large quantities of booty were taken, while the *Libyan leader fled in disgrace.

The conflict is recorded in Egyptian sources: a long inscription in the Temple of Karnak, a stela from Athribis, and a great granite stela, usurped from *Amenophis III and set up in Merneptah's Theban funerary temple. The latter is of great interest because it not only recalls the relief experienced by the Egyptians at their enemies' defeat, but it also includes the only known reference in Egyptian texts to Israel, which was apparently already an established entity in Palestine by Year 5 of Merneptah's reign.

Until the discovery of this Israel Stela in 1896, scholars had believed that Merneptah was the pharaoh of the Exodus, but since Israel was already established so early in his reign, it has since been necessary to date the Exodus somewhat earlier and it is now usually placed in the reign of *Ramesses II. In addition to this conflict, the *Libu also fermented trouble in Nubia, in order to distract the Egyptians while they attempted to invade through the Delta. Although the plan did not work, Merneptah was forced to follow up his defeat of the *Libyan coalition with a campaign of suppression against the *Nubians.

Since he was already an elderly man, Merneptah had little time to undertake an extensive building programme. His temple and palace at Memphis no longer survive and his Theban funerary temple, built of stone taken from *Amenophis III's temple, has also disappeared.

It is assumed that he was buried in his Theban tomb but the mummy was later moved by the priests to the tomb of *Amenophis II for safekeeping, and here, as part of the cache of royal mummies, it was finally rediscovered by V, Loret in 1898.

The king's burial service was conducted by an unknown prince (presumably a royal son by a minor wife), who was named Amenmesse. The order of the succession is confused at this point, but the throne was possibly seized at Merneptah's death by Amenmesse while the crown prince, Sethos, was away. Amenmesse may have had a brief reign and then the kingship passed to Sethos II (who was probably the afore-mentioned Crown Prince of Merneptah).

Although he only inherited the throne late in life, Merneptah was an affective and energetic king who continued to uphold the traditions that had been established at home and abroad during his father's reign.

BIBL. Holscher, W. *Libyer und Agypter*. Gluckstadt: 1937; Smith, G. E. Report on the unwrapping of the mummy of Menephtah.. *Ann.Serv*.8 (1907) pp 108-12; *CAH* ii,ch xxviii; Wainwright, G. A. Merneptah's aid to the Hittites. *JEA* 46 (1960) pp 24 ff.; Kitchen, K. A. *Ramesside Inscriptions*. Vol. 4. Oxford: 1968.

Meroites Third century BC - AD Fourth century.

To the south of Egypt there lay the independent kingdom of Meroe, which had come into existence when the 'Ethiopian' kings of the Twenty-fifth Dynasty were driven out of Egypt by the *Assyrians. These rulers returned to Napata in the south where, under *Psammetichus III of the Twenty-sixth Dynasty, the Egyptians campaigned, probably to prevent a resurgence of the power of the Nubians and any renewed attempt to reconquer Egypt.

The Nubian kingdom finally moved its capital from Napata further south to the new city of Meroe. They had by now disassociated themselves from Egypt and went on to develop their own Meroitic kingdom on the upper reaches of the Nile in virtual isolation. The northern boundary of this kingdom was probably established at Pnubs, south of the Third Cataract. Meroe possessed good resources: cattle could be raised and there were ample deposits of iron. As Egyptianised *Nubians, the Meroites retained Egyptian culture, and temples and art forms reflected the continuation of Egyptian religion which survived here until the fourth century AD. Although Napata remained a religious centre, the royal cemetery moved to the new capital of Meroe and flourished there between the third century BC and the fourth century AD; here pyramids were built and used for royal burials long after they had ceased to be constructed in Egypt.

The pottery of the Meroitic kingdom displays both African and Mediterranean influences, for contact with the north was continued through the Roman punitive expeditions that are described in Classical writers such as *Strabo, *Pliny and Dio Cassius. The Roman governor of Egypt, Petronius, led one of these expeditions in 23 BC and sacked Napata. When the Roman emperor *Diocletian withdrew all troops from the area and established Egypt's southern frontier at Philae, Meroe began a gradual decline; it was finally destroyed by King Aeizanes of Axum in Ethiopia (AD 325-75) in c. AD 350.

When the Meroites first severed their links with Egypt, they retained the classical language, Egyptian hieroglyphs, for their formal inscriptions, but gradually this became increasingly unintelligible. From Egyptian hieroglyphs, they evolved an alphabetic script for writing their native language and another linear type of writing. These scripts are both known as Meroitic and have been the subject of intense study.

BIBL. Shinnie, P. *Meroe, a Civilisation of the Sudan.* : 1967; Dunham, D. *The Royal Cemeteries of Kush.* (five vols) Boston, Mass.: 1950–63; Laming Macadam, M. F. *The temples of Kawa.* (two vols) Oxford, 1949, 1955.

Meshwesh c.1417 - c.720 BC.

The Meshwesh first appear in Egyptian records in the reign of *Amenophis III, but they are mentioned most frequently in connection with the *Libyans and *Sea-peoples in the battles against the Ramesside kings.

Hunger seems to have forced them, with their neighbours the *Libyans, to attempt to invade and settle in the Delta during the reign of *Ramesses II. When *Merneptah ruled, they joined the *Libyans and a coalition of *Sea-peoples to attack the Delta, but were repulsed by the Egyptians, and in Year 5 of *Ramesses III's reign they formed part of a *Libyan coalition which attacked Egypt, apparently in objection to pharaoh's choice of their new leader. Utterly defeated again, in Year 11 they nevertheless led a much larger coalition against Egypt, which gained some initial success but was finally crushed. On this occasion, their chief, Mesher, was taken prisoner and his father's appeals for mercy met with no response.

Descendants of the prisoners captured in these battles and those who voluntarily settled in Egypt later on were eventually rewarded with land there, in return for military service for Egypt. They became so numerous that by c.950 BC, the 'Chiefs of the Meshwesh' were able to become the kings of Egypt, establishing the Twenty-second Dynasty (c.945-730 BC).

BIBL. Kitchen, K. A. *3rd Int;* Wainwright, G. A. The Meshwesh. *JEA* 48 (1962) pp. 89 ff.; Holscher, W. *Libyer und Agypter.* Gluckstadt: 1937.

Mitanni   Kingdom of   Second millenium BC.

The kingdom of Mitanni was one of the major powers Egypt encountered in the Eighteenth Dynasty, first as an enemy and then as an ally. In the second millennium BC, the Hurrians had established several kingdoms on the Euphrates and the Habur, having branched out from their homeland in the region to the south of the Caspian Sea from c.2300 BC onwards. In one of these kingdoms, Mitanni, the Hurrian population was ruled by an aristocracy of Indo-Aryan origin: their kings had Aryan names, they worshipped Indian deities, and they had brought a special knowledge of horse-breeding which was ultimately transmitted to the peoples of Western Asia.

In the early Eighteenth Dynasty, Mitanni provided the major threat to Egypt. It was probably mentioned in the hieroglyphic texts as early as the reign of *Amenophis I, and it was recorded that *Tuthmosis I crossed the Euphrates into Nahrin (the 'River Country' – the terms Mitanni and Nahrin are used synonymously in the Egyptian texts) and slaughtered many of the enemy, taking the others as prisoners.

During *Hatshepsut's reign, many of the princelings of Palestine and Syria had been gathered into Mitanni's sphere of influence, and *Tuthmosis III dedicated much of his military prowess to fighting against the Mitannians, leading vigorous campaigns to drive them back beyond the Euphrates. In Year 33, in his eighth campaign, he crossed the Euphrates and inflicted a defeat, albeit temporary, on the Mitannian king. In the reign of his grandson, *Tuthmosis IV, there was a marked change in relations between the two kingdoms. Recognising that neither could successfully and permanently expel the other from northern Syria, they made peace and King Artatama I gave his daughter in marriage to *Tuthmosis IV. It was probably she who became his Great Royal Wife, *Mutemweya, and the mother of his heir, *Amenophis III.

*Amenophis III enjoyed cordial relations with his Mitannian contemporaries, the kings *Shuttarna and *Tushratta. *Shuttarna sent his daughter *Ghilukhepa to marry *Amenophis III and later, *Tushratta's daughter, *Tadukhepa, also became his wife. She was passed on to his son, *Akhenaten, and there has been speculation that she in fact became *Nefertiti, *Akhenaten's Great Royal Wife. However, it is more probable that *Nefertiti was of non-royal but Egyptian origin.

When *Amenophis III became a sick old man, *Tushratta sent an image of the goddess Ishtar of Nineveh to Thebes to aid his recovery. The relations between Egypt and Mitanni during these reigns are documented in the Amarna Letters, the archive of clay tablets discovered at Tell el Amarna. With the accession of *Suppiluliumas as king of the *Hittites, the new king set out to attack Mitanni. *Tushratta was murdered, dissension and foreign intervention split the kingdom, and Mitanni ceased to be a great power. The alliance of Egypt, Babylonia and Mitanni, supported by the mutual friendship of the rulers and their diplomatic and marriage ties, now disappeared, and the *Hittites replaced Mitanni as the main rival, and ultimately as the chief ally, of the Egyptians

BIBL. Mercer, S. A. B. *The Tell el Amarna Tablets.* (two vols) Toronto: 1939; Cavaignac, E. L'Egypte, le Mitanni, et les Hittites de 1478 à 1350. *Revue Hittite et Asianique* 1 (1931) pp. 61-71.

Montemhet   Fourth Prophet of Amun   c.680 - 650 BC.

In the later periods of Egypt's history, the role of Divine Wife of Amun was held at Thebes by the king's daughter and was designed to prevent the emergence of a rival to the king. Montemhet (who was the Fourth Prophet in the Temple of Amun at Karnak), managed to gain considerable practical if not outright political power at Thebes, at the side of the Divine Wife Shepenopet II, who was King *Piankhy's daughter and the successor of *Amenardis I as the God's Wife.

Egypt was currently passing through troubled times and the Ethiopian rulers were in combat with the *Assyrian forces in Egypt during the Twenty-fifth Dynasty. Montemhet was mentioned in the Rassam cylinder of *Ashurbanipal as 'King of Thebes', but although he undoubtedly wielded considerable influence there, no evidence indicates that he attempted outright to seize royal power. He came from a distinguished family (his grandfather was Vizier), and he built extensively at Thebes. He was a dutiful subject: a scene in the Temple of Mut at Karnak shows him, with his father and son, following the figure of King *Taharka as they worship the goddess Mut. Nevertheless in the accompanying inscription, he takes full credit for the programme of construction and repair of the divine buildings which customarily would have been ascribed to the king's own initiative.

Montemhet's tomb, one of the largest private tombs in the Theban Necropolis (no.34), is located in front of Deir el Bahri and is currently under restoration.

BIBL. Legrain, G. *Rec. trav.* 33 (1911) pp. 180-92; 34 (1912) pp. 97-104, 168-75; 35 (1913) pp. 207-16; 36 (1914) pp. 57-68, 145-52.

Moses „Jewish Prophet, reign of *Ramesses II (?), c.1250 BC.

According to the Biblical account, the descendants of the tribe of Israel whom *Joseph had brought into Egypt centuries earlier ultimately became part of those

81

groups of itinerant labourers who were press-ganged into various building projects; their particular task was to make mudbricks for the royal Delta cities of Pithom and Ramses. The persecution of the Children of Israel was probably part of the general stern measures which the Ramesside rulers of the Nineteenth Dynasty introduced against the peoples who lived on the borders of Egypt.

The Bible relates how Moses, the child of Hebrew slaves resident in Egypt, was rescued from the bulrushes by an Egyptian princess and was brought up in the palace. When grown, he defied Pharaoh and led the Hebrews out of Egypt, probably starting the journey from the district near the city of Ramses. In Sinai, Moses received God's covenant in the form of the Ten Commandments, and finally the Hebrews reached their destination and settled in the land that was to become known as Israel.

Although the Exodus marked a milestone in the religious and political history of the *Jews, and Moses was later regarded as a great spiritual leader, no reference to these events has been found in Egyptian records. This is not surprising since the Egyptians would have regarded this as a relatively unimportant uprising on the part of their workforce. It was also not the practise to document a pharaoh's failures. Despite the fact that Moses is not mentioned in Egyptian records he would have been totally acceptable at the Royal Court of the Nineteenth Dynasty, for many foreigners then held high positions. His Egyptian education would also have prepared him well for his role as a leader and law-giver.

It is generally accepted that the Exodus took place in the Nineteenth Dynasty, but no exact date can be established. Some evidence indicates that the persecution occurred under *Ramesses II and *Merneptah and that the Hebrews escaped during the latter's reign. However, the Israel Stela, which *Merneptah usurped from *Amenophis III and which is a major source for Egypt's Libyan War, also mentions Israel as an already established geographical place by the middle of *Merneptah's reign. This is the only known reference to Israel in an Egyptian inscription, and it is important in this context because it indicates that *Ramesses II and not *Merneptah was the king in whose reign the Exodus occurred, probably c.1290 BC.

The lengthy sojourn spent in Egypt undoubtedly influenced *Jewish thought: associations can be shown between some legal and liturgical elements in the Mosaic laws and in Egyptian examples, and some interesting parallels can be drawn between the two literatures, with particular reference to the Egyptian Wisdom Texts and the Hymn to the Aten. (*The Book of Proverbs* and *Psalm 104* respectively.)

BIBL. The Bible, Exodus, ch.1-20; Kitchen, K. A. *Ancient Orient and Old Testament.* London: 1966 pp. 57 ff., 156 ff; Freud, S. *Moses and Monotheism.* New York: 1967.

Mutemweya, Queen, reign of *Tuthmosis IV, 1425-1417 BC.

Diplomatic alliance between Egypt and *Mitanni in the middle of the Eighteenth Dynasty had prompted the *Mitannian ruler, Artatama I, to send his daughter to become the wife of *Tuthmosis IV. This foreign princess has tentatively been identified as *Tuthmosis IV's Chief Queen and the mother of his heir, *Amenophis III, since this woman (Mutemweya) is never entitled 'King's Daughter' or 'King's Sister' as she would have been if she were a direct member of the Egyptian royal family before her marriage. Another suggestion is that Mutemweya was Egyptian in origin and that she held her pre-eminent position at Court because she had borne the king's heir. One theory maintains that she may have been the sister of *Yuya, who later became important as the father-in-law of *Amenophis III.

Mutemweya appears in the wall-scenes in a room behind the colonnaded court in *Amenophis III's temple at Luxor, where his divine birth is depicted. These scenes emphasise the king's divine parentage and birth and closely resemble those in the temple of *Hatshepsut at Deir el Bahri. Mutemweya is shown as the consort of the god Amun, who assumes the form of her husband *Tuthmosis IV, and she is led to the birth-chamber by the deities Isis and Khnum. The queen may also be represented in the group of sculptured figures associated with the Colossi of Memnon (the great statues which once stood at the entrance to the funerary temple of *Amenophis III in western Thebes).

BIBL. Campbell, C. *The miraculous birth of Amon-hotep III and other Egyptian studies.* Edinburgh: 1912.

Muwatallis   King of the *Hittites   1306 - 1282 BC.

The territoral conquests which *Tuthmosis III had made in Syria were lost during the reign of *Akhenaten, having fallen to the *Hittites, but during the Nineteenth Dynasty *Sethos I and *Ramesses II sought to redress the balance.

Muwatallis, the grandson of *Suppiluliumas and son of Mursilis II, inherited a stable kingdom in northern Syria, surrounded by vassal states He was determined to uphold the treaties that had been made with these princes and to deal with the new threat posed by *Ramesses II.

The conflict between the *Hittites and *Ramesses II came to a head in Years 4/5 (1286/5 BC) of the latter's reign, when Egypt pushed northwards to recover Kadesh, which had fallen to the *Hittites. The Egyptian record, preserved in an epic poem – 'The Battle of Kadesh' – inscribed on the walls of various temples, indicates that *Ramesses II enjoyed a resounding victory, for although he found himself surrounded by the *Hittites, he was able to rout the enemy aided only by his bodyguard. The Boghazkoy Tablets (found in the *Hittite archive) present a very different picture: according to *Khattusilis III (Muwatallis' brother), the Egyptian king was conquered and driven into retreat near Damascus, allowing Muwatallis to take possession of the neighbouring district of Aba.

Muwatallis left a stable kingdom and an undisputed succession. Although he had no direct heir the throne passed to Urhi-Teshub, his son by a concubine.

BIBL. Gardiner, A. H. *The Kadesh Inscriptions of Ramesses II.* Oxford: 1960; Breasted, J. H. *The Battle of Kadesh.* Chicago: 1903.

Mycerinus (Menkaure)   King   c.2528 - 2500 BC.

Mycerinus (the Graecised but better known name of Menkaure) was the king who built the third pyramid at Giza. Much smaller than the monuments of his father, *Chephren, and his grandfather *Cheops, the pyramid of Mycerinus covers less than half the area of the Great Pyramid. If it had been completed this would have been an impressive monument which incorporated red granite brought from Aswan. However, much was left unfinished, including the task of covering the walls of the associated mortuary temple with stone casing, and *Shepseskaf (Mycerinus' successor) completed the complex in mudbrick and added the Valley Temple. It seems that Mycerinus died prematurely, a detail recorded by *Herodotus, who also related that the king's daughter committed suicide on account of Mycerinus' misdeeds.

*Herodotus compares Mycerinus favourably with his predecessors, *Cheops and *Chephren, and comments on his piety, his kindly and just disposition, and his beneficence as a ruler. Another tale relates how the oracle at Buto (a town in the Delta) prophesied that he had only six years to live, so in order to confound this prediction, he enjoyed life day and night, by the light of a candle, and thus gained another twelve years of pleasure.

His pyramid complex was excavated by G. A. Reisner. One of the major discoveries was the magnificent royal statuary found in the funerary temple; together with the sculpture from *Chephren's pyramid complex, this provides the most important evidence of royal art during the Old Kingdom. The finest piece from the Mycerinus complex is a superb life-size slate pair-statue of the king and his wife, Queen Khamerernebty II, which is now in the Boston Museum. This statue displays the finest qualities of Old Kingdom sculpture and shows the regal bearing of the king and the supportive attitude of his queen, who places her arm around his waist.

Archaeologists also discovered a series of smaller slate triads, each representing the king, standing between the goddess Hathor and one of the nome-deities. Egypt was originally divided into forty-two nomes or administrative districts, and although only four of these triads have survived, it is possible that there were originally forty-two of these statue-groups in the temple.

Mycerinus was the last great ruler of the Fourth Dynasty; his successor (who was probably also his son), *Shepseskaf, broke with tradition and rejected a pyramid in favour of a unique mastaba-tomb.

BIBL. Reisner, G. A. *The temples of the Third Pyramid at Giza.* Cambridge, Mass.1931.

N

Nabopolassar   King of Babylon   626 - 605 BC.
It was the growth of Babylon under Nabopolassar and their alliance with the Medes that persuaded the Egyptian king *Psammetichus I of the Twenty-sixth Dynasty to side with Egypt's erstwhile enemy, *Assyria. The *Assyrian capital of Nineveh fell in 612 BC, and the contest continued unresolved for many years.

In 610 BC, *Necho II inherited the Egyptian throne and, according to Biblical tradition, he became Nabopolassar's main enemy when he set out to fight the Babylonians. *Necho II interfered in the politics of Syria/Palestine and fought against King Josiah of Judah, when he tried to intervene in the conflict by barring Necho's way past the walls of Megiddo. Josiah was killed and *Necho II finally placed a ruler of his own choice in charge at Jerusalem.

The Egyptains then defeated the Babylonians at sites on the Euphrates, south of Carchemish, but, according to the Babylonian Chronicle, Nabopolassar's son *Nebuchadrezzar inflicted a major defeat on the Egyptians at the Battle of Carchemish in 605 BC. The major force withdrew, but the Babylonians pursued and destroyed the Egyptians in the district of Hamath, as they fled, bringing about a resounding victory for the Babylonians; ultimately, they seized all Egypt's northern possessions. A couple of months after this great Babylonian victory, Nabopolassar died and *Nebuchadrezzar inherited his empire.

BIBL. Wiseman, D. J. *Chronicles of Chaldaean Kings.* London: 1956 pp 5 ff.

Nakht, Astronomer and Royal Scribe, reign of Tuthmosis IV, 1425 - 1417 BC.
Nakht was a priest of Amun, with special duties as an astronomer and Royal Scribe. His beautiful and well-preserved tomb, situated in the district of Sheikh Abd el Qurna at Thebes, is justifiably famous on account of the quality of its wall-scenes. These include a series of agricultural themes, arranged in four registers, which show the peasants engaged in ploughing, sowing, harvesting and flax-cutting, in the presence of Nakht. He also appears in pursuit of fish and game in the marshes, and is shown accompanying his wife in the garden of their home and in a series of banqueting scenes in which they and their guests are entertained by dancers and musicians, including a blind harpist.

The name of the god, Amun, which occurs on the tomb walls was later hacked out during the reign of *Akhenaten, when the cult of the Aten (Amun's rival) became predominant.

BIBL. Davies, N. de G. *The Tomb of Nakht at Thebes.* New York: 1917.

Narmer (Menes)   King   c.3100 - ? BC.

The Egyptian King-Lists provide the name of 'Meni' as the first king of the First Dynasty, and Menes is the Greek form of this name. It is recorded in the later writings of *Herodotus and *Diodorus Siculus, who have preserved legends of this king. It was said that he was the first law-giver and that he brought civilisation to Egypt; also, as a creator-god, he was accredited with the building of the first town and, according to *Herodotus, he drained the plain of Memphis and built the 'White Wall' there, which surrounded the first capital of a united Egypt. At the centre of this town (later known by its Greek name of Memphis), Menes also constructed a temple to the god Ptah. According to Egyptian mythology, the creation of the world was followed by the establishment of a line of god-rulers and they in turn were succeeded by a dynasty of semi-divine kings which culminated in the reign of Menes, the first human ruler.

Today, historians identify Menes as the king who united Upper and Lower Egypt, bringing together the south and the north, originally ruled as two separate kingdoms, the White Land and the Red Land. In c.3100 BC, Menes (ruler of the southern kingdom) probably completed a process of conquest of the north that had been started by his predecessors, including King *Scorpion. Menes is therefore the symbol of the unification of the Two Lands, and is almost certainly to be identified with King Narmer, who is represented wearing the crowns of both the Red and White Lands. There has been discussion over this identification, since there was also the possibility that Menes could have been King 'Aha, who had a substantial funerary monument at Saqqara, the necropolis of Memphis.

The so-called Narmer Palette is one of the most famous and artistically interesting pieces from this period. These large sculptured slate palettes (of which only thirteen survive) were probably votive offerings, and they provide the earliest known examples of hieroglyphic writing. The Narmer Palette, discovered in the Temple of Hieraconpolis in 1897 and now in the Cairo Museum, has scenes carved on both the obverse and reverse; these commemorate the conquest of the north by the southerners and the subsequent unification of the Two Lands under King Narmer.

On one side of the palette, the king wears the Upper Egyptian White Crown and holds aloft a macehead, with which he is about to club the head of a kneeling enemy whom he grasps by his forelock. There is a group of hieroglyphic signs associated with these figures which seem to be an embryonic attempt to convey the meaning of the scene: the king's capture of the inhabitants of the Delta. On the verso, there are two entwined composite animals, probably symbolising the union of the Two Lands, and in the uppermost register, the king, who wears the Red Crown, is shown in the company of a number of standards (which represent those confederates who have helped him achieve victory) as he inspects the decapitated corpses of his enemies.

BIBL. Borchadt, L. Das Grab des Menes. *ZAS* 36 (1898) pp 87-105; Newberry, P. E. Menes: the founder of the Egyptian monarchy, in Brunton, W. et al. *Great Ones of Ancient Egypt.* London:1929 pp. 35-53. Petrie, W. M. F. *Ceremonial State Palettes.* London 1953.

Nebamun and Ipuky   Sculptors   c.1320 BC.

Nebamun and Ipuky were two sculptors who lived towards the end of the Eighteenth Dynasty and were buried in a tomb situated in the area of Asasif at Thebes. The tomb contains wall-scenes showing the usual events: the funerary and burial rites for the deceased, the journey of pilgrimage to Abydos, and the tomb-owners' prayers to *Osiris, god of the dead. There are also scenes of special interest; one shows the deified *Amenophis I and his mother Queen *Ahmose-Nefertari as the recipients of the deceased's prayers, emphasising the role of this royal couple as gods who received a special cult from the royal necropolis workmen of Thebes as the founders of their community at Deir el Medina. Other scenes illustrate the craftsmen (carpenters, goldsmiths and jewellers) whom the tomb-owners supervised in life, and these provide valuable information about crafts and techniques.

Bibl. Davies, N. de G.*The Tomb of Two Sculptors at Thebes*. New York: 1925.

Nebuchadrezzar II   King of Babylon   605 - 562 BC.

Babylonia had replaced *Assyria as Egypt's great enemy when *Assyria fell to the Medes and the Babylonians with the sack of Nineveh, in 612 BC. The kings of the Twenty-sixth Dynasty now faced a new threat, and although *Necho II of Egypt had strengthened his country's hold on Syria/Palestine in the early years of his reign, it is recorded in a Babylonian Chronicle, that the Egyptian army was completely defeated at Carchemish in 605 BC. Here, Nebuchadrezzar had fought on behalf of his father, *Nabopolassar, and had succeeded in taking all Egypt's territorial possessions in the area and destroying her Asiatic empire.

Shortly after this victory, *Nabopolassar died and Nebuchadrezzar returned to Babylon to claim the throne, before he marched again to campaign in Syria. In 604 BC, he attacked and sacked Askelon, whose people appealed to Egypt for help, but there is no record that any aid was sent.

In 601 BC, it is reported that Nebuchadrezzar once again set out to deal with Egypt, but he encountered heavy losses and probably returned to Babylon so that the conflict between the two powers was delayed for some time. *Necho II's successor, *Psammetichus II, pursued a peaceful policy, but when he was followed as king by *Apries in 589 BC, Zedekiah of Judah rebelled against Nebuchadrezzar and Egypt was again involved in the conflict.

In 587 BC, the Babylonians captured and destroyed Jerusalem, Zedekiah was taken prisoner, and a large proportion of the city's population was deported to Babylon. Some of those left behind went to Egypt and the prophet Jeremiah accompanied them.

None of *Apries' actions in this conflict are clearly reported in any of the records, and the military entanglements between the Babylonians and the next Egyptian king, *Amasis, are equally obscure. A cuneiform fragment in the British Museum recalls that Nebuchadrezzar engaged *Amasis in further hostilities in 568-567 BC. Nebuchadrezzar defeated Tyre in 574 BC, and was successful in creating a strong Babylonian influence in Syria/Palestine, but his country's power waned under his weak successors.

The last Babylonian king, Nabonidus, was overthrown in 539 BC by Cyrus II (the Achaemenid ruler) who had already conquered Media, Lydia and the cities of the Ionian coast. When Cyrus occupied Babylon, he dealt kindly with Nabonidus and exiled him to Carmania.

BIBL. Wiseman, D. J. *Chronicles of Chaldaean Kings*. London: 1956, pp 5 ff; Kienitz, F. K. *Die politische*. pp. 18 ff.

Necho I Prince of Sais 672 - 664 BC.

Necho, Prince of the Delta city of Sais, was installed as ruler by the *Assyrian conqueror *Esarhaddon, who followed a policy of giving limited authority to those native Egyptian princes whom he could trust. Necho became the foremost of these and wielded power not only in Sais but also in Memphis; he went on to possess a large kingdom in the western Delta and to adopt the pharaonic style in his own title. He probably began to rule as a local king in Sais in 672 BC and was confirmed as ruler by *Esarhaddon in 671 BC.

As the chief vassal of the *Assyrians in Egypt, Necho became a prime target for Tanuatamun, the nephew of King *Taharka of the Twenty-fifth Dynasty. On *Taharka's death, Tanuatamun claimed the kingship of *Nubia and of Egypt (664-656 BC), briefly regaining the country from the *Assyrians and their vassals. He sailed northwards to Thebes and eventually went on to the Delta and Memphis where he killed Necho I, whom the *Assyrians had appointed as local ruler. This power was short-lived; *Psammetichus I (son of Necho I) seized control and established himself as king of Egypt and the founder of the Twenty-sixth Dynasty.

Necho I left few monuments; his main role was to enable his descendants to gain power and establish themselves as the native rulers of an independent Twenty-sixth Dynasty.

BIBL. Kitchen, K. A. *3rd Int*. pp 145-7;.Yoyotte, J. Nechao. *Supplement au Dictionnaire de la Bible*, vi, col. 365.

Necho II King 610 - 595 BC.

The son and successor of *Psammetichus I, Necho II is not well represented by the monuments; in Egypt his main chronicler is the Greek writer *Herodotus. It is recorded that he was responsible for digging a canal to re-establish a waterway between the Nile and the Red Sea, which had the effect of increasing trade and commerce. He also provided Egypt with a fleet of triremes and sent his *Phoenician sailors around Africa on a voyage that lasted for three years, going from the Red Sea around the Cape and then returning by Gibraltar.

His foreign policy brought him into the centre of world events. The *Assyrian empire had fallen to the Medes and the Babylonians and Necho II now became the main adversary of the Babylonian kings. Like many of his predecessors, Necho II interferred in the politics of Syria/Palestine. He fought against Josiah, king of Judah, who tried to prevent him from passing the walls of Megiddo, and when Josiah was killed, Necho II installed a compliant ruler in Judah. His ambition for international influence was short-lived, for within a few years, *Nebuchadrezzar (son of the Babylonian king, *Nabopolassar) defeated him in a great battle at Carchemish in 605 BC. In 601 BC, *Nebuchadrezzar (who was now king of Babylon) marched against Egypt, but suffered great losses and was forced to return home.

Despite his unsuccessful forays into foreign politics, Necho II was an internationalist, whose interests in both foreign and domestic spheres extended beyond Egypt itself.

BIBL. *Herodotus*, Bk.ii, 158, Bk. iv, 42; Wiseman, D. J. *Chronicles of Chaldaean Kings*. London: 1956; Posener, G. Le canal du Nil à la Mer Rouge avant les Ptolemees. *Chron. d'Eg*.13 (1968) pp. 258-73.

Nectanebo I (Nekhtnebef)   King   380 - 363 BC.

Nectanebo I and his successors came originally from the town of Sebennytos; as the rulers of the Thirtieth Dynasty, they provided Egypt with its last line of great independent kings.This dynasty built extensively; they constructed or consolidated towns and temples, and Nectanebo I's monuments give a superficial impression of stability. On the island of Philae, he built a pylon gateway in the Temple of Karnak (which may have replaced an earlier one erected by *Shoshenk I), and a mammisi (birth house) near the main Temple of Hathor at Denderah. He also donated land to the temple at Edfu, extended temples at Hermopolis, and enriched the domain of the goddess Neith at Sais.

According to *Diodorus Siculus (xv. 41-43), Nectanebo I faced danger from the *Persians who, under Artaxerxes III (404-358 BC), wished to re-establish supremacy over Egypt. Under the satrap Pharnabazus, the *Persians set out for Pelusium in 373 BC, together with the *Greek mercenaries under Iphicrates. When Pharnabazus and Iphicrates disagreed over tactics, Nectanebo I was able to encircle them in the Delta and force them to retreat.

For the rest of his reign, Nectanebo I experienced local rebellions. His son, Tachos (Teos), inherited the throne only briefly (362-361 BC), and then the last ruler, Nectanebo II, held the kingdom from 360 to 343 BC, when it again passed to the *Persians.

BIBL.Kienitz, F. K. *Die politische*.

Neferirkare (Kakai)   King   2473 - 2463 BC.

Neferirkare succeeded his brother *Sahure as the third king of the Fifth Dynasty. He is one of the three kings mentioned in the story preserved in the Westcar Papyrus, in which it is foretold that triplets (the offspring of the sun-god Re and the wife of one of his priests) would inherit the throne instead of the descendants of King *Cheops, and would establish Re's supremacy. Although the named kings (*Userkaf, *Sahure and Neferirkare) were not triplets (*Sahure and Neferirkare were the sons of *Userkaf and his queen *Khentkaues), the Fifth Dynasty certainly enhanced the status of the sun-god. The rulers built solar temples at Abu Ghurob and took the additional title of 'son of Re'.

*Sahure inaugurated the royal cemetery at Abusir and Neferirkare's pyramid and funerary complex were also constructed there, although he died before this could be completed. His valley and mortuary temples were finished by his successors, Neferifre and *Niuserre, and the incomplete Valley Temple was incorporated into *Niuserre's own monument.

In 1893, important papyrus fragments were discovered, dating to a reign towards the end of the dynasty, which provide important information about the accounts and administration of Neferirkare's funerary temple, and the offerings made to the king's statues and those of the queen-mother, *Khentkaues.

BIBL. *AEL* i. pp. 215-22; Borchadt, L. *Das Grabdenkmal des Konigs Nefer-ir-ke3-Re.* Leipzig: 1909.

Nefertari   Queen   reign of *Ramesses II, 1304 - 1237 BC.
Nothing is known of the background of Nefertari, but she was a member of the harem which *Sethos I presented to his heir, *Ramesses II, and she became one of his principal queens, accompanying him on royal occasions throughout much of his reign. She bore *Ramesses II several children, including his eldest son, Amen-hir-wonmef, who later changed his name to Amen-hir-khopshef, although it was the son of another principal queen, Istnofret, who finally succeeded to the throne.

Nefertari appears in scenes in the temples at Luxor and Karnak, but her most famous monuments are the exquisitely decorated tomb in the Valley of the Queens at Thebes, and the rock-cut temple that *Ramesses II built for her, adjacent to his own temple at Abu Simbel. This temple, cut into the cliff, was dedicated to Hathor, the goddess of love and beauty, and the facade was decorated with sculptured figures of the king and queen and some of their children. *Ramesses II and Nefertari, accompanied by their daughter Meryetamun, probably made the long journey southwards to inaugurate these famous temples in Year 24 of the reign.

Nefertari also played a role in international diplomacy. The conclusion of a peace treaty between *Khattusilis III, the *Hittite king, and *Ramesses II was followed by a cordial correspondence between the royal families, and Nefertari exchanged letters and gifts (including jewels and royal garments) with the *Hittite queen Pudukhepa.

BIBL. Goedicke, H. and Thausing, G. *Nofretari.*. Graz: 1971; Kuentz, Ch. and Desroches-Noblecourt, C. *Le Petit Temple d'Abou Simbel*, Vol. 1. Cairo: 1968; Corzo, M. A. (ed.) *Wall paintings of the tomb of Nefertari. EAO*, Cairo and Malibu: 1987.

Neferti, Literary 'sage', probably reign of *Ammenemes I, 1991 - 1962 BC.
The text known as the 'Prophecy of Neferti' is preserved on a Leningrad papyrus

(reign of *Tuthmosis III) and in schoolboy exercises of the Nineteenth Dynasty. In this, Neferti appears as a lector-priest from the Delta town of Bubastis. The scene is set in the Fourth Dynasty: King *Sneferu is at Court and when he seeks diversion his courtiers bring Neferti before him. In a 'prophecy', Neferti then foretells a time of chaos and political disaster similar to the events outlined by *Ipuwer in the 'Admonitions of a Sage'. The situation is saved by the advent of a great king, 'Ameny' by name, whose non-royal origin is underlined.

This text forms part of the so-called Pessimistic Literature but it is also an example of political propoganda, intended to glorify the first king of the Twelfth Dynasty (*Ammenemes I), who seized the throne from the legitimate ruler. The message of the text is that the destruction of the kingdom by civil war can only be prevented by a strong king who can restore unity and order. It is probable that the original composition dates to the reign of *Ammenemes I or that of one of his immediate successors, since its main aim is to justify the usurpation of the throne by this dynastic line. The chaotic events that are described are probably a poetic device rather than a historical description, intended to set the theme of the king as the defender of order, since the period immediately before *Ammenemes I's accession was relatively stable and free from major uprisings (although the reign of *Mentuhotep IV may have experienced some difficulties).

BIBL. *AEL* i. pp. 139-45; Helck, W. *Die Prophezeiung des Nfr .tj.* Wiesbaden: 1970.

Nefertiti   Queen   reign of *Akhenaten   1379 - 1362 BC.

The Chief Queen of *Akhenaten, Nefertiti has become renowned for her beauty, which is evident in her portraits on stelae, in temple reliefs, and in sculptors' trial pieces and models. The most famous of these heads were discovered in workshops at Tell el Amarna in 1914, and they are now in museum collections in Cairo and Berlin. Although her face is well known, there is little information about Nefertiti's origins. One theory – that she might have been the *Mitannian princess *Tadukhepa, who entered the harem of *Amenophis III – is now largely discounted.

Since she never claims the titles of 'King's Daughter' or 'King's Sister', she was not of royal birth, and, for some reason, *Akhenaten apparently did not follow the royal tradition of marrying his eldest sister. It is known that Nefertiti's nurse or tutor was Tey (*Ay's wife), and that she had a sister, Mudnodjme; one theory suggests that she might have been *Ay's daughter by a wife who died, and that she was subsequently reared by his other wife Tey.

Nefertiti became *Akhenaten's chief wife (although he had other wives including a woman named Kia), and she became the mother of six daughters, two of whom (*Meritaten and *Ankhesenpaaten) became queens. Reliefs show the royal couple with their daughters, often in domestic and intimate surroundings which had never been represented before. In other scenes they participate in ritual or ceremonial events: one scene in the Amarna tomb of the steward Meryre shows the royal family taking part in a great reception of foreign tribute in Year 12 of *Akhenaten's reign.

The Queen's political and religious roles are of particular interest. She was apparently appointed, together with Queen *Tiye and *Ay, as *Akhenaten's adviser at the beginning of his reign, and she is frequently shown at the king's side. She is always represented wearing a tall blue crown, which is not seen elsewhere in Egyptian art, and was presumably her unique crown.

The discovery of thousands of blocks of stone, carved with reliefs and inscriptions, at Karnak and Luxor has provided new insight into her religious role. These blocks had been used as infill in the pylons in the temples at Karnak and Luxor, but originally they belonged to *Akhenaten's Aten temples which were built at Thebes, before he moved his capital to Amarna. A modern study – 'The Akhenaten Temple Project' – has been able to use a computer to extract sufficient information from these blocks to reconstruct the original content of some of the temple wall-scenes. These indicate that Nefertiti played a major cultic role in the Aten rituals, holding equal status with the king, and gaining an unparallelled importance for a queen.

After Year 12, she disappears and is replaced by her daughter *Meritaten, who usurps her inscriptions and portraits. This has led to speculation that Nefertiti may have fallen into disgrace at Court, perhaps because she clung to Atenism when her husband had begun to accept at least a partial restoration of the rival god, Amun. She may have been exiled to the northern palace at Amarna, where she possibly had the opportunity to indoctrinate the youthful *Tutankhamun.

There is no real evidence to support this reconstruction of events, and it is unlikely that *Smenkhkare would have been given her name Nefernefruaten if she had been discredited. It is more conceivable that the Queen died, perhaps soon after the death of her second daughter, *Maketaten, and was buried in the Royal Tomb at Amarna, as *Akhenaten had decreed in the city's Boundary Stelae. Her mortal remains may later have been transferred, together with the bodies of other members of this family, from Amarna to Thebes, but neither her body nor her burial place has yet been found.

BIBL. Aldred, C. *Akhenaten and Nefertiti*. Brooklyn: 1973; Aldred, C. *Akhenaten, King of Egypt*. London: 1968; Harris, J. R. Nefertiti Rediviva. *Acta Orientalia* 35 (1973) pp. 5 ff; Nefernefruaten Regnans. *Acta Orientalia* 36 (1974) pp. 11 ff.; Akhenaten or Nefertiti? *Acta Orientalia* 38 (1977) pp. 5 ff.;Samson, J. Nefertiti's regality. *JEA* 63 (1977) pp. 88 ff; Smith, R. W. and Redford, D. B. *The Akhenaten Temple Project: Vol.1:The initial discoveries*. Warminster: 1977.

Neskhons   Queen   reign of *Pinudjem II, 985 - 969 BC.

It was during the Twenty-first Dynasty that the High-priests of Amun at Thebes came to exert great influence in the south, and at this time their wives also became very powerful. Neskhons was the wife of the Theban High-priest *Pinudjem II. She held a string of titles and religious offices and enjoyed great wealth and prestige. In an oracle, the god Amun decreed that she would be deified after her death but also warned her not to undertake evil actions nor to prematurely terminate the lives of her husband or relatives.

Her mummy and coffin were amongst those discovered in 1881 in the cache of royal and priestly remains at Deir Bahri.

BIBL. Kitchen, K. A. *3rd Int.* pp. 65-6; Cerny, J. Studies in the chronology of the Twenty-first Dynasty. *JEA* 32 (1946) pp. 25-6, 30.

Nitocris   Queen   2183 - 2181 BC.

With the death of the aged king *Pepy II, it is probable that there were problems over the succession, and Nitocris briefly took the throne. She was one of only a very few women to become queen regnant, the most famous example being Queen *Hatshepsut. According to *Manetho, Nitocris was the last ruler of the Sixth Dynasty and her name is also given in the Turin Canon. *Herodotus (ii.100) relates a time of conflict and tells the story of the queen's suicide, after she had taken revenge on her brother's murderers, who had tried to make her ruler in place of him.

BIBL . Newberry, P. E. Queen Nitocris of the Sixth Dynasty. *JEA* 29 (1943) pp. 51-4.

Nitocris   Divine Wife of Amun   656 - 586 BC.

The title of 'God's Wife' was originally held by the king's spouse, but from the Twenty-first Dynasty, it was the king's daughter who became 'Divine Wife of Amun' (the chief state god). The princess was installed at Thebes, the cult centre of Amun, where she had extensive powers, endowments and possessions which equalled those of her father in many respects except that her influence was limited to the Theban area. Also, as the god's wife, she was fobidden to take a human husband, and her role at Thebes was to prevent any other ruler from seizing power there and threatening her father's supremacy as king.

In the Twenty-fifth Dynasty, this role was extended further and each king's daughter who became God's Wife was obliged to adopt the next king's choice as her female successor at Thebes.

Nitocris, who was the daughter of *Psammetichus I, succeeded Shepenopet II (the sister of King *Taharka) as Divine Wife of Amun and was endowed with great wealth at Thebes. She ruled there for sixty years and, as her successor, she adopted the daughter of *Psammetichus II.

BIBL. Caminos, R. A. *JEA* 50 (1964) p. 74 and pls. 8-9; Kitchen, K. A . *3rd Int.* pp. 237-9, 403-4.

Niuserre   King   2453 - 2422 BC.

A tale in the Westcar Papyrus in the Berlin Museum emphasises the allegiance that the kings of the Fifth Dynasty had to the cult of the sun-god Re, and the historical facts support this claim. The kings of this dynasty adopted the epithet 'son of Re' as part of the royal titulary, and they constructed sun-temples where Re's cult was given unprecedented importance.

Although it is known that six kings of this dynasty built such temples, only those of Niuserre and *Userkaf have been discovered. With the patronage of Baron von Bissing, Borchadt and Schaefer excavated Niuserre's temple in 1898-1901, and they were able to demonstrate the main features of the building. Situated on the edge of the desert at Abu Ghurob, about a mile north of Abusir where Niuserre built his pyramid, his sun-temple probably copied the main elements of the original sun-temple to Re-Atum at Heliopolis.

It incorporated the same main features as a pyramid complex, having a Valley Building and a covered causeway but, instead of leading to the pyramid and an attached mortuary temple, this causeway gave access to a paved courtyard and a rectangular podium which originally would have supported an obelisk, the cult-symbol of Re. This was also modelled on the original squat obelisk at Heliopolis which was known as the Benben. At the foot of the podium there was an altar where animals were sacrificed as part of the temple ritual. The courtyard was open to the sky which enabled the sun-god to be present at his ceremonies but the causeway was covered and here and elsewhere there were magnificent sculpted and painted wall-reliefs which are now in the Cairo and Berlin Museums.

These reliefs depicted a range of subjects including representations of animals and plants created by the sun, and religious ceremonies such as the foundation of the temple and the celebration of the king's jubilee festival. The scenes showing the activities of the seasons of the year are particularly notable: the three seasons – Akhet, Peret and Shemu – are personified and accompanied by figures representing the nomes or districts of Egypt, and other personifications – the Nile, the Sea, Grain and Nourishment-bring their offerings to the sun-god.

The pyramids of Niuserre and other kings of this dynasty, *Sahure and *Neferirkare, were situated at Abusir. Niuserre's pyramid was excavated by Borchadt in 1902-8, and in the causeway corridor there were some interesting reliefs showing the king as a lion or a griffin, trampling his enemies underfoot.

These temple and pyramid reliefs demonstrate the high standard of art in this period, and the temple reliefs also preserve the names of the king's important courtiers, including *Ti who owned a fine tomb at Saqqara.

BIBL. von Bissing, F. W. *Das Re-Heiligtum des Konigs Ne-Woser-Re* (Rathures) Three vols. Leipzig: 1905-28; von Bissing, F. W. and Kees, H. *Untersuchungen zu den Reliefs aus dem Re-Heiligtum des Rathures.* Munich: 1922; Borchadt, L. *Das Grabdenkmal des Konigs Ne-user-Re.* Leipzig:1907; *AEL* i. pp. 215-22.

Nubians.

In ancient times the land to the south of Egypt was generally known as Nubia: the sub-province from Aswan to the Second Cataract on the Nile was Wawat (Lower Nubia) and beyond that was the sub-province of Kush (Upper Nubia). From earliest times, the Egyptian had sought to colonise and exploit Nubia to gain access to the region's products and to use it as a thoroughfare to obtain the commodities of central Africa.

By the Archaic Period, the Egyptians had annexed the region around Elephantine to Upper Egypt and fixed their own frontier at the First Cataract; King

*Djer of the First Dynasty led his army as far as the Second Cataract. In the Old Kingdom, the pharaohs sent an increasing number of commercial expeditions to Nubia, with supporting military force where necessary; inscriptions in the Aswan rock-tombs of the governors of Elephantine are particularly informative about these ventures.

One governor, Harkhuf, describes his trading expedition to Nubia, which was probably undertaken partly by river and partly overland by donkey, to bring back incense, ivory, ebony, oil and panther skins. Nubia was also an important source for the hard stone that the Egyptians required for their monumental buildings but, in the Middle Kingdom, the region began to be extensively exploited for its gold supplies. Even the name 'Nubia' is derived from the Egyptian word meaning 'gold'.

The expeditions of the Sixth Dynasty ceased during the troubled years of the First Intermediate Period but under the Middle Kingdom rulers, Nubia was properly colonised and Lower Nubia was conquered as far as Semna to the south of the Second Cataract. *Sesostris III is remembered particularly for his expeditions to Nubia and his consolidation of the area. *Sesostris I and *Sesostris III safeguarded the frontier with a string of brick fortresses between Semna South and Buhen at the Second Cataract.

The Nubians became powerful and independent when the *Hyksos ruled Egypt, and they assisted the *Hyksos in their attempt to hold Egypt. The kings of the Eighteenth Dynasty made the repossession of Nubia one of their top priorities on account of the importance of its raw materials. *Tuthmosis I extended Egypt's control to its furthermost point beyond the Fourth Cataract, and *Tuthmosis III established the last major outpost at Napata, near the Fourth Cataract. The new frontier required additional fortresses, since the old Middle Kingdom ones had now lost much of their military significance, and several were established including those at Sai, Sedeinga, Sulb and Napata.

The whole area south of the First Cataract was now administered for the pharaoh by a Viceroy,who was not a royal relative; in the mid-Eighteenth Dynasty his area also included the three southernmost nomes of Upper Egypt. In the reign of *Tuthmosis IV, the Viceroy became entitled 'King's Son of Kush.' His main duty was to obtain the natural resources of the area and to ensure that Nubia's yearly tribute was paid in gold and other goods such as ostrich plumes, leopard skins, animals, precious stones and slaves. The gold came mainly from the mines in Wawat and was worked by prisoners-of-war, slaves and convicted criminals. It was a government monopoly and arrived in Egypt as gold-dust stored in bags, or as bars or ingots.

Egyptian power in Nubia was now at its height and some kings, such as *Amenophis III and *Ramesses II, established their personal cults there and received divine worship in magnificent temples. The Nilotic people of Nubia adopted Egyptian religion, customs and writing and, for some time the pharaohs sent expeditions to Nubia only to fight the tribesmen on the desert fringes. For centuries, the Nubians provided auxiliary forces for Egypt's army, and as the '*Medjay', they helped to police Egypt.

In the New Kingdom, the Egyptians came into direct contact for the first time with the negro peoples of Central Africa and depicted them in their art. Ultimately the Nubians reversed the process of Egyptian conquest and colonisation when, in the Twenty-fifth Dynasty, they briefly became the rulers of Egypt.

BIBL. Save-Soderbergh, T. *Agypten und Nubien. Ein Beitrag zur Geschichte altagyptischer Aussenpolitik.* Lund: 1941; Giorgini, M. S. Soleb. *Kush* 6 (1958) pp. 82-98; 7 (1959) pp. 154-70; Reisner, G. A. *The Archaeological Survey of Nubia* (Report for 1907-8).(two vols) Cairo: 1910; Kirwan, L. P. Studies in the later history of Nubia. *Liverpool Annals of Archaeology and Anthropology* 24 (1937) pp. 69-105; Emery, W. B. *Egypt in Nubia.* London: 1965.

O

Osiris   God of the Dead.

Osiris was probably Egypt's best-known god and received worship for over two thousand years. According to mythology, he was originally a human ruler who had brought civilisation to his country and was later deified. He was the son of Geb (the earth-god) and Nut (the sky-goddess) and the brother of Isis (who was also his wife), Nephthys, and Seth.

Osiris had probably originated as a fertility god and the incarnation of Egypt and its vegetation, but he soon acquired other roles. His first cult-centre was at Busiris in the Delta, where he was identified with the local god Andjety, a god-king from whom Osiris probably adopted his characteristics as an early ruler. At Memphis, he took over the god Sokaris who was associated with the creator deity Ptah, and assimilated his funerary features. His main cult-centre was Abydos where, by the Fifth Dynasty, he had become identified with the local god Khentiamentiu, who was a god of the dead and of cemeteries.

As well as his role as a fertility god, mythology also represented Osiris as a human who had suffered treachery and death but who triumphed and was resurrected as a god. Although aspects of the god's mythology are preserved in Egyptian literary sources, the only complete version of his myth survives in the work of a Greek author, *Plutarch, in his *De Iside et Osiride*. According to this text, Osiris was murdered by his brother Seth, and his body was dismembered and scattered throughout Egypt. Isis, his devoted wife, reunited his limbs and posthumously conceived their son Horus (originally there had been a falcon-god of the sky with the same name in Egyptian mythology). Isis hid Horus in the marshes of Chemmis to save him from the wrath of his uncle Seth, but when he was grown, Horus set out to fight Seth in order to avenge his father's death. The conflict was fierce and eventually Horus and Seth sought judgement before the divine tribunal: the gods found in favour of Horus who became King of Egypt, while Seth was banished, and Osiris was resurrected as Judge of the Dead and King of the Underworld. This symbolised the triumph of good over evil, and Osiris could henceforth promise his followers a unique chance of individual resurrection and eternal life.

This story was easy to understand and held a definite message, compelling worshippers to follow Osiris. He acquired all the funerary aspects, such as the role of god of embalming and of the western necropolis, which had previously been held by Anubis. With regard to the afterlife, Osiris also overtook the solar cult, and by the end of the Fifth Dynasty, every king was believed to become an 'Osiris' on death and, as a living ruler, to be the incarnation of Horus, having received the throne from his father.

By the Middle Kingdom, there was a marked process of democratisation in funerary beliefs and practices, and Osiris became very important because he could offer eternal life to all true believers. At death, every worthy person could now expect to become 'Osiris.'

At Abydos (where it was believed that Osiris' head was buried), an annual festival and miracle play were held which enacted events in his life, death and resurrection. Pilgrims flocked to Abydos at the beginning of the fourth month of the Egyptian year when the Nile flood-waters had receded and the fields were ready for cultivation. They watched and participated in the miracle plays which enacted the myth of Osiris, but in the secret chambers of the temple the priests performed the mysteries which were designed to reproduce Osiris' functions as a god of vegetation and to ensure the advent of the annual rebirth of the vegetation which had been destroyed by the sun and drought. These rites included the 'Raising of the Djed-pillar' (the god's cult-symbol). This was performed to ensure the god's resurrection. All believers attempted to visit Abydos at least once in a lifetime or to have their mummified remains taken there after death, to enhance their chances of an individual resurrection and life in the after world.

The representations of Osiris showed him as a mummiform figure who wore a crown and carried the royal insignia. He was frequently mentioned in the Pyramid Texts (the world's earliest body of religious writings that have survived) and in the Books of the Dead. In the *Ptolemaic Period some of his characteristics were transferred to Serapis, the hybrid Graeco-Egyptian deity, who was introduced by *Ptolemy I.

Osiris enjoyed immense popularity at most periods, effectively combining the concept of individual rebirth with the physical reality of the annual resurgence of Egypt's vegetation.

BIBL.Faulkner, R. *The Ancient Egyptian Pyramid Texts*. Warminster: 1985; Gardiner, A. H. Was Osiris an ancient king subsequently deified? *JEA* 46 (1960) p.104 Brief Communications; Griffith, J. G. Plutarch, *De Iside et Osiride*. Cardiff: 1970.

Osorkon II   King   874 - 850 BC.

The Twenty-second Dynasty is sometimes known as the Bubastite Dynasty. Osorkon, one of its kings, tried to retain the unity of the country and prevent a secession of the priests at Memphis and Thebes, by placing members of his own family in these positions.

At Tanis and Bubastis – the two great Delta cities at this time – Osorkon II built extensively, using stone removed from the city of Pi-Ramesse, constructed years before in the reign of *Ramesses II. At Bubastis, the archaeologist Naville excavated a great granite doorway that was of particular interest because it was decorated with reliefs depicting royal events, including the jubilee festival celebrated by Osorkon II in Year 22 of his reign.

The most dramatic discovery from his reign was his burial chamber in the royal tombs at Tanis, which contained his magnificent sarcophagus, canopic jars and funerary statuettes. The quartzite chest that housed his canopic jars was re-used from the Middle Kingdom; the four canopic jars which had stored the king's mummified viscera were finely carved in limestone. The tomb had been opened twice in antiquity, first to receive the burial of Prince Amen-Re Hornakht (probably the son of Osorkon II), whose quartzite sarcophagus was also found there by the Professor Pierre Montet, and secondly, when it was ransacked by tomb-robbers.

BIBL. Montet, P. *La necropole de Tanis: les constructions et le tombeau d'Osorkon II*. Paris: 1947; Kitchen, K. A. *3rd Int*. pp. 313-26; Naville, E. *The Festival-Hall of Osorkon II in the Great Temple of Bubastis*. London: 1892.

P

Peleset   One of the *Sea-peoples   c.1198 - 1166 BC.

The Peleset are listed amongst the *Sea-peoples in the Egyptian records of the battles that were fought by *Ramesses III. They have been tentatively identified as those who immigrated, probably in two or three stages, into Palestine and became the Philistines. In the Egyptian scenes they are shown as clean-shaven and they wear a panelled kilt, decorated with tassels, and, as a chest protector, either a ribbed corselet or they are bandaged with horizontal strips of linen; on the head, they have a circle made of either upright reeds or leather strips. Their weapons include spears and sometimes a rapier sword and a circular shield.

It is evident that their families accompanied them on the journey to Egypt, transported in wooden carts with solid wheels that were drawn by oxen. These animals were clearly humped oxen, of a type bred in Anatolia but not in the Aegean nor in Palestine, and the carts are of an Anatolian style. It is also evident that these people had close connections with Anatolia and were associated in some way with the *Akawasha with whom they fought against *Ramesses III in Year 5 of his reign.

Biblical references suggest that their homeland was Caphtor which may have been Crete or, less probably, Cilicia. Part of the coast of Palestine was called the 'Cretan' south, and this seems to emphasise a link with Crete, but their pottery displays a marked similarity in its shape to Mycenaean examples.

The original homeland of the Peleset is therefore obscure, and it is even possible that either Crete or Caphtor were only places en route and that ultimately they came from another country or area.

BIBL. Chicago University, Oriental Institute *Medinet Habu.* (four vols) 1932-40; Edgerton, W. and Wilson, J. A. *Historical records of Ramesses III.* Chicago: 1936; Macalister, R. A. S. *The Philistines, their history and civilisation.* Chicago: 1965; *CAH* ii,ch xxviii.

Pepy I   King   2332 - 2283 BC.

Later generations venerated Pepy I as one of the great rulers of the Old Kingdom. It is probable that as the son of Queen Iput, he succeeded *Teti, although another king – Usekare – appears to have ruled briefly for a year, perhaps while Iput acted as regent for her son.

Pepy I married two sisters who were both named Meryreankhnes; one became the mother of the next king, Merenre, while the second sister produced *Pepy II who ultimately succeeded Merenre. It is likely that Pepy I married the second queen late in his reign, as *Pepy II was only a child when he succeeded to the throne. The sisters came from a non-royal background; they were the daughters of

Khui, a powerful hereditary governor of the Thinite nome, and their brother, Djau, became vizier. Earlier tradition had demanded that the king should marry his own full- or half-sister, but it was now more important to gain the support of the powerful provincial nobility.

During this reign, Weni – a man of humble origin – rose to become a judge, and his inscription from Abydos provides details of the events of his career: as judge, he heard in private the cases of conspiracy that had occurred in the royal harem, one of which implicated a queen of Pepy I. He also mentions his role in dealing with the incursions by the *Beduin on Egypt's north-eastern frontier, indicating that pressures were already building up in that area. Later, such harrassment would contribute to the downfall of the Old Kingdom.

Pepy I constructed a pyramid complex a short distance from Saqqara and although the temple has not been excavated, the pyramid is important because here, in 1881, Maspero first discovered the evidence that the interior walls of the pyramids of the later Old Kingdom were inscribed with the Pyramid Texts. These religious spells, which occur in several pyramids, comprise the earliest known body of religious and magical texts from ancient Egypt. Other major building activities of the reign included the king's sanctuary at Bubastis in the Delta; also during his reign expeditions were sent to Nubia and Sinai.

Towards the end of his reign, it is possible that the king associated his elder son Merenre with him on the throne, providing an early example of co-regency.

BIBL . Drioton, E. Notes diverses, 2. Une Coregence de Pepy Ier de Merenre (?). *Ann. Serv.* 44 (1945) pp. 55-6; Mercer, S. A. B. *The Pyramid Texts in translation and commentary.* (four vols) New York: 1952; Habachi, L. *Tell Basta.* Cairo: 1947, pp. 11 ff.

Pepy II King 2269-2175 BC.

Pepy II, the younger son of *Pepy I, came to the throne as a young child, following the untimely death of his brother, Merenre. He is accorded the longest reign in Egypt's history and was the last ruler of importance in the Old Kingdom; *Manetho stated that he acceded to the throne when he was only six years old and lived into his hundredth year. His mother acted as his regent in the early years of the reign.

In a wall inscription in the Aswan tomb of the official Harkhuf, the text of a delightful letter is preserved. Harkhuf had served the kings Merenre and Pepy II and, as Governor of Upper Egypt, he had led four expeditions to *Nubia on behalf of the king. Pepy II had apparently written this letter to Harkhuf at the time of one of these expeditions, when he was bringing a dancing pygmy back from the south for the young king. The royal child, eager to see the pygmy, exhorts Harkhuf to take great care and to bring him safely to the palace – '...Come north to the Residence at once! Hurry and bring with you this pygmy... ! '.

This inscription also provides the most significant source for knowledge of Egypt's relationships with *Nubia at this time. Broken alabaster vases bearing the names of Pepy II, *Pepy I and Merenre have been discovered at Kerma in the Sudan, possibly indicating that the Egyptians may have already established a trading centre far to the south. Vase fragments inscribed with the names of *Pepy I and Pepy II have also been found at *Byblos in Syria, and trading ventures to this city were probably regular events during this period. There were also expeditions to the mines in Sinai, and it is evident that foreign contacts were widely established.

By the time that Pepy II's long reign came to an end, the royal power had diminished as the cumulative result of various political, economic and religious factors. The provincial nobility no longer felt a strong allegiance to the king, for they now held their governorships on a hereditary basis; other factors included the widening circle of inheritance of some Crown land and the loss of taxation on the land that the king distributed to the nobility. In addition, the royal funerary monuments and the solar temples had placed an increasing burden on the king's limited resources. Pepy II was perhaps senile in the later years of his reign and incapable of vigorous rulership; he may well be the old king who is mentioned in the literary text known as the 'Admonitions of *Ipuwer' who, isolated in his palace, is unaware of the destruction of his kingdom.

There is also evidence in Pepy II's reign that the borders of Egypt were being harrassed. Hekaib (another Governor of Aswan) recorded how he was sent to deal with inter-tribal troubles in Nubia, and soon after the death of the king, the '*Asiatics' probably increased their incursions on Egypt's north-east frontier. Eventually the society of the Old Kingdom collapsed and was replaced by the chaotic conditions of the First Intermediate Period.

Pepy II was the last king of the Old Kingdom to build a classic pyramid complex; it is situated south of Saqqara and was excavated by Jequier between AD 1929 and 1936. It is a good example of the most advanced form of such a complex and displays the same standard of excellence as the pyramids of the Fifth Dynasty. In the pyramid mortuary temple, food and other requirements are depicted in the wall reliefs so that these could be magically activated for the king in his next life.Outside the enclosure wall of the complex there were three small pyramids, each with its own set of buildings; these were intended for three important queens, Neith, Iput and Udjebten.

Pepy II was succeeded by his son, Merenre II, but the end of the Old Kingdom when the centre of power would move away from Memphis, was imminent.

BIBL. Jequier, G. *Le monument funeraire de Pepi II.*(three vols) Cairo: 1936-40; Dixon, D. M. The Land of Yam. *JEA* 44 (1958) pp. 40-55.

Peribsen King c.2730 BC.

Peribsen was a ruler of the Second Dynasty whose connection with the despised god Seth has been the subject of discussion. Unlike other kings whose names were preceded by a Horus-name (indicating their allegiance to the god Horus), Peribsen's name was associated with a Seth-name, and he also used the name 'Seth-Re'. In addition, on one of his seal impressions, there occurs the inscription 'The Ombite (i.e.Seth) has given the Two Lands to his son Peribsen.'

Like other early rulers, Peribsen had a funerary monument (tomb or cenotaph) at Abydos which was excavated by Petrie; here jar-sealings were discovered that bore the names of Seth-Peribsen and Horus Sekhemib, and it has been suggested that these names both refer to one ruler who, for political and religious motives, changed his allegiance from Horus to Seth. It is equally possible that these names may in fact refer to two distinct men. The title of 'Conqueror of the foreign lands' which Peribsen bore may indicate that he had introduced the cult of Seth into the north-eastern Delta.

There is also confusion and difficulty over his relationship with *Kha'sekhem and *Kha'sekhemui; it is possible that he ruled concurrently with *Kha'sekhem over a divided Egypt, or that *Kha'sekhem may have succeeded him as ruler of the country, once again uniting the supporters of Horus with those of Seth. *Kha'sekhem perhaps then marked this unification by taking a new name–*Kha'sekhemui – although another interpretation is that *Kha'sekhemui succeeded *Kha'sekhem.

BIBL. Petrie, W. M. F. *The Royal Tombs of the earliest dynasties.* (two vols) London:1900-1; Petrie, W. M. F. *Abydos.* (three vols) London: 1902-4; Newberry, P. E .The Set Rebellion of the Second Dynasty. *Ancient Egypt* Vol.2 (1922) pp. 40-6; Griffiths, J. G. *The conflict of Horus and Seth.* Liverpool:1960.

Persians (in Egypt) 525 - 332 BC.

Egypt was conquered by the Persian king *Cambyses in 525 BC; thus annexed to the Persian Empire, Egypt experienced domination in this so-called First Persian Period (the Twenty-seventh Dynasty) which lasted until 401 BC when the country regained independence for a span of sixty years. A later Persian king, Artaxerxes III, then reconquered Egypt and the Second Persian Period (the Thirty-first Dynasty) lasted until the Macedonian king, *Alexander the Great, arrived in 332 BC.

Egypt thus became a satrapy of the Persian Empire, ruled by a governor (satrap), and the attitudes of the Persian rulers towards their possession varied considerably: later writers recorded that *Cambyses was an impious tyrant, while *Darius I apparently took an interest in Egypt, overhauling the legal system and restoring the ancient canal that ran from the Nile to the Red Sea.

There is no evidence that the Persians excessively exploited Egypt, and they apparently observed at least some of a Pharaoh's religious duties. Persia ruled Egypt for over one hundred and thirty years; numbers of foreigners came to the country, Egyptian soldiers fought in the Persian campaigns, and Egyptian artists and officials worked at the Persian capital cities. However, it seems that these conquerors had very little impact on the native civilisation of Egypt and that, as foreigners, they were unwelcome rulers.

BIBL. Posener, G. *La premiere domination Perse en Egype.* Cairo: 1936; Kienitz, F. K. *Die politische.* pp. 76-112, 231 ff.

Petosiris High-priest of Thoth c.300 BC.

At Tuna el Gebel in Middle Egypt there is the necropolis of the ancient city of

Hermopolis, which was a centre for the worship of the ibis-god, Thoth. In AD 1920, Lefebvre excavated here the family tomb of Petosiris, who was an important citizen of Hermopolis and the High-priest of the Temple of Thoth. He lived at the time when Egypt was ruled by *Ptolemy I, and the decoration of his tomb is of particular significance in terms of Graeco-Egyptian art.

Petosiris, his wife and one of his sons were buried in the shaft of this tomb, and his sarcophagus, which was discovered there, was taken to Cairo Museum. It is the vestibule and the chapel of the tomb which are of great importance, for it is here that wall scenes provide an excellent example of the hybrid art which was developing at that time. This emerged alongside the purely Greek forms which flourished mainly at Alexandria and the traditional Egyptian style which remained untouched by the pressures of Greek culture that now prevailed throughout Egypt.

The theme of the scenes in Petosiris' tomb remains true to the Egyptian tradition. However, the style – in terms of clothes, hairstyles and personal adornment of the figures – is Hellenistic, and the accompanying wall inscriptions include such elements as personal piety which do not usually occur in traditional Egyptian funerary texts. In the vestibule (a later addition, dedicated to Petosiris), the hybrid art is present in the wall scenes showing daily activities – harvesting, metal-working, carpentry and bringing offerings to the deceased. In the chapel (built by Petosiris for the cult of his father and eldest brother), the scenes are more traditionally Egyptian in style, and depict the funeral procession, the presentation of offerings, and the worship of the gods.

BIBL Suys, E. *Vie de Petosiris*. Brussels: 1927; Picard, C. Le influences etrangeres au tombeau de Petosiris: Grece ou Perse? *BIFAO* 30 (1931) pp. 201-7.

Phoenicians   c.1200 - 540 BC.

The *Greeks were the first to use the name 'Phoenicians' for all the Canaanites; later, the term came to refer to those people who occupied the coastal area of Syria/Palestine and retained an independent status.The early inhabitants of Syria/Palestine had political and trading contacts with Egypt, through the coastal town of *Byblos, from at least as early as the Old Kingdom. When Egypt undertook its great territorial expansion in the Eighteenth Dynasty, the petty princes of the area became Egyptian vassals and the pharaohs ensured that these city-states were ruled by their favoured candidates. As the Egyptian empire declined during the reign of *Akhenaten, local rulers such as *Rib-Addi, the governor of *Byblos, and Abimilki of Tyre, wrote in vain to the Egyptian capital, begging for Egyptian assistance. In the Nineteenth Dynasty the campaigns of *Sethos I and *Ramesses II against the *Hittites once again restored Egyptian influence in the Phoenician coastal area.

It was only in the latter half of the second millennium BC that the Phoenicians became a distinct and separate entity. By 1200 BC, the Canaanites were squeezed in the south by the Philistines and the Hebrews, and in the north by the *Hittites and Amorites, so that they were able to retain only the central coastal strip which became known as Phoenicia.

The Egyptian kingdom, divided in the Twenty-first Dynasty, rapidly declined and the *Hittites also lost their power; with these great influences removed, several kingdoms now developed and flourished in Syria/Palestine – Phoenicia, Philistia, Israel, Moab and Edom. The Phoenicians, as great explorers and colonisers, soon spread their commercial and political influence throughout the Mediterranean and beyond. Their naval prowess was also recognised in later periods and, together with *Greeks and *Carians, they were used to fight as mercenaries for the Egyptian kings of the Twenty-sixth Dynasty, whose fleet they modernised and over whom they gained great influence.

Eventually, the Phoenicians were taken by *Nebuchadrezzar of Babylon but when he in turn was conquered by the *Persians in 539 BC, Phoenicia with Syria and Cyprus became the fifth satrapy (governate) of the *Persian Empire, and Phoenician naval power was adopted as one of the greatest forces in the *Persians' sea battles.

No documentary evidence has yet been discovered on the Phoenician sites which provides any commentary on their own view of their relationships with their great neighbours – Egypt, *Assyria, *Persia and the *Greeks. Thus to some extent it has only been possible to interpret their history from the literature of other societies.

BIBL. Leclant, J. in Ward, W. A. (ed.) *The role of the Phoenicians in the interaction of Mediterranean civilizations*. Beirut: 1968, pp. 13 ff; Harden, D. *The Phoenicians*. Harmondsworth:1971.

Piankhy (Piye)   King   747 - 716 BC.

Piankhy was the ruler of a kingdom which developed to the south of Egypt, with its capital situated at Napata. These people worshipped the Egyptian god Amen-Re and preserved many elements of the Egyptian culture of the Eighteenth Dynasty, and there has been some discussion of their possible origins; although some may have been descendants of priests of Amen-Re, who perhaps emigrated southwards, the later population undoubtedly also incorporated local elements.

Piankhy was the son of the Napatan chieftain or king, Kashta, and the brother of *Shabako. During the Twenty-second and Twenty-third Dynasties, Egypt was ruled by a number of princelings, and one – Tefnakht, Prince of Sais – attempted to expand southwards as far as Lisht.Piankhy, to prevent further advances by Tefnakht and also perhaps to re-establish some order in the homeland of his revered god, Amen-Re, marched northwards to attack these Libyan rulers of the Twenty-second and Twenty-third Dynasties.

*Manetho does not mention Piankhy, but a huge stela dating to Year 21 of Piankhy's reign, refers to his great campaign in c.730 BC. The inscription not only relates his prowess as a warrior, his capture of the cities of Egypt, and the resultant slaughter and capture of prisoners, but also emphasises his great piety regarding the Egyptian gods, particularly Amen-Re. Although it is evident that Egypt was divided into many principalities, Piankhy appears to have conquered the south and received submission from the northern rulers. After this great victory, Piankhy returned to his own kingdom and the local princes resumed their rulership in Egypt, with Tefnakht's descendants forming the Twenty-fourth Dynasty. Piankhy was buried in the south at Kurru, in the first true pyramid to be built there (many years after the Egyptian rulers themselves had ceased to use pyramids). His successor, *Shabako, returned to campaign in Egypt (715 BC) and to remove Tefnakht's successor, Bakenranef; he ultimately established the Twenty-fifth Dynasty and his daughter, Shepenopet II, was adopted as the Divine Wife of Amun.

BIBL. Von Zeissl, H. *Athiopen und Assyrer in Agypten*.Gluckstadt: 1944; Kitchen, K A *3rd Int.* pp 363 ff; Dunham, D. *El Kurru*. Cambridge:1950.

Pinehas   Viceroy of Ethiopia   reign of *Ramesses XI, 1113 - 1085 BC.

Pinehas held the titles of 'Viceroy of Ethiopia' and 'King's Son of Kush' and was a powerful and important person in the reign of *Ramesses XI. Among other sources, he is mentioned in the documents relating to the tomb-robbery trials of the Twentieth Dynasty.Although the details remain unclear, it appears that, perhaps at the king's request, he fomented some kind of armed rebellion against Amenhotep, the High-priest of Amun at Thebes, whose increasing power may have prompted him to claim authority over Ethiopia.

It is probable that Pinehas seized power at Thebes and established control over the city and its surrounding area, thus crushing the centre of Amenhotep's power. Eventually, Pinehas may have returned to the south and continued his resistance from there; a tomb was prepared for him at Aniba in *Nubia, which may have been his original home.

*Herihor took over Pinehas' place at Thebes; he became High-priest of Amun but also adopted the title of King's Son of Kush and annexed the offices and powers that were part of that position.

BIBL . Reisner, G. A. The Viceroys of Ethiopia. *JEA* 6 (1920) pp. 28-55, 73-88; Lefebvre, G. *Histoire des grands prêtres d'Amon de Karnak jusqu'à la XXIe dynastie.* Paris: 1929; Peet, T. E. *The Great Tomb-robberies of the Twentieth Dynasty.* (two vols) Oxford: 1930, pp. 124; Cerny, J. *Late Ramesside Letters.* Brussels :1939 pp. 7-8.

Pinudjem I, High-priest of Amun 1064 - 1045 BC; 'King' 1044 - 1026 BC.

Smendes (the first king of the Twenty-first Dynasty) moved the capital from Thebes to Tanis, and reached an agreement with *Pinudjem I, the High-priest of Amun at Thebes and Governor of the South, regarding the division of power within the kingdom: Pinudjem I was to recognise Smendes as Pharaoh and Smendes would regard Pinudjem as the effective ruler of the south, and both would agree to mutual rights of succession.

*Pinudjem I was the descendant of *Herihor, who had inaugurated this dynastic line of powerful High-priests at Thebes and, in contemporary inscriptions, Pinudjem I was usually mentioned only as a High-priest.There is one instance during his lifetime where he used the royal title, and on his coffin he was called

'King of Upper Egypt.' In the same way King *Psusennes I and King Amenemope, at Tanis, also adopted the title of High-priest of Amun thus asserting their supremacy over Thebes.

Despite these rival claims, the Tanite and Theban ruling families remained on good terms, and princesses of Tanis married Theban High-priests so that from Pinudjem I's time onwards, the Theban High-priests, through their mothers, became descendants of the Tanite pharaohs.

Building projects that date to the time of Pinudjem I include the decoration of the Temple of Khonsu at Karnak, and the great town wall near the modern village of El Hiba which was perhaps intended as a defense against the local chiefs of the *Libyan mercenaries who settled nearby at Heracleopolis. Pinudjem I and his predecessor *Herihor were responsible for the order to rebury the royal mummies whose original burial places had suffered desecration at the hands of the tomb-robbers, but the task was completed by his descendant, *Pinudjem II.

BIBL. Kitchen, K. A. *3rd Int*. pp 258 ff.

Pinudjem II   High-priest of Amun   985 - 969 BC.

Pinudjem II, a High-priest of Amun at Karnak, was the grandson of *Pinudjem I and the son of Menkheperre who were both members of that dynastic line of High-priests who, in the Twenty-first Dynasty, ruled the south of Egypt from Thebes. His son *Psusennes II was also a High-priest and he assumed the kingship of the whole country when the pharaoh at Tanis finally died.

One of Pinudjem II's most enduring achievements was the rescue and reburial of nine kings and some of the queens and princes whose original tombs had suffered desecration. *Pinudjem I had given the order for this to be undertaken, but it was Pinudjem II who, in Year 5 of the reign of the Tanite king Siamun, organised the removal of the mummies and any of their surviving funerary goods and their reburial in the tomb of his wife, *Neskhons. In Year 10 of the same reign, the mummies of Ramesses I, *Sethos I and *Ramesses II were added to the group in this tomb which lay to the south of Deir el Bahri. The tomb also contained *Neskhons' own burial and the mummies of Pinudjem II and Masahert – the only Theban High priests to be discovered here – when the cache was revealed in 1881. All these bodies and their associated funerary goods were ultimately taken to the Cairo Museum.

BIBL. Kitchen, K. A. *3rd Int*.; Maspero, G. *Les Momies royales de Deir el Bahari*. Cairo: 1889; Reeves C.N. *Valley of The Kings*. London: 1990. Smith, G. E. *The Royal Mummies*. Cairo: 1912.

Pliny the Elder   Classical Author   AD 23 - 79.

Pliny's *Historia Naturalis* provides a less important study of Egypt's geography than the account given by *Strabo, but he supplies some useful and interesting information.

107

His extensive collection of facts is compiled from the works of earlier authors; he refers not only to human inventions but also to all material objects that had not been manufactured by man and, with regard to Egypt, he comments on the monuments within the country but also on those – such as obelisks – which had been brought out of Egypt, at the Roman emperor's decree, and transported to Rome. He also gives an account of the process of mummification, thus providing a third commentary on this subject by a Classical writer, the others being given by *Herodotus and *Diodorus Siculus.

BIBL. Pliny. *Selections from the History of the World commonly called the Natural History of C.Plinius Secundus*.Transl. by Turner, P., Carbondale, Ill: 1962.

Plutarch Classical Author Before AD 50 - after AD 120.

The works of the *Greek writer, Plutarch of Chaeronea, have preserved, in its fullest form, one of Egypt's greatest myths, although the same story occurs earlier in the writings of *Diodorus Siculus.

This myth, *De Iside et Osiride* ('On Isis and Osiris'), relates the story of *Osiris who was originally believed to have been a human ruler who brought civilisation to Egypt. He was subsequently murdered by his brother Seth, his body was dismembered and his limbs scattered throughout the land. His devoted wife, Isis, reunited his limbs and posthumously conceived their son, Horus, who in adulthood, fought Seth in a famous conflict to avenge his father's death. The gods sat in judgement on their case and, when they found in favour of Horus, he became King of the Living while Osiris was resurrected as Judge of the Dead and King of the Underworld; Seth, was banished. The Myth expressed in graphic terms the eternal triumph of good over evil and the success of life over death, as well as the continual ability of the countryside and the vegetation to renew their vitality after the Nile's annual inundation. It was a potent story that symbolised in vivid and easily understood imagery the roles of Seth as the 'Evil One' and of *Osiris as the god of the dead, who could promise his followers the chance of individual resurrection and eternal life.

Although there is no extant Egyptian account of the Myth, Plutarch's version undoubtedly recounts the story as it existed in popular mythology and it agrees to a considerable degree with the references and allusions which are preserved in the Egyptian religious texts found on temple walls and in papyri. Plutarch probably provides an authentic outline of the Myth, but his account almost certainly presents an analysis of the Myth's meaning and significance which reflects a *Greek rather than an Egyptian outlook.Nevertheless, even with its inaccuracies, Plutarch and the other Classical writers provided one of the few detailed accounts of Egyptian religion which was available to Western scholars during the Middle Ages and the Renaissance. Only with modern archaeological excavation of the sites and monuments and the decipherment of Egyptian hieroglyphs, could scholars obtain firsthand information about Egyptian civilisation which enabled Classical sources to be reassessed.

BIBL. *Plutarch's Moralia.* (fourteen vols) Vol. 5. Cambridge, Mass.:1936; Griffiths, J. G. Plutarch, *De Iside et Osiride*. Cardiff: 1970.

Psammetichus I King 664 - 610 BC.

The Egyptian local princes who had intrigued with *Taharka, the Ethiopian ruler of Egypt, against the *Assyrians were removed to Nineveh. One of these – *Necho I, the Prince of Sais – and his son Psammetichus were returned to Egypt by the Assyrian king, *Ashurbanipal. *Necho then became *Assyria's vassal ruler at Sais and Memphis, while Psammetichus was appointed ruler of Athribis (c.665 BC) under his *Assyrian name of Nabu-shezibanni.

Psammetichus followed *Necho I as ruler of Sais and Memphis and, as Psammetichus I, became the true founder of the Twenty-sixth Dynasty. At first, he probably ruled concurrently with Tanuatamun (664-656 BC), the last Ethiopian ruler of Egypt, after the deaths of Tanuatamun's predecessor, *Taharka, and Psammetichus' father, *Necho I. While Tanuatamun ruled in the south, Psammetichus I established a strong position in the Delta. By Year 8 of his reign, Psammetichus I had probably become the effective overlord of the Delta, bringing rivals under his control and establishing his leadership of the 'Dodecarchy' of native princes to whom *Herodotus refers (ii,147).

*Herodotus (ii,152) also mentions Psammetichus' use of *Greek mercenaries, who undoubtedly helped him to gain mastery over the other Delta princes, while in Middle Egypt he had the support of a powerful ally, Pediese. By Year 9 (656 BC), Psammetichus had gained recognition as ruler in Upper Egypt and his daughter, *Nitocris, was sent to Thebes to be adopted by Shepenopet II, the God's Wife of Amun, and her heir apparent, Amenardis II, as their future successor. There is a detailed account of this journey on a stela found at Karnak and in a set of reliefs in the Temple of Mut at Karnak. *Nitocris received great riches and possessions, including some two thousand acres of land. Sixty years later, the process was repeated when she in turn adopted as her successor the daughter of *Psammetichus II. At Thebes, Psammetichus I left the old officials in place, including the Mayor of Thebes and High-priest of Amun, *Montemhet. However, as they died, he replaced them with his own men so that by 654 BC he was the strong and effective ruler of the whole country.

In this powerful position Psammetichus I ceased to pay tribute to *Assyria, although in 616 BC he decided that it was prudent to form an alliance with *Assyria against the new threat posed by the joint forces of the Babylonians and the Medes. By 655 or 654 BC, he had also made an alliance with *Gyges of Lydia who sent troops to assist him in Egypt; generally,although it is probable that he sent a punitive expedition to Nubia early in his reign, Psammetichus I focused his attention mainly on Western Asia and his northern neighbours.

At home, an increasing number of foreigners began to reside in Egypt, coming either as mercenaries in the army or as traders, and this began to cause concern amongst the indigenous population; consequently it was necessary to introduce certain measures to confine foreigners to particular areas. Nevertheless, the dynasty was based on these foreign military skills and the kings also made good use of *Greek naval expertise and trading ability. As a parallel development, there was a revival of national spiritin and in art and in religion it is possible to determine a pronounced archaism and a reassertion of the essentially Egyptian values of the earlier periods. In particular, animal worship – which was a distinctively Egyptian concept – became increasingly popular and was seen as a focus for nationalistic sentiments.

BIBL. Kienitz, F. K. *Die politische*. Caminos, R. A. The Nitocris Adoption Stela. *JEA* 50 (1964) pp. 71-101, pls. 7-10.

Psammetichus II   King   595 - 589 BC.

The reign of Psammetichus II, the son and successor of *Necho II, was brief but not uneventful; more monuments have survived from his time than from the reigns of his two predecessors.

Stelae from Tanis and Karnak and *Greek inscriptions left behind on one of the colossal statues at *Ramesses II's temple at Abu Simbel (the graffiti of Psammetichus' *Greek, *Carian and *Phoenician mercenaries) have preserved details of this king's campaign which penetrated deep into *Nubia. *Amasis, who later became pharaoh, was a general on this campaign which may have been part of a policy against the Ethiopians; in this reign there is also the first evidence that, on their monuments, the names of the Ethiopian rulers of the Twenty-fifth Dynasty were damaged and erased.

Psammetichus II died in 589 BC when King Zedekiah of Judah was rebelling against *Nebuchadrezzar of Babylon, and Psammetichus' son and successor, *Apries, quickly became involved in the problems of this region.

BIBL. Kienitz, F. K. *Die politische*.

Psammetichus III   King   526 - 525 BC.

*Amasis died in 526 BC and his throne was briefly inherited for a few months by his son, Psammetichus III.

*Cambyses, King of *Persia, had invaded Egypt in 525 BC: the Egyptians fought the Battle of Pelusium with great tenacity, but were eventually forced back to Memphis where, after a period of siege, they surrendered. Psammetichus III was put to death and *Cambyses established Egypt as part of the *Persian Empire.

The reign of Psammetichus III thus brought the Saite or Twenty-sixth Dynasty to an end, and marked the conclusion also of a brief period of nationalism when the Egyptians, ruled once again by kings of native origin, had sought renewed strength and pride from their earlier culture, gaining inspiration in particular from the achievements of the Old and Middle Kingdoms.

BIBL. Kienitz, F. W. *Die politische*.

Psusennes I   King   1063 - 1037 BC.

The kings of the Twenty-first Dynasty chose to make Tanis, a Delta city, the place of their main Residence, although Memphis probably remained Egypt's administrative centre. Psusennes I was an early king of this dynasty and was apparently also its most important ruler. Upon the death of *Ramesses XI, Nesbenebded (who had gained great power in the north, while the High-priest of Amun ruled concurrently in the south) became Pharaoh of Egypt and, as Smendes, founded the Twenty-first Dynasty. Psusennes I was a successor of Smendes; his great achievements were centred at Tanis which probably replaced Pi-Ramesse as Egypt's major northern port, and here he built a great mudbrick enclosure wall to protect the temples that he constructed to the honour of Amun, Mut and Khonsu, and the royal tomb. Outside Tanis, very little evidence of his work has survived and in fact, his activities were probably limited to the northern part of Egypt.

The history of this period is particularly obscure: the sequence of the reigns of the seven kings whom *Manetho assigns to this dynasty is uncertain, and the exact length of these reigns is also unclear. It is evident that while the kings ruled at Tanis in the north, a line of High-priests of Amun – the descendants of *Herihor – maintained great independence at Thebes in the south. Nevertheless the Tanites and Thebans remained on good terms, and they were joined by marriage when a daughter of Psusennes I, Esemkhebe, became the wife of one of the Theban High-priests; their descendants could thus claim descent from both the Tanite and Theban ruling families. Psusennes I took the unprecedented step of adopting the title of High-priest of Amun (in the way that the Theban priests had taken on royal attributes), and thus asserted the Tanite supremacy over the Theban priests. His wife, Mudnodjme (who was also his sister), adopted the titles of the female counterpart of the High-priest of Amun, and at Tanis Psusennes I built temples to the Theban deities, choosing to emphasis the cult of Amun and to provide an alternative centre for this god's worship.

The French archaeologist, Montet, discovered the intact tomb of Psusennes I at Tanis in 1940; although the mummified body and organic material have not survived (being less well preserved in this Delta site than in the more favourable conditions of the south), the gold and silver vessels, the jewellery, the solid silver coffin and solid gold face mask provide a magnificent funerary group which can be compared with the goods found in the tomb of *Tutankhamun at Thebes. The tomb contained chambers not only for the burial of Psusennes I and his chief queen (whose mummy and equipment were later removed and replaced by the burial of the next king, Amenemope), but also an ante-room and side-rooms which were eventually filled with other royal and noble burials. The body of Psusennes I was placed in its silver coffin inside a black granite sarcophagus which was in turn enclosed in a red granite sarcophagus – because of the scarcity of stone in the Delta, both sarcophagi were usurped from earlier owners.

BIBL. Montet, P. *La necropole de Tanis*, Vol.2: *Les contributions et le tombeau de Psousennes à Tanis*. Paris: 1951; Daressy, G. Les rois Psousennes. *Rec. trav.* 21 (1899) pp. 9-12.

Psusennes II King 959 - 945 BC.

After the death of *Ramesses XI, Smendes pronounced himself the first king of the Twenty-first Dynasty and moved the capital from Thebes to Tanis in the Delta, where he established a line of kings who, although they were recorded as the only legitimate rulers of Egypt at this period, in practice exercised their powers only in the north. In the south, centred at Thebes, a line of powerful High-priests of Amun dominated their own region, although they apparently retained cordial relations with the pharaohs at Tanis and the two families became joined by marriage.

Towards the end of this period, Psusennes, the son of a Theban High-priest named *Pinudjem II, took over the kingship of the entire land when the Tanite king died. He moved to Tanis, where he was included in the line of kings as Psusennes II, thus uniting the north and south and the two concurrent lines of legitimate pharaohs at Tanis and High-priests at Thebes.

After his death, the throne passed to a new family, headed by *Shoshenk I who inaugurated the Twenty-second Dynasty; this line descended from the chiefs of *Libyan origin who had settled at the Delta city of Bubastis.

BIBL. Montet, P. *La necropole de Tanis. Vol.2:Les constructions et le tombeau de Psousennes à Tanis.* Paris: 1951; Daressy, G. Les rois Psousennes. *Rec. trav.*21 (1899) pp. 9-12; Kitchen, K. A. *3rd Int.*pp. 283-6.

Ptah-hotep   Vizier   reign of Isesi, 2414 - 2375 BC.

Ptah-hotep, a vizier in the Fifth Dynasty, is famous on account of his tomb at Saqqara; this, and the tomb of *Ti, provide some of the finest wall-reliefs of the Old Kingdom, illustrating activities of everyday life which the deceased owner hoped to experience and enjoy again in the afterlife. Ptah-hotep's tomb also incorporated a funerary chapel for his son, Akhet-hotep. The Instructions in Wisdom attributed to Ptah-hotep are amongst the earliest examples of this type of literature, although this text may in fact have been composed later, in the Sixth Dynasty.

The Instructions are couched in terms of maxims which Ptah-hotep, the elderly, wise vizier, hands on to his son; they provide advice on personal conduct and on the ethics and behaviour of one who will hold a high public office. The maxims – a total of thirty-seven – emphasise the importance of obedience to one's father or superior and extol the virtues of self-control, modesty, humility, truthfulness, tact and good manners. The recipient of this advice would one day hold an important position in society, and therefore the Instructions provide guidance on how he should deal fairly and generously with his superiors, peers and inferiors, and show justice and kindness even to the poor.

Egyptian society was hierarchical, but the Instructions indicate there was a considerable emphasis on individual justice and equality and that standards set for civil servants were obviously of the highest level.

Four copies of this text have survived: the only complete version is on Papyrus Prisse (now in Paris) which dates to the Middle Kingdom, while two other papyri (both in the British Museum) date to the Middle and New Kingdoms. The other source is an inscribed wooden tablet (Carnarvon Tablet 1 in the Cairo Museum) which also dates to the New Kingdom.

The later versions are copies made by schoolboys; the Wisdom Instructions were favourite school exercises, because they not only provided advice on good behaviour and acceptable conduct, but, particularly with Ptah-hotep's maxims, they were also regarded as models of fine language and literary expression which would influence and improve the schoolboys' own writing style.

BIBL. *AEL* i. pp 61-80; Zaba, Z. *Les Maximes de Ptah-hotep.* Prague: 1956; Gunn, B. *The Instruction of Ptah-hotep and the Instruction of Ke' gemni.* London: 1918; Paget, R. and Pirie, A. *The Tomb of Ptah-hotep.* Vol. 2. London: 1898; Davies, N. de G. *The mastaba of Ptah-hetep and Akhethetep at Saqqara.* (two vols) London: 1900-1.

Ptolemies Kings c.323 - 30 BC.

The Ptolemies ruled Egypt from the accession of *Ptolemy I to the death of *Cleopatra VII and the fall of the country to Rome in 30 BC.

*Ptolemy I, the general whom *Alexander the Great left in charge of Egypt, was also Macedonian in origin, and he and his successors imposed Hellenistic culture on Egypt: large numbers of *Greeks came to settle in Egypt and the Greek language and customs of the conquerors became predominant, although the native population continued with their own language and traditions. Alexandria, the city founded by *Alexander the Great, became the capital and a great centre of culture and intellectualism, and other Greek cities were established throughout Egypt.

Nevertheless, it was essential that the Ptolemies should uphold the tradition that they were pharaohs, and thus they built or reconstructed great temples to the Egyptian gods in which the wall-scenes show them as kings of Egypt, making offerings and doing obeisance to the native deities. This gave them the religious legitimacy to rule the country, but they used this power to impose heavy taxes and drain the natural resources; not surprisingly native opposition to the Ptolemies flared up on two occasions (208-186 BC and 88-86 BC) in the district around Thebes.

BIBL. Fraser, P. M. *Ptolemaic Alexandria.* Oxford: 1972; Bevan, E. *A History of Egypt under the Ptolemaic Dynasty.* London: 1927.

Ptolemy I Soter King 305 - 283 BC.

When *Alexander the Great died in 323 BC and his empire was divided, his Macedonian general, Ptolemy the son of Lagos, became the satrap of Egypt, first under Alexander's half-brother, Phillip Arrhidaeus, and then under his son, Alexander IV. In 305 BC, Ptolemy assumed the kingship of Egypt in his own right and established the Ptolemaic rulership of the country. He ensured the stability of his line by associating his son with him as co-regent and by introducing the concept of consanguineous marriages: his son married his full-sister.

Ptolemy I regarded himself as the regenerator of the country and took the name 'Soter' which meant 'Saviour'. He re-organised Egypt and began a programme of building and restoring the native Egyptian temples, a concept which later *Ptolemies developed to enforce their religious right to rule Egypt. Ptolemy I also intoduced a new god – Serapis – who was a hybrid deity combining features of the Egyptian *Osiris with those of various Hellenistic gods. He also founded a cult of

113

*Alexander the Great at Alexandria and, eventually, a temple for his own personal cult was built at Koptos. He founded the Museum and Great Library in the palace quarter at Alexandria, and the Greek city of Ptolemais in Upper Egypt. As the first Ptolemy, he established the basis for a powerful and wealthy kingdom in Egypt, which would also have influence throughout the Mediterranean world.

BIBL. Bevan, E. *A History of Egypt under the Ptolemaic Dynasty*. London: 1927; Skeat, T. C. *The reigns of the Ptolemies*. Munich:1969.

Ptolemy II Philadelphus King 283 - 246 BC.
*Ptolemy I associated his son Philadelphus with him as co-regent in 285 BC, and he inherited the kingdom in 282 BC. During his reign Egypt reached the zenith of her power under the *Ptolemies. Philadelphus married his full-sister, Arsinoe II, thus establishing the Ptolemaic custom of royal consanguineous marriages; his name 'Philadelphus' means 'sister-loving', and he set up an official cult of Arsinoe and himself, thus introducing the concept of a dynastic cult.

Ptolemy II also inaugurated a detailed system of financial administration in Egypt, and introduced *Greek farming communities in the Fayoum district; under his Revenue Laws, there was also close monitoring of industries such as papyrus-manufacture and oil-production. His reign was the most prosperous of the *Ptolemaic Period, and his finance minister, Apollonius, wielded great power.

Ptolemy II also intervened to begin the abolition of the native aristocracy which his father had allowed to survive and, under his rulership, the intensive Hellenisation of Egypt began. He was active in many other spheres: under his kingship, the canal between the Red Sea and the Nile was restored, to facilitate trade and communication. As a patron of the arts, Ptolemy II enlarged the Great Library at Alexandria and encouraged scholars from many parts of the world to visit the city. According to one tradition, he brought seventy scholars from Jerusalem to Alexandria to translate the Pentateuch into Greek, so that the copy could then be placed in the Library. He was also responsible for the addition of many buildings in Alexandria, including the Pharos, and spectacular processions and games were introduced in his reign.

BIBL. Bevan, E. *A History of Egypt under the Ptolemaic Dynasty*. London: 1927; Skeat, T. C. *The reigns of the Ptolemies*. Munich:1969.

Ptolemy III Euergetes I King 246 - 221 BC.
The son of *Ptolemy II, Ptolemy III married Berenice II, the daughter of the Ptolemaic governor of Cyrene, Ptolemy Magas. It is recorded that they were great benefactors to temples and cults in Egypt, particularly those of the sacred Apis and Mnevis bulls, and this is reflected in the king's name – Euergetes – which means 'benefactor'.

Ptolemy III achieved some military success with his conquest of the Seleucid empire in Asia Minor and his advance on Babylonia, but he was forced to return to

Egypt because of native unrest. Consequently Seleucus repossessed much of his lost territory.

In Egypt Ptolemy III added to the Temple of Karnak, and began the Temple of Horus at Edfu in 237 BC. This is one of the finest examples of those native temples that the *Ptolemies either substantially reconstructed or built as a new monument. The building programme at Edfu was interrupted because of the native rebellions in the Theban district, and the temple was only completed in 57 BC.

BIBL. Bevan, E. *A History of Egypt under the Ptolemaic Dynasty.* London: 1927; Skeat, T. C. *The reigns of the Ptolemies.* Munich: 1969.

Ptolemy IV Philopator   King   221 - 204 BC.

The son of *Ptolemy III, Ptolemy IV took the name of 'Philopator' which means 'father-loving'; according to the custom of this dynasty, he married his sister, Arsinoe III.

He defeated Antiochus III of Syria at the battle of Raphia in 217 BC, after Antiochus had threatened Egypt's frontier, but this success may have contributed to the problems that he had to face at home. A large contingent of native Egyptians had fought well at Raphia, and this victory may have encouraged them to become involved with nationalistic riots in the region of Thebes. These began in 207-206 BC, and their aim was to re-establish native rule in Egypt; to some extent this was achieved when, for nineteen years, a line of Egyptian 'pharaohs' seized some control which enabled them to rule the Theban district.

Under Ptolemy IV, problems began which were associated with the government and administration of the country and in succeeding reigns, these difficulties would become even more acute.

BIBL. Bevan, E. *A History of Egypt under the Ptolemaic Dynasty.* London:1927; Skeat, T. C. *The reigns of the Ptolemies.* Munich:1969.

Ptolemy V Epiphanes   King   204 - 180 BC.

Ptolemy V came to the throne at the age of five, as the result of a dynastic intrigue. During his reign the serious native revolts that had broken out at Thebes in the time of his predecessors, and resulted in the establishment of a line of native 'pharaohs' controlling the Theban area, continued. These were crushed in 186 BC and Ptolemy V regained control of the south, but similar uprisings occurred later in the next century, in 88-86 BC.

In foreign affairs, Egypt lost most of her possessions in Asia Minor, Palestine and the Aegean, and managed to retain only Cyprus and Cyrene. Ptolemy V took a foreign wife – the daughter of the Seleucid king Antiochus III – and she became Queen Cleopatra I.

Building projects at home included a chapel for the deified *Imhotep on the sacred island of Philae. A Decree (issued on March 27,196 BC) commemorates the religious ceremonies that took place at the king's coronation at Memphis, but this has become famous not so much for its content as for the contribution that it made to the decipherment of Egyptian hieroglyphs. Known today as the Rosetta Stone (since it was discovered at Rosetta in 1798), the Decree was inscribed in hieroglyphs, Demotic and Greek; this triple version enabled scholars,who knew Greek, to begin deciphering the corresponding Egyptian scripts.

BIBL. Bevan, E. *A History of Egypt under the Ptolemaic Dynasty*. London: 1927; Skeat, T. C. *The reigns of the Ptolemies*. Munich:1969.

Ptolemy VIII, Euergetes II, Physcon   King   145 - 116 BC.

Nicknamed 'Physcon' which meant 'pot-bellied', Ptolemy VIII was a violent and ruthless man. He fought against his brother, the good and pious Ptolemy VI Philometor, and briefly seized power (164-163 BC). He later became king in 145 BC, but dynastic conflict was continued during his reign by his sister and his neice who both became his wives. They issued an Amnesty Decree in 118 BC which recorded their conciliation and the benefits that this would bring to their subjects.

Ptolemy VIII was typical of the cruel and degenerate ruler who controlled Egypt in the later years of the *Ptolemaic era, but he retained interest in some projects abroad and sent an expedition to attempt to discover the route to India.

BIBL Bevan, E. *A History of Egypt under the Ptolemaic Dynasty.London:* 1927; Skeat, T. C *The reigns of the Ptolemies*. Munich: 1969.

Punt, People of

The Land of Punt was situated somewhere to the south-east of Egypt, probably on the east coast of Africa near the south end of the Red Sea. The Egyptians had known of its existence at least as early as the Fifth Dynasty and they probably made voyages there in the late Old Kingdom, some expeditions possibly setting out from Memphis and crossing over in the north, near Suez. The expeditions continued intermittently. In the Eleventh Dynasty, the Chief Steward, Henenu, led three thousand men on the king's behalf, taking the route which was used throughout the Middle and New Kingdoms. This involved crossing from Koptos to the harbour of Quseir, on the Red Sea coast, and then taking ships along the coast to Punt.

Henenu's expedition obviously re-established the trade that had presumably lapsed at the end of the Old Kingdom, after the expeditions that the local governors of Elephantine had formerly undertaken for the king, had ceased. Henenu's journey was obviously well-planned and organised: men were sent ahead across the desert from Koptos to clear the ninety-mile route of marauding nomads and to dig fifteen wells to provide a water supply. Each member of the expedition was equipped with a staff and a leather canteen and had a daily ration of two jars of water and twenty biscuits. A donkey train also carried spare sandals to replace the men's worn footwear.

At a place on the Red Sea coast (probably near the modern Wadi el Gasus), a special type of craft (known as *Byblos-ships) was built and the expedition set sail for Punt. On their return, they had to disembark and load the produce of Punt on to donkeys to take the overland journey back to the Nile Valley; this was a tiresome necessity since, at this date, there was no navigable waterway between the Nile and the Red Sea.

Main sources for the current knowledge of Punt date to the Middle and New Kingdoms. It was apparently the land of tree-gum (myrrh or frankincense), which the Egyptians wished to obtain for use in their temple rituals. The most famous account is recorded on the walls of Queen *Hatshepsut's funerary temple at Deir el Bahri, where domestic projects are given an unprecedented emphasis because of the absence of military exploits during the queen's reign.

This expedition occurred in Year 9 of her reign, and *Hatshepsut claimed (inaccurately) that it was the first of its kind. The scenes and accompanying inscriptions relate how the Egyptain ships arrived in Punt and how the envoys were greeted there by the bearded chief of Punt and his wife. The scene graphically illustrates the apparent physical deformities of this woman. It is also evident that the Puntites lived near a river in round-domed huts which were built on piles and had to be reached by ladders, and that the landscape included palm-trees and such animals as cattle, dogs, apes, giraffes and hippopotami.

The Egyptian envoys appear to have traded with the Puntites by means of barter, and relations were obviously cordial, for they brought gifts of beer, wine, meat and fruit and, in exchange, obtained myrrh trees packed in baskets for planting in the Egyptian temple groves, as well as ebony, ivory, leopard skins and baboons.The cargo was weighed and measured, and loaded on to the Egyptian ships for the homeward journey.

The Egyptians clearly regarded Punt and its inhabitants as exotic and mysterious and the Land of Punt is mentioned in some of the Egyptian love poems and popular tales as a faraway and romantic setting.

BIBL. Naville, E. *The Temple of Deir el Bahari.* (seven vols) London: 1894-1908; Lucas, A. Cosmetics, perfumes and incense in ancient Egypt. *JEA* 16 (1930) pp. 41-53.

R

Ramessenakhte, High-priest of Amun, reign of Ramesses IV, 1166 - 1160 BC.
Ramessenakhte held the important position of High-priest of Amun at Karnak
during the reign of Ramesses IV.

An inscription in the Wadi Hammamat dating to Year 3 of this reign states that
the High-priest was responsible for the temples and statues which the king
presented to the local gods and, as 'Superintendent of Works', Ramessenakhte
played an important role in obtaining building stone from the quarries.

He is most significant as the man whose descendants became the hereditary
holders of the High-priesthood of Amun at Karnak; his son Nesamun first took this
over and it was then passed to another son, Amenhotep, who achieved an almost
equal status with his king, *Ramesses IX, and was shown in art representations as
the king's equal in size. This increased importance of the High-priests
foreshadowed the events of the Twenty-first Dynasty when Egypt became a
divided kingdom, with the kings ruling at Tanis while the High-priests controlled
the area around Thebes in the south.

BIBL. Couyat, J. and Montet, P. *Les inscriptions hieroglyphiques et hieratiques du Ouadi
Hammamat.* Cairo: 1912; Kitchen, K. A. *3rd Int.*

Ramesses II   King   1304 - 1237 BC.
Perhaps the best-known of Egypt's kings, Ramesses II was a noted warrior and a
prolific builder. He was the son of *Sethos I and, as his co-regent, he took part in a
number of campaigns. In the Great Dedicatory Inscription that he caused to be
placed in his father's temple at Abydos (which Ramesses II completed), it is
indicated that Ramesses II devoted the early years of his reign to restoring order at
home. In Year 4 he set out to repeat his father's successes in Syria, reaching Nahr
el Kelb, a few miles beyond modern Beirut, and the following year he embarked
on his most notable military undertaking – to attack the *Hittites and repossess the
town of Kadesh that *Sethos I had briefly gained.

Ramesses II's account of this battle is preserved in an epic poem which is
repeated in eight inscriptions in the temples of Karnak, Luxor, Abydos and the
Ramesseum, as well as in a shorter version known as the 'Report'. This account
emphasises his personal prowess and bravery in achieving a single-handed victory,
but the *Hittite record, inscribed on tablets in their capital city of Boghazkoy,
relates a different story.

It is clear that the Egyptians retired homewards, having suffered a strategic
defeat, although in later years Ramesses II did achieve success in quelling revolts
in the Palestinian states and in penetrating the *Hittite territories. Egypt came to

realise the difficulty of holding these far-distant gains, and in Year 21, Ramesses II signed a Peace Treaty with the *Hittites, bringing to an end some sixteen years of sporadic fighting. The treaty was made between Ramesses II and *Khattusilis III as equal powers and it was a pact of perpetual peace and brotherhood. It formed the basis of an alliance with reciprocal provisions: there was an agreement of non-aggression between Egypt and the *Hittites; they recognised a mutual frontier and agreed to a joint defensive pact against outside aggressors and to deport refugees from each other's country. The two lands became amicable allies; the royal families exchanged regular letters and they were formally united by marriage ties when, in Year 34, Ramesses II took as his wife the eldest daughter of *Khattusilis III. This princess became his Great Royal Wife and she may have been joined later by another *Hittite princess.

The situation with the *Hittites improved in this reign but Ramesses II had to contend with another problem. The tribes in the western Delta – the *Tjemhu, *Tjehnyu, *Meshwesh and *Libu – were driven by hunger to invade and attempt to settle in Egypt, so that it was necesary for Ramesses II to take measures to control them, which included the construction of a series of forts along the western coast road.

Although Thebes remained the state and religious capital, the administrative centre was now Memphis, and Ramesses II also built a Delta residence city at Pi-Ramesse. His building programme was extensive, and he constructed more temples than any other king. The most important were the Temple of Ptah at Memphis, the temple at Abydos, his mortuary temple (the Ramesseum) at Thebes, and his completion of the Hypostyle Hall at Karnak and of his father's temple at Abydos. The most celebrated of all are the two rock-cut temples at Abu Simbel which in modern times have been saved from the effects of the construction of the High Dam at Aswan. The larger temple here was dedicated to Re-Harakhte, Amun and Ramesses himself, while the smaller one belonged to the goddess Hathor and was built in honour of *Nefertari, the favourite queen of Ramesses II.

Ramesses had five or six major queens and many concubines by whom he fathered over one hundred children. In addition to *Nefertari, favoured queens included the *Hittite princess Manefrure, his own daughter Bint-Anath who became his consort, and Istnofret whose son, *Merneptah, succeeded Ramesses II as king. *Merneptah was the thirteenth son of Ramesses II but he outlived his elder brothers and eventually inherited the throne.

Ramesses II was buried in the Valley of the Kings, but his mummy was amongst those discovered in the cache of royal bodies at Deir el Bahri. It has been the subject of an intensive programme of scientific investigation and conservation which was carried out in France. Ramesses II, who was probably almost one hundred years old when he died, may have been the pharaoh associated with the Exodus. His schemes at home and abroad were grandiose, and although the quality of the art and architecture during his reign does not match its quantity, he nevertheless was the last of Egypt's truly great rulers. His funerary temple (the Ramesseum), which was erroneously known as the 'Tomb of Ozymandias', has received frequent visitors over the centuries and was immortalised by Percy Bysse Shelley in his famous sonnet, written in 1817, although Shelley had never actually visited the temple.

BIBL. Kitchen, K. A. *Pharaoh Triumphant:The life and times of Ramesses II*. Warminster: 1981; Langdon, S. and Gardiner, A. H. The Treaty of Alliance between Hattusili, King of the Hittites, and the Pharaoh Ramesses II of Egypt. *JEA* 6 (1920) pp. 179 ff; Kitchen, K. A. Some new light on the Asiatic wars of Ramesses II. *JEA* 50 (1964) pp. 47 ff.; Breasted, J. H. *The Battle of Kadesh*. Chicago: 1903; Balout, L. and Roubet, C. *La Momie de Ramses II*. Paris: 1985.

Ramesses III   King   1198 - 1166 BC.

The son of Setnakhte and his queen Tiye-merenese, Ramesses III was the last great warrior-king of Egypt, although his military actions were largely defensive. He conciously modelled himself on *Ramesses II with regard to his titles, the names of his children and his wars; also, his funerary temple at Medinet Habu imitated *Ramesses II's temple, the Ramesseum, and at Medinet Habu he included a chapel for the cult of *Ramesses II's barque-image.

In Year 5, Ramesses III faced his first great conflict. The *Libyans had recoverd from their war against *Merneptah and were seeking land in the Egyptian Delta; as an excuse for hostilities, they used their dislike of the new ruler whom Ramesses III had imposed upon them. Their forces included the three tribes of the *Libu, Sped and *Meshwesh, but the coalition was utterly defeated and the captives were taken to become forced labourers in Egypt.

In Year 8, Egypt faced an even greater threat. A confederation of northerners (known collectively as the *Sea-peoples) had brought down the *Hittite Empire and they now advanced down the Syrian coast, bringing their women, children, ox-carts and possessions, with the intention of settling permanently in Syria, Palestine and Egypt. *Merneptah had repulsed a similar group who had allied with the *Libyans. The new association included the *Sheklesh, *Sherden, Weshwesh and three new groups – the *Peleset, Tjekker and Denen. This land-march was accompanied offshore by a formidable fleet, and the Egyptians had to meet the enemy on both fronts. Ramesses III managed to hold the land attack successfully, mobilising his forces in Palestine while he prepared his troops in Egypt. The Egyptians also trapped the enemy fleet in one of the mouths of the Nile, and successfully destroyed it. The third attack, in Year 11, came again from the *Libyans, and was also defeated.

Wall-scenes in Ramesses III's temple at Medinet Habu and additional information in the Great Harris Papyrus provide a graphic account of these significant dangers that threatened Egypt. Other scenes, which show Ramesses III engaged in campaigns against *Hittite and Syrian towns, are probably anachronistic and merely copy scenes of the original, genuine, expeditions undertaken by *Ramesses II, the hero of Ramesses III.

After Year 11 there was peace; the Great Harris Papyru (which was apparently written on the day of the king's death to ensure that he joined the gods) was almost certainly compiled at the behest of his son, Ramesses IV. It is the most extensive state archive yet discovered and probably formed part of the funerary temple archive. It lists the benefactions that the dead king had bestowed on the gods' temples, with Amen-Re of Karnak receiving the largest share. The Papyrus also provides a survey of the events of the reigns of the king and his father, and expeditions to *Punt for incense and to Sinai to obtain turquoise and copper are mentioned. The prosperity of this reign is also attested by the size and quality of the king's funerary temple at Medinet Habu, with its unique architectural feature of a gateway in the style of a Syrian fort; by the additional temples at Karnak; and by the king's large tomb in the Valley of the Kings.

There were obviously troubles in the latter part of the reign; in Year 29, the monthly rations to the royal workforce, building the king's tomb, were delayed and strikes and riots resulted. The situation was only temporarily restored when the vizier intervened and food supplies appeared. At some point in the reign, there was an attempt to assassinate the king and to place a usurper (the child of a secondary wife, Tiy) on the throne. Tiy gained the support of the harem women and of some officials and they plotted to foment a rebellion; even a troop-commander from Kush, the brother of one of the harem women, was implicated. The conspiracy also drew on magical resources, using spells and waxen images, but it was uncovered and the offenders were brough to trial. The Conspiracy Papyri – now in Turin – are the state record of these trials, compiled under *Ramesses V, although the procedures were carried out in his father's reign.

The defendants were found guilty. The more socially prominent were allowed to take their own lives, while the rest were put to death. Five of the judges originally chosen to hear the cases were also arrested and tried for carousing with the accused harem women. This assassination attempt was almost certainly unsuccessful, since the mummy of Ramesses III, discovered in the Deir el Bahri cache, shows no evidence of a violent death.

Ramesses III's great queen was Ese and he had many children from his wives; his son Ramesses IV finally succeeded him.

BIBL. Erichsen, W. *Papyrus Harris*. Brussels: 1933; Chicago University, Oriental Institute *Medinet Habu*. (four vols) Chicago: 1932-40; de Buck, A. The Judicial Papyrus of Turin. *JEA* 23 (1927) pp. 152 ff; Edgerton, W. and Wilson, J. A. *Historical records of Ramesses III*. Chicago: 1936; Edgerton, W. F. The strikes in Ramses III's twenty-ninth year. *JNES* 10 (1951) pp. 137 ff.; *CAH* ii, ch xxviii; Schaedel, H. *Die Listen des grossen Papyrus Harris*. Gluckstadt: 1936.

Ramesses V King 1160 - 1156 BC.

Ramesses V was probably the son of Ramesses IV and, although he reigned for only a short time, two important documents date to his reign.

The Turin Papyrus provides a list of serious accusations against a number of people but particularly against a priest in the Temple of Khnum at Elephantine, whose misdeeds included embezzlement, theft and offences of a religious nature. The crimes apparently continued from the reign of *Ramesses III to that of Ramesses V, and this indicates that there were serious oversights in administration and laxity in dealing with offences during that period.

The other document is the Wilbour Papyrus which was compiled in Year 5 of the reign. This is an official document, the only extant copy of its kind, and thus of great importance to the study of land-holding and taxation in Egypt, although many of the details remain unclear. It consists of a measurement and assessment of the fields in an area of Middle Egypt, covering from a point near Crocodilopolis to the region in the vicinity of the modern town of El Minya, a distance of some ninety miles. The papyrus provides information about each piece of land and refers to the landowner as the plot-holder; it supplies facts about the position and size of the land and the calculated yield in terms of grain. It does not state to whom the taxes would have been paid, but it is probable that the Temple of Amun at Karnak rather than the king was the recipient.

In his short reign, Ramesses V prepared a tomb in the Valley of the Kings which was unfinished at the time of his death, although he was actually buried there; later, this tomb was usurped and annexed by his successor, Ramesses VI, who completed its decoration.

There is also other evidence that suggests that there was a conflict between Ramesses V and Ramesses VI (who was a son of *Ramesses III); this may have involved civil war in which some factions supported Ramesses VI and may have deposed Ramesses V before his death, to place Ramesses VI on the throne. Ramesses V was presumably reburied in another tomb, although its location remains unknown, but his body was ultimately found amongst the royal mummies reburied by the ancient priests in the tomb of *Amenophis II in the Valley of the Kings. This mummy is of particular interest because medical examination has shown that he died at a relatively early age, probably from smallpox.

BIBL. Pleyte, W. and Rossi, F. *Papyrus de Turin.* (two vols) Leiden: 1869-76; Gardiner, A. H. *The Wilbour Papyrus.*(Three vols.) Oxford: 1941-8, Faulkner, R. O. Vol. 4*: Indices.* Oxford: 1952; Peet, T. E. A historical document of Ramesside age. *JEA* 10 (1924) pp. 116 ff.; Smith, G. E. *The Royal Mummies.* Cairo: 1912. p. 91.

Ramesses IX   King   1140 - 1121 BC.

The later Ramesside kings (Ramesses IV to XI) ruled over a country in which society was experiencing a slow disintegration, with a constant pattern of corruption, failing food supplies, strikes and tomb-robberies.

By Year 10 of the reign of Ramesses IX, Amenhotep-the High-priest of Amun at Thebes-had acquired a considerable degree of personal power, controlling the god's wealth and estates. This position had become hereditary and, apart from their titles, these priests now equalled the powers of the kings in the north. An unprecedented example is set by Amenhotep who, in two temple wall-reliefs, is shown as a figure equal in size to the king, thus indicating his relative status and importance.

The records relating to the community of royal workmen who lived at Deir el Medina indicate that in the later years of Ramesses IX, the workers were terrorised by foreigners at Thebes. It is unclear whether these were incursions by a new group or whether the descendants of the prisoners-of-war were now fomenting rebellion there. Because of famine in Egypt, the food rations of the work-force were delayed and the consequent unrest led to a series of strikes and tomb-robberies in which workmen were implicated.

Various papyri – particularly Papyri Abbott, Amherst and Mayer A – provide detailed information about the tomb-robberies and the great state trials which began in Ramesses IX's reign and lasted for many years. It is evident that the king took a close interest in the proceedings of these trials which he had inaugurated. No deterrent action was successful, because in times of hardship and hunger the lure of the royal tombs with their rich treasure was always compulsive.

In foreign policy, Egypt was left with only her southern possessions, Kush (Ethiopia) and Wawat (*Nubia), since the Asiatic provinces had been lost soon after *Ramesses III's death.

BIBL. Cerny, J. *A. community of workmen at Thebes in the Ramesside Period.* Cairo: 1973; Peet, T. E. *The Great Tomb-robberies of the Twentieth Egyptian Dynasty.* (Two vols) Oxford: 1930.

Ramesses XI   King   1113-1085 BC.

Ramesses XI, the last king of the Twentieth Dynasty, managed to hold his kingdom together although it was during his reign that the country virtually divided into two parts.

The king continued to rule in the north, but the High-priest of Amun, Amenhotep, had gained considerable power at Thebes. Perhaps at the king's behest, *Pinehas (the Viceroy of Nubia and King's Son of Kush) intervened against Amenhotep, taking Thebes and claiming for himself the resources of the district and supreme command of the army. *Pinehas now became the effective ruler, although still nominally under Ramesses XI, of Upper and Middle Egypt as well as *Nubia, but he fell into disgrace at Thebes where a new man of unknown origin, *Herihor, emerged as High-priest of Amun. He not only held this position but also claimed *Pinehas' titles as King's Son of Kush and Overseer of the Southern Lands, becoming the first man ever to combine great military power, the High-priesthood at Thebes and control over Nubia. *Pinehas held on to Nubia, where he had now become a rebel, and refused to submit to *Herihor, so that Nubia finally broke away from Egypt.

In Year 19 of Ramesses XI's reign, 1080 BC, the 'Renaissance Era' was proclaimed. Such periods, known as a 'Repetition of Birth', had been announced in other reigns to mark the start of a great new era. On this occasion, the 'Renaissance' saw the emergence of three rulers − *Herihor ruled in the south, Smendes (the Nesbenebded in the Story of *Wenamun) ruled concurrently in the north, and both were nominally subject to the pharaoh, Ramesses XI. Smendes may have been *Herihor's son and possibly married a younger daughter of Ramesses XI; upon the king's death, Smendes became the king of all Egypt and the first ruler of the Twenty-first Dynasty.

*Herihor died before Ramesses XI and was succeeded in the south by his son Piankh. Despite his great power, *Herihor never assumed the kingship of Egypt but was always subordinate to Ramesses XI. In the Temple of Khonsu at Karnak, in those areas erected and decorated in the time of Ramesses XI and *Herihor, the latter is shown in the wall-scenes officiating with the king; he appears to hold an equal status to the king, and in some instances he even uses the royal titulary in the inscriptions, but this excessive bombast is only evident in Thebes, the centre of his own power and influence. Ramesses XI's reign marked the end of the New Kingdom. He was possibly the last king to be buried in the Valley of the Kings at Thebes, and it was during his reign that the royal necropolis workers' village at Deir el Medina was abandoned. By now, Egypt had no possessions in Syria/Palestine and under Ramesses XI, Nubia broke away from Egypt and continued on its own course for many years.

BIBL Kitchen, K. A. *3rd Int.* pp. 248-54.

Ramose   Vizier   reigns of *Amenophis III and *Akhenaten, c.1417-1375 BC.

Ramose was Governor of Thebes and Vizier under *Amenophis III and also served his son *Akhenaten (Amenophis IV) during the early years of his reign when Thebes was still the capital. Thus, he lived through the period of transition when Amenophis IV was introducing his revolutionary worship of the sun-disc, the Aten. Ramose's tomb is situated at Sheikh Abd el Qurna, Thebes, and it was excavated and restored by Mond; it is of great interest both historically and artistically because it is one of the few monuments that represent this transitionary period before Amenophis IV (*Akhenaten) left Thebes to found his new city of Akhetaten (Tell el Amarna).

The wall-scenes in the tomb vividly contrast traditional art and the new art forms introduced under *Akhenaten; most of the reliefs depict Amenophis IV in the conventional style but there is a dramatic change in the scene that shows the king and his queen, *Nefertiti, standing on a balcony, beneath the sun-disc and its descending rays, presenting Ramose with gold collars. This scene is typical of the so-called Amarna art, both in terms of the subject matter, which is parallelled in scenes at Amarna, and in the representation of the figures; these appear in the near caricature style of Amarna art which distorts the human figure.

The tomb was unfinished and the fate of Ramose (along with other Theban officials who held positions of authority before the Court moved to Amarna) is unknown.

BIBL. Davies, N. de G. *The tomb of the Vizier Ramose.* London: 1941; Aldred, C. *Akhenaten, King of Egypt.* London: 1988.

Rekhmire   Vizier   reign of *Tuthmosis III, 1504-1450 BC.

Rekhmire was Governor of Thebes and Vizier under both *Tuthmosis III and *Amenophis II, thus becoming one of the country's most powerful officials during an important and expansive period.

His tomb at Sheikh Abd el Qurna, Thebes, is important because it provides details of the nature and extent of his duties, thus extending knowledge of the role of a vizier in the Eighteenth Dynasty. In the wall-scenes he is shown in a range of activities: holding audiences, collecting taxes brought in the form of commodities by the district officials, and inspecting the temple works. The latter included the building of a pylon (temple gateway) and the activities of the temple workshops where leather goods and vases were being made and carpenters and goldsmiths plyed their crafts in the service of the god. The text of two inscriptions are important; one describes the installation of a vizier and the other gives details of his duties, both augmenting knowledge of the functions of the vizier's office.

The scenes also illustrate the presentation of foreign tribute to Egypt, which is received by Vizier Rekhmire; this is a useful source of information regarding the countries Egypt dealt with at this time, and the commodities that they provided. The 'Peoples of the South' are shown, and the Cretans who bring fine vases, as well as the *Nubians whose tribute includes exotic animals, skins and gold; the Syrians are also represented, bringing chariots, horses, an elephant and a bear.

BIBL Sethe, K. *Die Einsetzung des Veziers unter der 18.Dynastie. Inschrift im Grabe des Rekh-mi-re zu Schech Abd el Gurna* (Unters. 5,2). Leipzig: 1909; Davies, N. de G. *The tomb of Rekh-mi-Re at Thebes*. New York: 1943.

Rib-Addi   Governor of *Byblos   reigns of *Amenophis III and *Akhenaten, c.1417-1370 BC.

Rib-Addi was the Governor of Byblos, a vassal state of Egypt during the Eighteenth Dynasty; he is known from the extensive correspondence he carried on with the Egyptian king, and the letters are preserved in the state archive at Amarna, the city built as a capital by *Akhenaten.

There are nearly seventy letters in this particular correspondence and since these greatly outnumber letters from any other source, it has been suggested that the Amarna archive must be incomplete, preserving only limited examples from other correspondents. Some of Rib-Addi's letters were duplicates that he had sent out from Byblos by different messengers in the hope that at least one of his pleas for help would reach the Egyptian Court and receive some attention.

His letters have been used to illustrate the situation which appears to have existed in Syria/Palestine during the reigns of *Amenophis III and *Akhenaten, when loyal vassals pleaded in vain for Egyptian assistance and military support against their northern enemies. Particularly in *Akhenaten's reign, this is regarded as evidence of the continuing decline of Egypt's influence in the area. Rib-Addi repeatedly requested Egypt to help him hold *Byblos against the attacks of Abdi-Ashirta of Amurru, but the pleas went unanswered and Rib-Addi and his city eventually succumbed to the enemy.

BIBL. Mercer, S. A. B. *The Tell el Amarna Tablets*. (two vols) Toronto: 1939; Kitchen, K. A. *Suppiluiuma and the Amarna Pharaohs*. Liverpool: 1962; *CAH* ii, ch li.

Romans   Rulers of Egypt   30 BC - c.AD 600.

When the Romans conquered Egypt in 30 BC, the mass of the people at first experienced few obvious changes. Unlike other major Roman provinces, Egypt was not governed directly by members of the Roman Senate, but became the personal possession of Octavian *Augustus, who appointed a viceregal governor entitled Prefect who was directly responsible to him. Thus, Egypt no longer had its own king or capital city, and it was no longer an independent nation but merely a district whose main purpose was to supply grain for the people of Rome.

The administrative system which had been set up by the *Ptolemies was basically retained and the principal magistrates kept their posts. The administration's main function now was to collect taxes and in return for this tribute, Egypt received little benefit and the country generally experienced a continuing decline. There was no long-term investment in Egypt's future, although, in the atmosphere of political stability that Roman rule provided, the economy flourished in terms of the goods – corn, papyrus, and glass – which were produced for Rome.

*Greek was still the official language, as it had been under the *Ptolemies, and Hellenistic culture continued to predominate in the Greek cities of Egypt. The Roman emperors carried on the *Ptolemaic policy of representing themselves as pharaohs, since this gave them the religious authority to rule Egypt and, as far as they were concerned, to exploit its resources. Some Roman emperors completed Egyptian temples for the same reasons: additions were made to the temples at Denderah, Esna, Philae and Kom Ombo, and wall-scenes show the emperors as pharaoh in the company of the Egyptian gods.

Christianity was adopted throughout Egypt, and the Edict of *Theodosius I (AD 384) marked the end of the ancient religion; it formally declared Christianity to be the religion of the Roman Empire and ordered the closure of temples to other gods.

In AD 395, the Imperial possessions were divided into eastern and western portions and Egypt, as part of the eastern empire, now came under the control of Byzantium.

BIBL. Bell, H. I. *Egypt from Alexander the Great to the Arab Conquest.* Oxford: 1956; Hoffman, A.K. *Egypt after The Pharoahs: 332 BC-AD 642 from Alexander to the Arab Conquest.* London 1986. Jones, A. H. M. *The Later Roman Empire,* 284-602. Oxford: 1964.

S

Sahure   King   2487 - 2473 BC.

Sahure was the son and successor of *Userkaf, the founder of the Fifth Dynasty; he and his brother *Neferirkare were both the children of Queen *Khentkaues. Sahure was mentioned in the folktale preserved in the Westcar Papyrus, as one of the triplets born to the sun-god Re by the wife of a priest of Re; the tale relates that these children were destined to exercise the kingship throughout Egypt.

Sahure continued his father's policy of promoting the sun-cult, and he also inaugurated the royal cemetery at Abusir to the north of Saqqara, where his successors, *Neferirkare, Neferifre and *Niuserre, also built their pyramids. Sahure's pyramid is the most complete pyramid of the Fifth Dynasty to be excavated and published and it displays a high level of artistic achievement. The plain, rectangular pillars found in earlier pyramid temples are replaced here by columns which represent papyrus stems bound together, and the capitals imitate the leaves of the palm.

Fine limestone was used for the sculptured wall-reliefs, and although some of these have been badly damaged, the remainder illustrate a wide range of subject matter dealing with the king's relationship with the gods, and his public duties. These include scenes of hunting in the desert, baiting hippopotami in the river, and historical events such as a campaign against the *Libyans. In these, Seshat, the goddess of writing, lists the animals captured in the desert hunt, and the foreign chieftains and their families are shown coming in submission to Egypt. A parallel scene on another wall depicts ships returning from Syria; these have sailors and *Asiatics on board, who raise their arms in praise of pharaoh; this probably represents a trading expedition returning from *Byblos, the port that supplied the Egyptians with their cedarwood. It is known from the Palermo Stone that during this reign expeditions were also sent to Sinai in search of turquoise and to *Punt on the Red Sea coast to obtain incense and spices.

BIBL. Borchadt, L. *Das Grabdenkmal des Konigs Sa3hu-Re.* (three vols) Leipzig: 1910-13.

Scorpion   King   before 3100 BC.

The Scorpion Macehead, discovered at Hieraconpolis and now in the Ashmolean Museum at Oxford, provides evidence relating to one of the earliest kings of Egypt for whom any historical information has been found. With the *Narmer Palette, this macehead preserves the earliest examples of hieroglyphic writing that have yet been uncovered.

The names of only two kings of the predynastic period – Ka and Scorpion – are known, and the latter is represented by a hieroglyph which depicts a scorpion.

The Scorpion Macehead is decorated with scenes in relief which are arranged in three registers: the top one probably commemorates the king's action (together with the leaders of a group of southern districts) of subjugating foreigners in the deserts, the oases, and some part of Lower Egypt possibly as far north as the apex of the Delta. The middle and bottom registers are probably concerned with the agricultural measures that the king took after his military victories, for here he is shown digging a canal, perhaps to initiate a major irrigation project.

It is generally considered that Scorpion was a southern ruler who took early steps to conquer the northern kingdom – a process of unifying the Two Lands which his successor, *Narmer, successfully concluded.

BIBL Arkell, A. J. Was King Scorpion Menes? *Antiquity* 37 (1963) pp. 31-5; Emery, W. B. *Archaic Egypt*. Harmondsworth: 1972.

Sea-Peoples   reigns of *Merneptah and *Ramesses III, c.1236 - 1166 BC.

The confederation of peoples or tribes, who attacked Egypt in the reigns of *Merneptah and *Ramesses III, were referred to as 'Sea-peoples' in the Egyptian record of the conflicts, preserved on the temple walls at Karnak and Medinet Habu, as well as in the Great Harris Papyrus. These people may have come from a number of different homelands, but they seem to have been driven southwards by hunger and possibly by displacement. At least one group – the *Sherden – were known in Egypt as early as the reign of *Amenophis III when they acted as Egyptian mercenaries.

After the turn of the thirteenth century BC, the Sea-peoples attacked the *Hittites, Cyprus and the coastal cities of Syria; they flooded down through Palestine and joined cause with the *Libyan tribes, to mass against Egypt from the west. They brought with them their families and domestic possessions in ox-drawn carts, and they obviously intended not simply to raid the Egyptian coast but to invade and settle in Palestine and the Egyptian Delta. *Ramesses III finally defeated them by blocking their land entry into Egypt with his garrisons in Palestine and by destroying their fleet in a sea-battle in one of the mouths of the Nile. It is evident that some of the Sea-peoples fought both for and against the Egyptians in these conflicts, and two of the tribes – the *Peleset and the Tjekker – stayed on and settled in Palestine, eventually forcing the Egyptians to relinquish their sovereignty there. Others settled in Egypt, where they became soldiers in the army and, eventually, landowners.

The Sea-peoples are of great historical interest because some of their names have a close similarity to, and have been tentatively identified with, later racial groups who lived in the Mediterranean countries and islands.

BIBL. Wainwright, G. A. Some Sea-peoples and others in the Hittite archives. *JEA* 25 (1939) pp. 148 ff; Wainwright, G. A. Merneptah's aid to the Hittites. *JEA* 46 (1960) pp. 24 ff; Chicago University, Oriental Institute. *Medinet Habu.*(four vols) Chicago: 1932-40; Edgerton, W. and Wilson, J. A. *Historical Records of Ramesses III*. Chicago: 1936; Sandars, N. K. *Sea Peoples*. London 1985. Wainwright, G. A. Some Sea-peoples. *JEA* 47 (1961) pp. 71 ff; CAH ii, ch xxviii.

Senenmut   Royal Courtier   reign of *Hatshepsut, 1503 - 1482 BC.
Senenmut entered the royal household during the reign of *Tuthmosis II, but
became Chief Steward of *Hatshepsut, the famous queen regnant of the
Eighteenth Dynasty. He came from an undistinguished background, but amassed
great power and wealth as the queen's favoured courtier, holding twenty different
offices of which the most influential were the Steward of Amun and the Tutor to
the royal heiress, Neferure. There are six statues which show him holding the
young princess, and in one statue inscription he claims that he was responsible for
*Hatshepsut's building programme at Thebes.
   Hatshepsut's most famous monument was the mortuary temple at Deir el Bahri,
and here Senenmut had his figure represented in partially concealed wall-scenes in
the chapel niches, where he is shown praying for the queen. Most of these images
have been mutilated, as have his portraits in the burial chamber he prepared for
himself under the temple court. His fate is not known, but he disappears from
power several years before the end of *Hatshepsut's reign.

BIBL.Werbrouck, M. *Le temple d'Hatshepsout a Deir el Bahari.* . Brussels: 1949; Winlock,
H. E. *Excavations at Deir el Bahri.* New York: 1942, pp. 145-53; Hayes, W. C. *Ostraka
and Name Stones from the Tomb of Sen-Mut (no.71) at Thebes.* New York: 1942. Dorman,
P. *Monuments of Senenmut: Problems in historical methodology.* London: 1988.

Sennacherib   King of Assyria   705 - 681 BC.
In the reign of Sennacherib, Egypt's involvement with *Assyria was renewed,
particularly with relation to their conflict over the vassal-states in Syria/Palestine
who were now requesting Egyptian support against the expansionist policies of
*Assyria.
   In his third campaign Sennacherib set out to subdue the *Phoenician coastal
towns. After another series of events, Hezekiah, King of Judah, appealed to Egypt
for help; the combatants met at El-tekeh and there was a great defeat for the joint
Egyptian and Ethiopian forces (Egypt was now ruled by a dynasty of Ethiopian
kings) at the hands of the *Assyrians. This may have been the only time that the
Egyptians came into direct conflict with Sennacherib, but a Biblical reference (II
Kings, xix, 8-35) suggests that their forces were due to meet on another occasion
but that many of the *Assyrian soldiers were slain in the night through God's
intervention and were forced to return to Nineveh.
   Ultimately, Sennacherib was assassinated at Nineveh, but his contest with the
Egyptians was pursued with even greater vigour by his successors, *Esarhaddon
and *Ashurbanipal.

BIBL. Luckenbill, D. D. *Annals of Sennacherib.* Chicago: 1924; Kitchen, K. A. *3rd Int.* pp.
154-6.

Sennedjem   Chief Craftsman   reign of *Sethos I, 1318 - 1304 BC
Sennedjem was the Chief Craftsman of the royal necropolis workers at Thebes

during the Ramesside period; he lived and was buried at the workmen's town of Deir el Medina at Thebes.

His tomb is an excellent example of a necropolis worker's burial place. The royal workmen used their expertise and materials diverted from the tombs they were preparing for the kings, to build and decorate their own tombs to a very high standard.

In Sennedjem's tomb, the burial chamber has a vaulted ceiling and is decorated with vivid wall-scenes. By this time such scenes no longer emphasise the everyday activities of the owner, as they had done in the Eighteenth Dynasty, but they concentrate instead on themes that relate to death and burial and on concepts taken from the Book of the Dead. Sennedjem's scenes show Anubis, the god of cemeteries and mummification, embalming his mummy and leading him forward to the Day of Judgement in the presence of the tribunal of gods; other representations depict Sennedjem and his wife working in the Fields of *Osiris (the land of the dead) and, in a ceiling painting, the goddess of the sycamore tree presents food and water to the tomb-owner and his wife.

The contents of this tomb, discovered in 1928, are now in the Cairo Museum and include Sennedjem's coffin, mummy, furniture and funerary statuettes. They provide valuable information about the funerary equipment of a craftsman.

BIBL. Bruyere, B. *Rapport sur les fouilles de Deir el Medineh.* (sixteen vols) Cairo: 1924-53; Cerny, J. *A community of workmen at Thebes in the Ramesside Period.* Cairo: 1973.

Sennufer   Mayor of the Southern City   reign of *Amenophis III, 1450-1425 BC.
Sennufer was the Mayor of the Southern City (Thebes) and Overseer of the Gardens of Amun, in the reign of *Amenophis III. His subterranean rock-cut tomb at Sheikh Abd el Qurna, Thebes, was beautifully and appropriately decorated. Approached down a steep flight of steps, the pillared hall of the tomb-chapel opens off the ante-chamber; the irregular, rock-cut ceiling is decorated with paintings consisting of a network pattern and of a vine hung with grapes. The figures of Sennufer and his wife/sister Merit are depicted in the wall-scenes and on the sides of the pillars, and thus appear to undertake their various activities beneath the vine painting on the ceiling. The funerary ceremonies are shown, a priest offers a sacrifice to the couple as they sit at a table and, on another occasion, he pours a libation over them. There is also a particularly fine scene that depicts the boats which transported the deceased's mummy to Abydos on a final pilgrimage before taking it to the Theban burial place.

Bibl. Zabern, P. von. *Sennefer: Die grabkammer des Bürgermeisters von Theben.* Mainz: 1990.

Septimius Severus   Roman Emperor   AD 193-211.
Lucius Septimius Severus was born in North Africa. Having successfully

campaigned against the Parthians in AD 198-9, he went on to visit Egypt (AD 199-200) before continuing to Syria.

In Egypt, he visited Alexandria where he inaugurated a number of major administrative reforms: a municipal constitution was established and the emperor issued a series of legal judgements which dealt with cases brought by people from both Alexandria and the countryside.

In AD 204, he issued an edict which prohibited all Roman subjects from embracing Christianity.

BIBL. Jones, A. H. M. *The later Roman Empire, 284-602*. Oxford: 1964; Birley, A. R. *Septimius Severus: the African emperor*. London: 1971.

Seqenenre Ta'o II King c.1575 BC.

Seqenenre Ta'o II succeeded his father Seqenenre Ta'o I as the ruler of Thebes in the Seventeenth Dynasty. Ta'o I's wife was Tetisheri who was apparently not of royal descent, and their children, Seqenenre Ta'o II and *Ahhotpe, married each other. Queen Tetisheri was venerated by later generations as a powerful influence in the fortunes of the dynasty and of the country.

Seqenenre II was probably the first Theban ruler who openly opposed *Hyksos rule; although the south was perhaps virtually independent of the *Hyksos in political terms, they nevertheless were obliged to pay them tribute. It was the Theban princes – Seqenenre II,*Kamose and *Amosis I – who eventually sought to drive the *Hyksos rulers out of Egypt.

Preserved in Papyrus Sallier I, there is a story that describes the beginning of the conflict. The Theban rulers had apparently revived the ancient ritual of harpooning hippopotami in a pool or canal at Thebes; this rite was designed to destroy the king's enemy through sympathetic magic and to ensure the safety of the Egyptian kingship. The *Hyksos king, *Apophis I, who was ruling at Avaris in the Delta took offence at this revival, probably because it was designed to threaten his political position, but also because the hippopotamus represented Seth, the god worshipped as a patron deity by the *Hyksos. In the papyrus, the excuse given by *Apophis I for his complaint to Seqenenre is that he cannot sleep because of the noise made by the hippopotami at Thebes – although this city was several hundred miles away from his capital!

He ordered Seqenenre to come away from the pool of the hippopotami, and this led to the start of their conflict. It is evident that the *Hyksos ruler wanted to provoke a fight; only the earlier part of the text is preserved, but it is assumed that the tale would have continued with an account of the struggle and of a victory for the Thebans. In reality the conflict was probably indecisive and although a limited truce may have been arranged, it was Seqenenre's successors, *Kamose and *Amosis, who fought on to defeat the *Hyksos.

Seqenenre II was nevertheless known as 'The Brave', and he may have lost his life in this struggle. His body was discovered in the cache of royal mummies at Deir el Bahri in 1881, and certain physical signs indicate that he may have died in battle. The body is twisted in the agony of death, there were wounds to the neck and the head, where a blow behind the left ear had been caused by a dagger. The Papyrus Sallier story also provides some interesting background information regarding the period of *Hyksos rule in Egypt: it makes it clear that *Apophis ruled as king at Avaris in the north, while the Thebans concurrently controlled the southern district, although they paid tribute to the *Hyksos.

BIBL. Gunn, B. and Gardiner, A. H. New renderings of Egyptian texts. II. The expulsion of the Hyksos. *JEA* 5 (1918) pp. 36-56; Save-Soderbergh, T. On Egyptian representations of hippopotamus hunting as a religious motive. *Horae Soederblomianae*, 3. Uppsala: 1953; Save-Soderbergh, T. The Hyksos rule in Egypt. *JEA* 37 (1951) pp. 53-71; Smith, G. E. *The Royal Mummies*. Cairo: 1912 pp 1-4.

Sesostris I King 1971 - 1928 BC.

*Ammenemes I associated his eldest son, Sesostris I, with him as co-regent in Year 20 of his reign, and thereafter Sesostris undertook all the major campaigns in Syria, *Nubia and *Libya. It was while he was away on one of these expeditions to Libya that he learnt of his father's assassination at his palace, and returned immediately to take control of the country and to avert a crisis. The events surrounding his accession are mentioned in two literary sources – the instruction of King *Ammenemes I for his son Sesostris (a propoganda exercise that was almost certainly composed by a scribe in the reign of Sesostris I himself), and the Story of *Sinuhe.

Using skilful propoganda and firm government, Sesostris I was able to restore the power and prestige of the monarchy, and to extend Egypt's influence abroad. He sent punitive expeditions against the *Libyans, and protected Egypt's northern border against incursions, but his general policy in the north was primarily defensive and diplomacy was his main method of dealing with Syria/Palestine. There is evidence that Egyptians settled in these areas and there were trading and other contacts with the region. In Sinai, mining operations were vigorously pursued, and Egypt's foreign policy was developed against a domestic background of stability, prosperity, and a firm centralised government.

In foreign policy, Sesostris I (together with his descendant, *Sesostris III) is remembered for his action in *Nubia where, in Year 18, he launched a ruthless campaign to conquer and occupy Lower Nubia. Sesostris I effectively subjugated and annexed the region so that the Egyptians now exercised a degree of control between the Second and Third Cataracts and were again able to obtain the gold, copper, diorite, granite and amethyst that *Nubia offered.

At home, Sesostris I pursued a prodigious building programme, enlarging and enhancing almost all the existing temples. Today, a single obelisk is all that remains of the great temple to Re-Atum that he built at Heliopolis; this obelisk was originally one of a pair erected there to mark his jubilee festival. At Karnak, it is still possible to admire his exquisite limestone chapel which was dedicated to Amun on the occasion of the king's jubilee; the reliefs that decorate this chapel are of the finest quality and indicate the standard of contemporary craftsmanship. His pyramid at It-towy (el Lisht) was more impressive than that of his father, and is the best preserved of the whole dynasty; it revived the layout of the Old Kingdom complexes, and the style of ten limestone statues of the king from the same site indicates that the Memphite art forms had also been reintroduced.

Even in the Twelfth Dynasty Sesostris I already received a divine cult, and in later legends he is remembered in the person of 'Pharaoh Sesostris' who performed great and miraculous deeds; this individual – representing the Egyptian ideal of an omnipotent king – was actually a compilation of three historical rulers – Sesostris I, *Sesostris III and *Ramesses II.

Sesostris I continued the policy of co-regency, used by this dynasty to ensure a smooth and troublefree succession, and associated his son and heir, *Ammenemes II, with him on the throne.

BIBL. *AEL* i.pp. 135-8,222-35; Gardiner, A. H. The accession day of Sesostris I. *JEA* 32 (1946) p 100; Simpson, W. K. The single-dated monuments of Sesostris I: an aspect of the institution of co-regency in the Twelfth Dynasty. *JEA* 15 (1956) pp. 214-19; Lacau, P. and Chevrier, H. *Une chapelle de Sesostris Ier a Karnak*. Cairo: 1956.

Sesostris II King 1897 - 1878 BC.

Sesostris II succeeded *Ammenemes II and continued to pursue a peaceful policy abroad and to improve agricultural and economic conditions at home. His reign saw no military expeditions, but Egypt maintained close contact with her neighbours. There is evidence that foreigners visited and settled in Egypt and that trade between Egypt and other countries flourished. Throughout the Twelfth and Thirteenth Dynasties, *'Asiatic' men and women from Syria/Palestine came in large numbers to live in Egyptian households as servants, and it is evident from the household goods and papyri found at Kahun, the pyramid workmen's town of this reign, that foreigners were engaged at the town as part of the workforce and as temple employees. Even in the contemporary tomb-scenes there is a cosmopolitan influence; one example is the tomb of the nomarch Khnumhotep at Beni Hasan in Middle Egypt, where scenes depict the arrival in Egypt of a *Beduin chief and his retinue.

In the Fayoum, Sesostris II may have inaugurated the great land reclamation project which was completed by and accredited to his grandson, *Ammenemes III. Here also, at Lahun, Sesostris II chose to build his pyramid; it incorporated a major innovation in that the entrance was placed outside the main pyramid structure in a vain attempt to deter robbers.

The king's pyramid was plundered, but the Sir Flinders Petrie made one of the greatest discoveries of Egyptian jewellery at this site in 1914. The jewellery was found in the shaft-tomb of the princess Sit-Hathor-Iunet, situated inside the pyramid complex enclosure walls. It included two exquisite pectorals and other pieces which are among the finest examples of Egyptian art. A similar discovery was made by another Egyptologist, de Morgan, at the pyramid enclosure of *Sesostris III at Dahshur in 1849.

Petrie also excavated the pyramid town and temple of Sesostris II which lay a short distance from his pyramid. The town is known today as 'Kahun', but in antiquity both the town and temple were called 'Hetep-Sesostris', meaning

'Sesostris-is-satisfied'. The town site is of great interest because it is one of the few examples of domestic, purpose-built architecture that have been uncovered in Egypt. The populace deserted this town in haste, for some unknown reason leaving behind their possessions, including furniture, jewellery, toys, tools and clothing with the result that this site provides a unique insight into living conditions in the Middle Kingdom. Papyri found in the temple and in the houses preserve temple accounts, letters, wills, household censuses, hymns, medical and veterinary treatments, and illustrate the strict administrative measures in force in such a community. The town housed not onlyworkmen (and their families) who were engaged in building and decorating the pyramid, but also officials and temple personnel and all those people required to organise and service such a community. There was also a small palace where Sesostris II rested on his visits to inspect progress on his pyramid.

BIBL. Petrie, W. M. F. *Illahun, Kahun and Gurob*. London: 1890; Petrie, W. M. F. *Kahun, Gurob and Hawara*. London: 1890; Griffith, F. Ll. *Hieratic papyri from Kahun and Gurob*. (two vols) London: 1890; Brunton, G. *Lahun, I.The Treasure*. London: 1920.

Sesostris III King 1878 - 1843 BC.

The Twelfth Dynasty probably reached its zenith with the reign of Sesostris III. 'Pharaoh Sesostris', the legendary hero who appears in later Classical accounts and combines the personalities of *Sesostris I, Sesostris III and even *Ramesses II, was probably based on folk-memory of the great Sesostris III.

One of his major achievements was to curtail forever the power of the provincial nobility. Since the Old Kingdom they had threatened the pharaoh's autocracy and in the First Intermediate Period had wielded great power as independent rulers. As the early rulers of the Twelfth Dynasty needed their support, they had allowed these nomarchs in Upper and Middle Egypt to retain a degree of independence and to continue building great rock-cut tombs in their own districts. Although his methods remain obscure, Sesostris III managed to abolish the nomarchs' ancient rights and privileges, and thus put an end to the feudal state. Royal power was enhanced and a new administration was introduced which placed the vizier, as the king's deputy, in overall control of the various departments. The demise of the hereditary nobility resulted in the beginning of a middle-class which consisted of craftsmen, tradesmen and small farmers; also, the great provincial tombs ceased to be built. By his action Sesostris III removed one of the greatest threats to pharaonic power.

Another great achievement was the king's energetic consolidation of Egypt's annexation of *Nubia. Troubles had begun to emerge in this region following the peaceful reigns of Sesostris III's two predecessors, and in Year 8 and on at least three other occasions, Sesostris III campaigned in *Nubia to rectify this situation. A new channel was cut in the First Cataract, near the island of Sehel, to provide a navigable waterway to link Upper Egypt to Lower Nubia and to allow the king's ships to gain access to *Nubia. The Egyptian frontier was now fixed at Semna, at the southern end of the Second Cataract, but Egyptian influence extended beyond this. To consolidate and control the area, Sesostris III built or extended at least eight brick forts between Semna South (at the border) and Buhen (at the northern end of the Second Cataract). These forts, situated on islands and promontories, provided an effective defence system and enabled the Egyptians to expand their exploitation of *Nubia, where Sesostris III was later deified and worshipped for many centuries.

In Palestine there was far less activity and only one military expedition is recorded, when the Egyptians took Sekmem, (probably Shechem in Mount Ephraim). In the Execration Texts, the names of a number of foreign rulers are included; these texts (the most important of which date to this reign or shortly afterwards) had a magical purpose. They included the names of enemies and dangers (both personal and of Egypt as a state). These were inscribed on pottery bowls which were then smashed and buried in the non-royal tombs at Saqqara and Thebes, with the intention of destroying the ability of a host of evils to harm the deceased.

Sesostris III's own pyramid was at Dahshur; it was investigated by de Morgan in 1894 and he discovered magnificent jewellery belonging to the queens and princesses of the royal family, who had been buried in a shaft-tomb within the pyramid enclosure. This compares closely with the other Middle Kingdom treasure discovered at Lahun by Petrie in 1914.

Other artistic and literary achievements of this reign include the temple built to Mont, the god of war, at Medamud near Karnak; the fine sculptured portrait heads of the king; and the hymn in praise of Sesostris III which was found amongst the papyri at Kahun, the pyramid workmen's town of *Sesostris II.

BIBL. Lansing, A. The Museum's excavations at Lisht. *Bull. MMA* 19 (1924). Dec., part 2, pp. 33-43;28 (1933). Nov., Section 2, pp. 4-38; 29 (1934). Nov., Section 2, pp. 4-40; Blackman, A. M. A reference to Sesostris III's Syrian campaign. *JEA* 2 (1915) pp. 13-4; Clarke, S. Ancient Egyptian frontier fortresses. *JEA* 3 (1916) pp. 155-79, pls. 24-32; Gardiner, A. H. An ancient list of the fortresses of Nubia. *JEA* 3 (1916) pp. 184-92.

Sethos I King 1318 - 1304 BC.

The son of Ramesses I, Sethos I's ambition was to restore Egypt's Syrian empire and to re-establish her prestige abroad, following the decline it had suffered during the Amarna Period. Ramesses I had been appointed by *Horemheb as his successor, but he died only sixteen months after his accession. His family had no royal blood; they came from the Delta and their personal god was Seth, the deity of Avaris. It was against this background, and probably to emphasise his political and religious legitimacy as ruler of Egypt, that Sethos I undertook certain actions. He not only sought to regain the empire, but also inaugurated a major programme to build and refurbish religious monuments at Thebes and Abydos. He took the additional title of 'Repeater of Births' to indicate that he regarded himself as the inaugurator of a new era.

His major campaigns are recorded in a series of scenes on the north and east walls in the Hypostyle Hall of the Temple of Karnak. In Year 1 of his reign, on his first campaign, the king led his forces out from the border fortress of Sile, along the military coast road from Egypt to Palestine, cleared the wells and entered

SETHOS

Gaza. Ultimately, this campaign probably took him further north to the southern end of the Phoenician coast. In a second campaign, he returned and progressed further north along the *Phoenician coast to launch an attack on the town of Kadesh. Then trouble in the western Delta forced him to return to Egypt to fight the *Libyans, before he could return to Syria. Here, in Year 5 or 6, he fought against the *Hittites; his brief possession of the land of Amurru and the town of Kadesh brought him into direct conflict with the *Hittites, but his Treaty with *Muwatallis, the *Hittite king, acknowledged that the Egyptians would cease trying to regain Kadesh and Amurru (which reverted to *Hittite control). It also stated that the *Hittites would recognise Egypt's interests, particularly with regard to the *Phoenician coastal towns.

Thus Sethos I had restored Egyptian authority in Palestine and even gained temporary control of part of Syria. He had imitated the actions of earlier pharaohs, particularly *Tuthmosis III, by establishing control first in Canaan and then gaining the *Phoenician coastal towns, from which it was possible to launch an attack into central and northern Syria. Further military action was necessary in another area, and in Year 8 Sethos I was forced to move against a *Nubian tribe – the Irem – who planned to revolt against their Egyptian overlords.

At home, Sethos I continued *Horemheb's policy of restoration, and this was best expressed in Sethos' magnificent religious monuments – the major construction and decoration of the Great Hypostyle Hall at Karnak; the magnificently decorated temple at Abydos; his mortuary temple at Qurna; the work undertaken on the temples of Re at Heliopolis and Ptah at Memphis; and his tomb, which is the finest in the Valley of the Kings. Descending over three hundred feet into the rock, the tomb is decorated with magnificent funerary scenes. It was discovered in AD 1817 by Belzoni, and the fine alabaster sarcophagus is now in the Sir John Soane Museum in London. The mummy of Sethos I was reburied by the priests in the cache at Deir el Bahri and is in the Cairo Museum; it is especially well-preserved, and it can be seen that the king was a strong and handsome ruler.

From his monuments, it is evident that although Sethos I was originally from the Delta, he maintained Thebes as his state and religious capital. His greatest building was his mortuary temple, built at Abydos, the cult-centre of the god *Osiris. It was designed as a national shrine to win him popularity and support, and includes seven chapels in the sanctuary area, which are dedicated to six major gods and to the deified Sethos himself; there is also a List of Kings giving the names of legitimate rulers from Menes (*Narmer) to Sethos I. The Nauri Decree records the king's endowment of this temple and the safeguards he gave to its staff and its property. The temple accommodated the rituals of the gods and also the king's own mortuary ritual. It was completed by Sethos I's son, *Ramesses II, who also finished other major buildings of Sethos I's reign.

Sethos I was himself a pious son, and he constructed a chapel for Ramesses I at Abydos. His reign was memorable because he effectively restored Egypt's power abroad and ensured stability at home.

BIBL. Kitchen, K. A. *Ramesside Inscrips.* Vol. 1. Oxford: 1968 1, pp 6-25 and 2, pp 25-37; Calverley, A. M. and Broome, M. F. *The Temple of King Sethos I at Abydos.* (four vols) London: 1933-58; David, A. R. *A Guide to religious ritual at Abydos.* Warminster: 1981; Faulkner, R. O. The wars of Sethos I. *JEA* 33 (1947) pp. 34 ff.; Griffith, F. Ll. The Abydos Decree of Seti I at Nauri. *JEA* 13 (1927) pp. 193 ff.

Shabako King 716 - 702 BC.

The brother of the great Ethiopian warrior, *Piankhy, Shabako returned to Egypt in 715 BC and established the Kushite or Ethiopian Twenty-fifth Dynasty. He deposed and took captive Bochchoris (Bakenrenef), the ruler of the Twenty-fourth Dynasty and a successor of Tefnakht, against whom *Piankhy had fought previously. By 711 BC, Shabako had established himself as the first *Nubian pharaoh and ruled Egypt in its entirety. He built and possibly established his capital at Thebes, although he was buried far to the south, in a pyramid at Kurru in his native land of Kush.

Shabako avoided intriguing with the states of Judah and Philistia against the new northern power, *Assyria, although his successors pursued an interventionist policy in this area which brought *Assyria to attack Egypt. He ruled for at least fourteen years; few monuments have survived from his reign, and he is not mentioned in contemporary Hebrew or *Assyrian sources, although *Herodotus (ii,137) refers to an Egyptian king Sabacos. Shabako was succeeded by Shebitku, and his reign was followed by that of *Taharka, the greatest ruler of this dynasty.

BIBL. Kitchen, K. A. *3rd Int.* pp 378-83; Dunham, D. El Kurru *in The Royal Cemeteries of Kush.* Vol. 1. Boston, Mass. 1950, pp 55-8.

Shalmaneser V King of *Assyria 727 - 722 BC.

Shalmaneser V, the son of *Tiglath-pileser III, continued his father's policy of ruthless expansion and annexation, thus forcing the vassal states of Syria/Palestine to seek help from Egypt. Hoshea rebelled openly against Shalmaneser, with the result that Samaria was captured and, three years later, in 721 BC, the population was taken away to *Assyria by Sargon II, Shalmaneser's successor; Hoshea was himself cast into prison. Biblical sources (II Kings,17:4) provide the information that Hoshea had involved Egypt in this conflict by sending messengers to 'So, King of Egypt' with requests for help. Attempts have been made to identify So with an Egyptian ruler but it seems more probable that this was the name of an Egyptian general.

BIBL. Kitchen, K. A. *3rd Int.* pp 372-4; von Zeissl, H. *Athiopen und Assyrer in Agypten.* Gluckstadt: 1944.

Sheklesh One of the Sea-peoples reigns of *Merneptah and *Ramesses III, c.1236- 1166 BC.

The Sheklesh were part of the confederation of *Sea-peoples who fought against the Egyptians in battles in Year 5 of *Merneptah's reign and Year 8 of *Ramesses III's reign.

The Egyptian temple scenes show them as bearded and wearing a pointed kilt with tassels; some wear a medallion suspended on a cord around the neck, and their chests are bound with protective strips of linen or leather. They apparently carried two spears, or a scimitar. According to these scenes, the Sheklesh, *Sherden, *Akawasha and Tursha were circumcised, and thus the hands (rather than the genitals) of the prisoners taken from these groups were presented to the Egyptian king as an enemy count. They may ultimately have arrived and settled as the Sicels in Sicily, where archaeological evidence indicates the arrival of a new people.

BIBL. *CAH* ii, ch xxviii; Wainwright, G. A. Some Sea-Peoples. *JEA* 47 (1961) pp. 71 ff.; Sheklesh or Shashu. *JEA* 50 (1964) pp. 40 ff.

Shepenopet I (Shepenwepe)   Divine Wife of Amun   c.754 - 714 BC.

Shepenopet I was the daughter of King Osorkon III, and held the position of Divine Wife of Amun at Thebes; according to the custom, she was obliged to adopt the daughter of King Kashta (*Amenardis I) as her 'daughter' and successor to this position. By the beginning of the Twenty-fifth Dynasty, the position of God's Wife of Amun had become a tool of great political importance, enabling the king to retain control of Thebes, through the status there of his daughter or other female relative.

Originally, this title had been borne by the king's chief wife, but from the Twenty-first Dynasty it was the king's daughter who assumed this position with its extensive power and possessions. She was required to live and die at Thebes and, as the consecrated wife of the god Amun, she was subject to the rule of chastity which also applied to her Court where the women were Amun's concubines, so that they too had to adopt their successors.

These Divine Wives of Amun played an important role in later history when their main function was to prevent the seizure of political power at Thebes by a man, who could then rival the pharaoh and cause a division between the northern and southern parts of the kingdom.

BIBL.Kitchen, K. A. *3rd Int.* Laming Macadam, M. F. *The Temples of Kawa.* Oxford: 1949, pp. 119 ff.

Shepseskaf   King   2500 - 2496 BC.

Shepseskaf was probably the son of *Mycerinus by a secondary wife. He was the last important ruler of the Fourth Dynasty whose reign witnessed the gradual disintegration of the dynasty and consequent political and religious upheaval. He completed the pyramid complex of *Mycerinus and dedicated the building for his father in a decree set up in the pyramid temple.

Shepseskaf broke away from Fourth Dynasty tradition by choosing south

Saqqara as his burial site and by building a tomb which was not a pyramid; this is the so-called Mastabat Fara'un which appears to revert to some of the architectural forms of earlier dynasties. Constructed as a mastaba-tomb, it is built with sloping sides, a bevelled roof and vertical ends, and has the appearance of a great rectangular stone sarcophagus. The internal burial chambers were also constructed with granite, but the outer court and causeway were built of mudbrick, and the monument was probably finished after the king's death. Queen Bunefer (who was probably his wife) apparently performed the funerary cult here for Shepseskaf, and she herself was buried in a rock-cut tomb at Giza.

Shepseskaf may have attempted to break away from the stranglehold that the priests of Re (the sun-god) increasingly imposed on the kings, and his tomb may reflect that independent stance. His decision to be buried in a mastaba-tomb may signify a rejection of the pyramid because it had close associations with the sun-cult. With his death, the Fourth Dynasty also passed away, and was replaced with a line of kings who clearly proclaimed their allegiance to Re's priesthood.

BIBL. Jequier, G. *Le Mastabat Faraoun*. Cairo: 1928.

Sherden   One of the *Sea-peoples   reigns of *Merneptah and *Ramesses III, c.1236 - 1166 BC.

The Sherden were amongst the *Sea-peoples who attacked Egypt in the Ramesside period, but they were first mentioned in Egyptian records during the reign of *Amenophis III, when they were described as pirates. In the reign of *Ramesses II, they came in war-ships from the midst of the sea and in the ensuing battle, many prisoners were taken. Later, they appeared amongst Pharaoh's bodyguard, and in the battles between *Ramesses III and the *Sea-peoples, they fought both for and against the Egyptians. Finally, they came to own and cultivate plots of land in Egypt, which presumably they had been awarded on account of their military service for Egypt. In the temple reliefs, they are shown wearing distinctive helmets which are ornamented with a large knob or disc at the apex and with projecting bull's horns; they carry round shields with handles and two-edged swords.

Although they were seafarers or pirates, they have also been tentatively associated with various land sites. The bronze-working population of Sardinia who built stone towers (nuraghi) seemed to arrive on the island suddenly, sometime between 1400 and 1200 BC, and they have left bronze statues there which show themselves with horned helmets and round shields similar to those of the Sherden. In Corsica, similar helmets are represented on figures that are depicted on the menhir-like tombstones. It is possible that Cyprus may have been the original homeland of these people, although Sardinia is probably the place where they ultimately settled, for according to the earliest *Phoenician inscription there, the name of the island was Shardan.

The Sherden fought against the Egyptians under *Merneptah as part of the coalition of *Libyans and *Sea-peoples, but in *Ramesses III's reign they occur not only in the enemy alliance but also as warriors on the Egyptian side.

BIBL. *CAH* ii, ch xxviii; Guido, M. *Sardinia*. London: 1963.

Shoshenk I   King   c.945 - 924 BC.

When the last ruler of the Twenty-first Dynasty, *Psusennes II, died with no male heir, the kingdom passed to Shoshenk, the powerful chief and army commander whose son was married to *Psusennes II's daughter. As Shoshenk I, the new ruler inaugurated the Twenty-second Dynasty, known also as the *Libyan or Bubastite Dynasty. Shoshenk I and his descendants came from the line of *Libyan chiefs who had once fought against the Egyptians; Bubastis was Shoshenk's family seat.

As the ablest ruler since early Ramesside times, he attempted to restore unity and stability in Egypt, although his success was short-lived. Previously, he had been closely associated with the kings of the royal line at Tanis and the high-priests of Ptah at Memphis, and his rulership was readily accepted by them. His accession was more reluctantly acknowledged at Thebes, but unification of the north and south was gradually brought about by royal appointments and marriage alliances. His second son, Iuput, was appointed as High-priest of Amun at Karnak, and thus Thebes was brought under the king's control. He established his capital at Tanis where he made additions to the great temple, and it is possible that he was buried there; certainly his descendants had their tombs at Tanis.

Once the unity of the realm had been established, Shoshenk turned his attention to foreign affairs. He renewed links with the city of *Byblos and again opened up *Nubia to Egyptian influence and trade. He also gave asylum to Jeroboam who fled from the wrath of King Solomon, thus laying the foundations for any future action in Palestine that might be useful to Egypt. This opportunity came when Solomon died in c.931/2 BC, and Jeroboam was recalled to Palestine by his supporters to challenge Rehoboam, Solomon's son and heir.When the realm was consequently divided into the two kingdoms of Judah and Israel in 930 BC, Egypt used the excuse of a border skirmish to launch a campaign in Palestine. Although the course of this campaign is unclear, the Biblical account recalls that King 'Shishak' removed a large amount of tribute from the temple and palace at Jerusalem; he did not attempt to extend his attack into Syria but returned to Egypt in triumph.

At home, work commenced on Shoshenk I's greatest building achievement – a forecourt and gateway (the so-called 'Bubastite Portal') at the front of the Temple of Amun at Karnak. Here, next to the Bubastite Gate, there was a triumphal scene with inscriptions, commemorating the king's Palestine campaign and showing him in the act of smiting his enemies. A partially destroyed list is given of the names of towns in Edom, Judah and Israel.

Shoshenk's monuments had not been completed when he died in the following year and was succeeded by his son, Osorkon I. In general, his reign had been a brief attempt to restore Egypt's internal stability and her prestige abroad.

BIBL.*The Bible* I Kings, 14: 25-6; II Chronicles, 12: 2-9; Kitchen, K. A. *3rd Int.* pp 72-6, 287-302.

Shoshenk II   Co-regent   c.890 BC.

With the death of *Psusennes II, the throne passed to a new family who were descended from the *Libyan chiefs who had settled at Bubastis in the Delta. The reign of *Shoshenk I, who was a member of this family, ushered in the Twenty-second Dynasty and heralded a period of renewed Egyptian ambitions abroad. However, even *Shoshenk I's abilities were unable to create a unified country to hand on to his descendants, and Osorkon I and Shoshenk II could not establish a strong kingdom.

Their capital continued to be at Tanis in the Delta and here, in 1929 to 1940, Montet and his colleagues excavated the site, discovering the burials and funerary treasure of a number of kings and officials of this period, including Shoshenk II.

Unlike the Valley of the Kings at Thebes, the Tanite royal burials were not placed in a separate necropolis away from the city, but occupied a site within the city, in the south-western corner of the temenos of Amun. The associated funerary temples were probably built directly above the tombs.

BIBL. Montet, P. *La Necropole royale de Tanis.* (three vols) Paris: 1947-60; Kitchen, K. A. *3rd Int.* pp. 117 ff.

Shoshenk III   King   c.825 - 773 BC.

Shoshenk III, a descendant of those *Libyan chiefs who had established the Twenty-second Dynasty, was no more capable of holding the kingdom together than his predecessors had been, and in c.800 BC there were two rival royal claims. Pedubast I established himself as pharaoh at Leontopolis and founded the Twenty-third Dynasty, while Shoshenk III continued the Twenty-second Dynasty at Tanis. Some years later the competition for the kingship had become even more intense and there were another two lines of pharaohs in Upper Egypt as well as a motley collection of principalities throughout the Delta, ruled by the descendants of the *Libyan chiefs. It was only the invasion from the south, establishing the Twenty-fifth or Ethiopian Dynasty, that succeeded in restoring unity to Egypt.

Shoshenk III had taken the kingdom in place of Prince Osorkon, son of King Takeloth I, and he used royal titles based on those of *Ramesses II, but his reign witnesses further disintegration and anarchy. He managed to remain ruler for at least fifty-two years and was eventually succeeded by King Pemay.

The burial of Shoshenk III was discovered at Tanis by Montet in 1939, and King Farouk was present at the opening of the coffin. It was believed that this would hold the remains of *Psusennes I, but instead it was found to belong to Shoshenk III.

BIBL. Montet, P. *La Necropole royale de Tanis.* Vol.3, Chechanq III. Paris: 1960; Kitchen, K. A. *3rd Int.* pp. 334-47.

Shuttarna, King of *Mitanni, reign of *Amenophis III, 1417 - 1379 BC.

The Amarna Letters – the royal archive found at the site of Tell el Amarna – preserve the correspondence between the rulers of *Mitanni and the Egyptian kings, *Amenophis III and *Akhenaten.

A marriage was arranged between *Amenophis III and *Ghilukhepa, the daughter of Shuttarna, and she came to Egypt accompanied by over three hundred attendants. The son and successor of King Shuttarna – *Tushratta – continued to pursue diplomatic relations with Egypt.

BIBL. Mercer, S. A. B. *The Tell el Amarna Tablets*. (two vols) Toronto: 1939; Engelbach, R. A 'Kirgipa' commemorative scarab of Amenophis III presented by His Majesty King Farouk I to the Cairo Museum. *Ann. Serv.* 40 (1941) pp. 659-61.

Sinuhe   Literary character   Middle Kingdom, c.1980-1930 BC.

The 'Story of Sinuhe' is regarded as a masterpiece of world literature and perhaps the greatest literary achievement of the Egyptians. It was written in the Middle Kingdom and is preserved in numerous fragmentary copies, the most complete being two papyri of Middle Kingdom date which are now in the Berlin collection. It was a very popular text and a good example of literary skill, combining prose and poetry, and thus it became a classic which was copied as an exercise by schoolboys hundreds of years after its composition.

The text takes the form of an autobiographical inscription of the kind that was placed in tombs, and it relates the events in the life of a court official named Sinuhe. It may represent the life experiences of a real person, although this is uncertain, but it clearly provides an accurate historical setting at the time of the death of *Ammenemes I and the subsequent reign of his son,*Sesostris I. The story relates that Sinuhe, brought up at the Royal Court in Egypt, fled from the country at the death of *Ammenemes I, because he feared that he might be drawn into the political troubles which he believed would happen over the succession. The Wisdom Instruction of *Ammenemes I also mentions this difficult period.

Sinuhe escaped across the Delta and the Isthmus of Suez into the desert regions where he faced death from thirst but was rescued by *Beduin tribesmen. He became a wanderer in this desert, but eventually achieved the status of chieftain of a tribe, and his travels took him as far as *Byblos on the Syrian coast, where he met the Prince of Retenu. This resulted in prosperity and wealth, for the Prince gave Sinuhe his daughter in marriage and allowed him to choose some of his land.

Despite personal honours, Sinuhe longed to return to Egypt where he could ensure that he would be buried with the correct traditions. A decree of pardon from the new king, *Sesostris I, invited him to return to Egypt; he started his homeward journey and, at the frontier, he was met with ships laden with goods. Eventually, travel-stained and unkempt, he reached the capital city, It-towe, and here he was led into the king's presence. Prostrating himself before the pharaoh, Sinuhe received kind words of welcome from *Sesostris, and was able to establish a new life in Egypt; he was even accorded the great honour of a magnificent tomb prepared for him close to the burial places of the king's own children.

The story was designed primarily to show that *Sesostris I was a benign and forgiving ruler. It also provides us with valuable insight into the political conditions in the Middle Kingdom, when Egypt's international prestige was high and Sinuhe was well-received outside his country. This provides a vivid contrast to the 'Story of *Wenamun' who, when he travelled abroad as the royal envoy hundreds of years later, met with many frustrations and humiliations from foreign officialdom because Egypt no longer exercised world power.

BIBL. *AEL* i. pp. 222-35; Blackman, A. M. Some notes on the Story of Sinuhe and other Egyptian texts. *JEA* 22 (1936) pp. 35-44; Gardiner, A. H. *Notes on the Story of Sinuhe.* Paris: 1916.

Siptah King c.1209 - 1200 BC.

Siptah was probably the son of Sethos II and his third wife, Tio, although his parentage is uncertain. The heir apparent – Sethos II's son by *Tewosret – died before his accession, and Siptah became king; as he was still a child, his step-mother *Tewosret and the Chancellor, Bay, acted as his regents. Indeed, Bay was such a powerful courtier that he was able to prepare his own tomb in the Valley of the Kings and to claim, in his inscriptions, that it was he who 'established the king upon the seat of his father.' In a few inscriptions of the reign, Bay is closely associated with Siptah, and it is possible that the courtier was of Syrian origin.

The exact order of succession is uncertain at this period, and a ruler named Amenmesse may have briefly usurped the throne during Siptah's reign. In Year 3, Siptah (born Ramesses-Siptah) changed his name to Merneptah-Siptah, and this may have been to mark his successful repossession of the throne from Amenmesse. Siptah, however, was dead by Year 6 and, as he had no heir, *Tewosret assumed the rulership of the country as queen regnant. Later generations did not regard Siptah as a legitimate ruler, although the reason for this is unclear. His funerary monuments suffered damage after his death, and in his tomb in the Valley of the Kings,his royal cartouches were excised, while his Theban funerary temple (which had perhaps never been completed) was destroyed.

BIBL. Aldred, C. The parentage of King Siptah. *JEA* 49 (1963) pp. 41 ff.; Von Beckerath, J. Queen Tewosre as guardian of Siptah. *JEA* 48 (1962) pp. 70 ff.; Gardiner, A. H. Only one King Siptah and Twosre not his wife. *JEA* 44 (1958) pp. 12 ff.

Smenkhkare King c.1364 - 1361 BC.

In Year 12 of *Akhenaten's reign, Queen *Nefertiti disappeared from the records, perhaps due either to her death or to a fall from favour. One of her names – Nefernefruaten – was subsequently given to Smenkhkare and he was also called 'Beloved of *Akhenaten'; he was probably made co-regent in Year 13 and the coronation perhaps took place in the great extension built to the Royal Palace at Amarna. His right to the throne was confirmed by his marriage to *Meritaten, the royal heiress.

Few facts are known of Smenkhkare or his brief reign. It is probable that he was the son of *Amenophis III, either by Queen *Tiye, or by Sitamun, or another minor wife, and the medical examination of the body found in Tomb 55 at Thebes (now attributed to Smenkhkare) has indicated that he was probably a full brother of *Tutankhamun and that he died around the age of twenty.

The details of his reign are obscure, particularly relating to the existence of a co-regency with *Akhenaten and the possibility of a brief period of sole rule. The only known date of Smenkhkare's reign occurs in a hieratic graffito in the Theban tomb of Pere, which gives a regnal date of Year 3 and also indicates that the cult of the god Amun was again in evidence. This possibly shows that Smenkhkare, as an independent ruler, was the first to move away from the Aten heresy, but other interpretations have suggested that *Akhenaten himself may have realised the failure of his revolution and sent his co-regent to Thebes to re-establish contact with the supporters of Amun, or that *Akhenaten and Smenkhkare may have disagreed fundamentally over the religious issues, with the result that Smenkhkare alone returned to orthodoxy.

There is evidence that Smenkhkare planned to be buried at Thebes, for he built a mortuary temple there which would suggest that he also intended to construct a tomb nearby. It is likely that *Meritaten predeceased him and that he then married the next royal heiress, *Ankhesenpaaten, but there were evidently no heirs because he was succeeded by the boy-king *Tutankhamun, who was probably his brother.

Events surrounding the death of Smenkhkare are also confusing. In Tomb 55 in the Valley of the Kings, a body and funerary equipment were discovered, and various interpretations of this evidence have been suggested. The body, examined on different occasions by several experts, has been variously identified as that of Queen *Tiye, of *Akhenaten and, most recently, of Smenkhkare. It has been shown to belong to a young man, aged about twenty at death, and it has an unusual but not abnormal platycephalic skull, similar to that of *Tutankhamun. The body was also enclosed in a coffin which bears a close resemblance to that of *Tutankhamun, but it was originally prepared for *Meritaten, Smenkhkare's wife, and it seems that both the coffin and the associated canopic jars (for containing the viscera) were later adapted for Smenkhkare. In a similar re-allocation of funerary equipment, some of Smenkhkare's goods were subsequently used in the tomb of *Tutankhamun, whose unexpectedly early death must have caused problems for those preparing his burial.

There is no simple explanation of Tomb 55 and its contents, and it is also unclear whether Smenkhkare owed his allegiance to the Aten or to Amun. Indeed, his very identification and existence have been questioned, and one theory has suggested that the inscriptions can be interpreted to indicate that 'Smenkhkare' was not a separate person at all, but that *Nefertiti herself took over a new name which perhaps marked some major development during her reign with *Akhenaten. In this case, there would have to be an alternative explanation for the body in Tomb 55 – that it belonged to some other, as yet unidentified member of the royal family.

BIBL. Aldred, C. *Akhenaten, King of Egypt*. London: 1988; Aldred, C. Year 12 at El-Amarna. *JEA* 43 (1957) pp. 114-17; Davis T. M. *The Tomb of Queen Tiyi*. London:1910. Gardiner, A. H. The so-called Tomb of Queen Tiye. *JEA* 43 (1957) pp. 10-25; Roeder, G. Thronfolger und Konig Smench-ka-Re. *ZAS* 83 (1958) pp. 43-74; Derry, D. E. Note of the skeleton believed to be that of Akhenaten. *Ann. Serv.* 31 (1931) pp. 115-19; Harrison, R. G. An anatomical examination of the pharaonic remains purported to be Akhenaten. *JEA* 52

(1966) pp. 95-119; Harrison, R. G. et al. The kinship of Smenkhkare and Tutankhamun demonstrated serologically. *Nature* 224 (1969) pp 325-6; Harris, J. R. Nefertiti Rediviva. *Acta Orientalia* 35 (1973) pp. 5 ff; Nefernefruaten Regnans. *Acta Orientalia* 36 (1974) pp. 11 ff; Akhenaten or Nefertiti? *Acta Orientalia* 38 (1977) pp. 5 ff; Samson, J. Nefertiti's regality. *JEA* 63 (1977) pp. 88 ff.

Sneferu King c.2613 - 2589 BC.

Sneferu, the successor of *Huni, inaugurated the Fourth Dynasty and ushered in a new era. Later generations remembered his importance, and he was one of the few kings accorded a cult, receiving worship in particular at the turquoise mines in Sinai.

Details of only six years of his reign (he ruled for over twenty-four years) are preserved on the Palermo Stone and on the large Cairo fragment: great ships were built of cedar and other coniferous wood, and forty shiploads of cedar were brought to Egypt, some of which was used to make the doors of a palace. The cedar probably came from *Byblos, the port on the Syrian coast with which the Egyptians had established sea-trade from early times.

In a successful raid against the *Nubians, Sneferu claimed to have brought back seventy thousand captives and two hundred thousand head of cattle, and his activity probably helped to subdue *Nubia and to establish a situation which enabled his successors to obtain hard stone from the south for their monumental building projects. Sneferu was also active in Sinai and, in a rock-carving in Wadi Maghara, he is shown smiting a local chieftain. He and his successors followed a tradition of raids which allowed the Egyptians to gain control over the turquoise mines of this area. He also campaigned against the *Tjehnyu Libyans and brought back a large quantity of booty.

Sneferu's claim to the throne was probably enhanced by his marriage to the princess *Hetepheres who became the mother of his heir, *Cheops. Sneferu's mother, Meresankh, was a minor queen of *Huni but she had sufficient influence to ensure her son's succession to the throne.

Later generations remembered Sneferu as a liberal, well-intentioned and beneficent ruler, in contrast to his descendants, *Cheops and *Chephren. In the Westcar Papyrus, the story relates the ways in which magicians sought to entertain various rulers of the Old Kingdom, and Sneferu was portrayed as a good-humoured individual who was drawn out of his boredom when he was rowed on the palace lake by a team of beautiful girls. His most enduring monument is supplied by the two or possibly three pyramids that are attributed to him; more than anything else, these emphasise his great political and economic power.

The pyramid at Medum (about thirty-three miles south of Saqqara) is the earliest of these, and in fact may have been started by *Huni but completed by Sneferu. It was first constructed as a Step Pyramid but subsequently the eight steps were filled in to attempt to achieve a smooth, four-sided structure. A short distance from Saqqara, at Dahshur, Sneferu built two substantial pyramids. The southern one is known as the Bent or Rhomboidal Pyramid because, at a point halfway along its height, the angle of the incline is suddenly reduced. In the associated

Valley Building, excavations have revealed an important series of wall-reliefs which show female offering-bearers; these personified the king's funerary estates in the various districts of Egypt and indicate that the administrative system was already well-established.

The northern monument is the first example of a true pyramid; it rises to over three hundred and ten feet in height but the angle of incline is approximately the same as that of the upper section of the Bent Pyramid.Although various suggestions have been offered, there is no conclusive explanation as to why one ruler built two or even three pyramids.

BIBL. Le Maystre,C. Les dates des pyramides de Sneferou. *BIFAO* 35 (1935) pp. 89 ff; Petrie, W. M. F. *Meydum*. London: 1892; Fakhry, A. *The Bent Pyramid of Dahshur*. Cairo: 1954; Mendelssohn, K. A building disaster at the Meidum Pyramid. *JEA* 59 (1973) pp. 60-71; Batrawi, A. The skeletal remains from the Northern Pyramid of Sneferu. *Ann. Serv.* 51 (1951) pp. 435-40.

Solomon   King of Israel   971/970 - 931/930 BC.

Although there are no contemporary Egyptian records to confirm Solomon's relations with the Egyptian kings, the Bible provides some information. Hadad, an Edomite prince, fled to Egypt after Joab, who was in command of King David's forces, laid waste to Edom and slaughtered the entire male population. The Bible records that Hadad grew up in Egypt and eventually married Tahpenes who was a sister of the Egyptian queen, and that he became a committed enemy of Solomon.

Other references in the Bible indicate that Solomon enjoyed cordial relations with Egypt: he married one of pharaoh's daughters, and when the Egyptian king captured Gezer, where he slaughtered many Canaanites, he presented this region as a gift to this daughter. It is probable that this Egyptian ruler was one of the kings of the Twenty-second Dynasty.

Egypt also exerted influence in other ways, for when Solomon began to organise the Jewish kingdom, the pattern of a long-established and highly organised bureaucracy already existed in Egypt for him to copy.

BIBL. Kitchen, K. A. *3rd Int.* pp. 279-83.

Strabo   Geographer   c.64 BC.

Strabo was born at Pontus, but spent some years at Alexandria in Egypt; in the seventeenth and last book of his *Geographia* (which was written in Greek), he gives a short account of the geography of Egypt and other details about the country occur elsewhere in his writings.

It is mainly geographical facts which are presented in his work, and these are generally considered to be accurate. He describes Alexandria and the surrounding district in some detail and he provides a topographical survey that lists some ninety-nine towns and other settlements, with information particularly about the Delta area. He and his friend, the Roman Prefect Aelius Gallus, probably made a journey as far as the First Cataract in 25/24 BC, and this apparently aroused his interest in many subjects. He refers to buildings, including the pyramids, tombs and temples, and he comments on the religious cults and some historical details. However, as with other Classical authors, it is necessary to assess these 'facts' with some caution.

Strabo followed *Herodotus in the tradition of a Classical author writing about Egypt, and some of his comments are of considerable interest. For example, he mentions his visit to the Theban tombs in 27 BC and also the famous Nilometer at Elephantine, which was used for measuring the annual level of water in the river. Strabo was also the first to comment on the phenomenon of the singing stones in the Colossi of Memnon, which he visited when he travelled to Thebes. The Colossi – two great statues that originally stood at the entrance to the mortuary temple of *Amenophis III – were always an impressive sight, but after 27 BC, there was additional interest in them, because the northernmost statue was reputed to emit a singing noise at dawn; this 'wonder' was heard and commented upon by Classical writers, but Strabo was rightly sceptical about the 'singing statue'. Modern science has subsequently explained that this phenomenon was the result of an earthquake which occurred in 27 BC; it split the statue so that it broke in two at the waist and, when sudden changes in the humidity and temperature occurred at dawn, this brought about an internal action which set up a vibration in the stone. The statue ceased to sing when it was repaired in 199 BC, on the order of the Roman Emperor, *Septimius Severus.

BIBL. Strabo *The Geography of Strabo* transl.by Jones, H. L. (eight vols) London: 1932; Bowersock, G. W. *Augustus and the Greek world*. Oxford: 1965, pp. 123 ff.

Suppiluliumas   King of the *Hittites   1380 - 1340 BC.

The son of Tudhaliyas III, Suppiluliumas became king of the *Hittites in 1380 BC, and his reign introduced a new era of expansion and military power.

He conducted a brilliant campaign, overthrowing the rival kingdom of *Mitanni in 1370 BC, and eventually brought the whole of northern Syria as far as Kadesh under *Hittite control. It is possible that he would have held the *Hittite boundary as the River Orontes, but the ruler of Kadesh (who was an Egyptian vassal) entered into battle with the *Hittites and was defeated, so that Suppiluliumas' army went as far as Abina near Damascus. The *Hittite king was recalled by problems at home, but he returned to campaign in Syria in 1340 BC.

Suppiluliumas' progress in the area was made easier because *Akhenaten (to whom Suppiluliumas had sent a letter of congratulation on his accession) was preoccupied with his religious reforms in Egypt. Towards the end of *Akhenaten's reign, the kingdom of Amurru in central Syria had been forced into an alliance with the *Hittites and thus Egypt had lost another province; gradually, the *Hittites undermined Egypt's empire throughout Syria/Palestine.

Against this background of hostility and mistrust, it is therefore even more surprising to discover that an Egyptian queen (almost certainly *Ankhesenpaaten/ Ankhesenamun) wrote to the *Hittite king, Suppiluliumas, beseeching him to send a prince to marry her. Suppiluliumas was obviously wary of this request, and sent an envoy to Egypt to investigate further. The envoy returned with a reiteration of

147

the queen's plea, and Suppiluliumas eventually sent a son to Egypt, but he was murdered on arrival, probably by the agents of the rival faction in Egypt who did not wish to see their country handed over to their arch-enemy through the agency of a royal marriage.

This murder of a *Hittite prince had repercussions; there was immediate retaliation by Suppiluliumas who sent his armies against Egypt's Syrian vassals and, in the longer term, there was a period of distrust and warfare between Egypt and the *Hittites. Suppiluliumas died of a pestilence only a few years after his ill-fated son.

BIBL. Kitchen, K. A. *Suppiluliumas and the Amarna Pharaohs*. Liverpool: 1962.

Syncellus Historian c.AD 800.

George the Monk, known as Syncellus, wrote a book entitled, 'History of the World from the Creation to Diocletian', in which he provides the last transmission, although only in a partial form, of the major work (the *Aegyptiaca*) of the Egyptian priest, *Manetho. Other sources that partially preserve *Manetho's *History* are the earlier writers *Josephus, *Africanus and *Eusebius.

T

Tadukhepa   *Mitannian princess   reign of *Amenophis III, 1417 - 1379 BC.
In the correspondence (preserved in the Amarna archive) between King *Tushratta of *Mitanni and *Amenophis III, there are several letters which are concerned with the protracted negotiations over the dispatch of Princess *Tadukhepa to become the wife of *Amenophis III. He had earlier received another royal wife (*Ghilukhepa, *Tushratta's sister) from *Mitanni, but *Tushratta now insisted that his daughter Tadukhepa should not only become *Amenophis III's wife but that she should also be 'Mistress of Egypt'. Eventually, she arrived in Egypt with a great assortment of costly gifts, but *Amenophis III was probably old and sick by then and Tadukhepa was ultimately transferred to the harem of his son, *Akhenaten (Amenophis IV), who was addressed as Napkhuria by the *Mitannians.
    At one time it was suggested that *Akhenaten's famous queen, *Nefertiti, was the re-named Tadukhepa; the famous head of *Nefertiti in Berlin, it was argued, represented a woman of non-Egyptian and possibly Indo-Aryan origin. Evidence that relates to other members of *Nefertiti's family would indicate that she was of Egyptian, although unknown, parentage.

BIBL. Mercer, S. A. B. *The Tell el Amarna Tablets*. (two vols) Toronto: 1939.

Taharka   King   690- 664 BC.
The brother of Shebitku, *Nubian ruler of Egypt in the Twenty-fifth Dynasty, Taharka was summoned with his other brothers from Napata to join Shebitku at Thebes. They came with an army and accompanied Shebitku to Lower Egypt.
    Taharka and his brothers may have been present when *Sennacherib defeated Egyptian and Ethiopian forces at El-tekeh in 701 BC, after Egypt had interfered in the policies of Ekron (a Philistine town) and Judah. There is another reference to a possible conflict between *Sennacherib and Egypt in the Bible (II Kings, 19:8-35), when King Tirhakah of Egypt came out to fight *Assyria, but the *Assyrian forces were slain by the angel of God in the night and *Sennacherib returned to Nineveh. In *Herodotus (ii,141), a slightly different version relates that the *Assyrians were forced to retreat because their bows and quivers were eaten by mice.
    Taharka succeeded Shebitku as king of Egypt and Nubia, and was crowned at Memphis. Five great stelae that were excavated at Kawa recount the events of his early reign as well as the donations he made to the local temple. There were momentous events in Year 6 (c.685 BC): a very high Nile inundation and rainfall in *Nubia was followed by a rich harvest; the king began an extensive building programme at the Kawa temple; and his mother, Abar, came to Memphis,

providing the first opportunity for them to meet since Taharka had left *Nubia to join Shebitku.

The earlier years of the reign were peaceful and great building programmes were initiated throughout the country: a colonnade was added in the Bubastite forecourt of the Temple of Karnak and other additions were made at Buhen, Kasr Ibrim, Napata and Sanam. Taharka's daughter, Amenardis II, was adopted at Thebes as the God's Wife of Amun by the incumbent, Shepenopet II. The new *Assyrian ruler, *Esarhaddon, regarded Egypt's interference in the affairs of his vassal states in Palestine and Syria as intolerable, and this brought *Assyria to Egypt. In 674 BC, *Esarhaddon tried to invade Egypt and was repulsed by Taharka, but a second attack in 671 BC drove Taharka out from Memphis. In 669 BC, there was danger of further trouble in Egypt, and *Esarhaddon set out again to deal with this, but fell ill and died at Haran on the way.

Taharka re-established himself at Memphis and occupied it until the next *Assyrian ruler, *Ashurbanipal, drove him out in 667/666 BC. He fled to Thebes and when the *Assyrians reached there, he escaped further south to Napata. *Ashurbanipal returned to Nineveh, having first obtained the allegiance of the Delta princes. They soon decided that they preferred *Nubian rule and began to intrigue with Taharka at Napata. This conspiracy was discovered and the Delta princes were dispatched to Nineveh; two of them − *Necho of Sais and his son *Psammetichus − were sent back to Egypt and reinstated by *Ashurbanipal as the local rulers.

In the meantime, Taharka died at Napata and was buried in a pyramid at Nuri; he had chosen his nephew, Tanuatamun, as his successor.

BIBL. Laming Macadam, M. F. *The Temples of Kawa*.(four vols) Oxford: 1949, 1955; Dunham, D. *The Royal Cemeteries of Kush. Vol.2: Nuri*. Boston, Mass.: 1955, pp. 6 ff.; Kitchen, K. A. *3rd Int.*

Teresh   One of the Sea-peoples   reign of *Merneptah, 1236 - 1223 BC.

The Teresh (Tursha) formed part of the confederation of *Sea-peoples who fought against Egypt in the reign of *Merneptah.

The temple wall-reliefs show them as bearded and wearing pointed kilts with tassels; some also have a medallion suspended around the neck and their chests are protected with a bandaging of strips of linen or leather; they also carry a pair of spears or a scimitar. The Teresh were circumcised, and they have been tentatively identified with the Tyrsenoi, the ancestors of the Etruscans. There is as yet no evidence in Italy to suggest that the Etruscans arrived there at such an early date.

BIBL. *CAH* ii, ch xxviii.

Teti   King   c.2345 - 2333 BC.

The Fifth and Sixth Dynasties are separated by events which remain obscure, but the transfer of power to Teti, the first king of the Sixth Dynasty, does not appear to have involved a major upheaval or conflict. Indeed, the titles borne by his chief queen, Iput, indicate that she carried the royal line from one dynastic family to the next, and it is probable that she was a daughter of *Unas, the last king of the Fifth Dynasty.

Little further evidence remains of Teti's reign, although foreign contacts were obviously continued with *Byblos, Syria and *Nubia. The country was stable and affluent and the courtiers continued to build fine tombs around the king's pyramid at Saqqara; one particularly impressive tomb belonged to the vizier Mereruka, who was also the king's son-in-law.

Teti's pyramid was conventional in style; on the inside walls the inscriptions provide a selection of magico-religious texts ('The Pyramid Texts'), which were intended to ensure the king's safe passage into the next world and his acceptance there by the gods. Nearby, he built a pyramid for two of his queens, Iput and Khuit.

According to *Manetho, Teti was murdered by his bodyguard, although there is no historical corroboration of this statement. He was briefly succeeded by a king named Userkare, and then by *Pepy I, his son by Queen Iput.

BIBL. Firth, C. M. and Gunn, B. *The Teti Pyramid Cemeteries.* (two vols) Cairo: 1926.

Tewosret   Queen   c.1202 - 1200 BC.

Tewosret was the chief queen of Sethos II and bore the heir apparent, but this son died prematurely and it was the child of another queen, Tio, who succeeded Sethos II on the throne. The young king (named Ramesses-Siptah) was probably chosen by Chancellor Bay, the Syrian courtier who wielded great influence, and he may have forced this decision on Queen Tewosret, for she and Bay briefly acted as regents for *Siptah.

By Year 6 of his reign, *Siptah was dead, and Tewosret seized power for herself, assuming the full kingly titles. She was only the fourth woman in Egypt's history to take control of the country as a queen regnant. She ruled briefly for two years and left a funerary monument to the south of the Ramesseum at Thebes; she was buried in a tomb in the Valley of the Kings at Thebes, an honour previously bestowed on only one woman – Queen *Hatshepsut. Her successor Setnakht (whose origins are unknown) apparently seized her tomb and destroyed the queen's mummy, although her funerary jewellery had already been removed to a place of safety, where it was discovered by Theodore Davis.

When Tewosret's reign ended, the line of direct descendants of *Ramesses II ceased to rule Egypt.

BIBL. Von Beckerath, J. Queen Tewosre as guardian of Siptah. *JEA* 48 (1962) pp. 70 ff; Gardiner, A. H. Only one King Siptah and Twosre not his wife. *JEA* 44 (1958) pp. 12 ff; Gardiner, A. H. The tomb of Queen Twosre. *JEA* 40 (1954) pp. 40 ff.

Theodosius I   Roman Emperor   AD 379 - 395.

Theodosius the Great was baptised a Christian soon after his accession. He was the emperor who formally declared Christianity as the religion of the Roman Empire. Heretics and pagans were persecuted, and there was a systematic destruction of heathen temples and monuments in Egypt and Syria. The Patriarch Theophilus carried out this work at Alexandria, and it was during this period that the Serapeum (the place where the god Serapis had been worshipped) was destroyed. Despite the Edicts of Theodosius I, the ancient religion of Egypt continued to be practised on the sacred island of Philae where the temples were not closed until the reign of Emperor Justinian (c.AD 540).

BIBL. Milne, J. G. *A History of Egypt under Roman rule*. London: 1924.

Thuya   King's mother-in-law   reign of *Amenophis III, 1417 - 1379 BC.

Thuya was the wife of *Yuya and the mother of Queen *Tiye. In the inscriptions on the commemorative scarabs issued in the reign of her son-in-law *Amenophis III, she is entitled 'Chief Lady of Amun's harem'.

The tomb of *Yuya and Thuya was discovered in AD 1905, in the Valley of the Kings at Thebes; perhaps because the tomb-robbers were disturbed, the two mummies and many of the funerary possessions survived intact and can now be seen in the Cairo Museum. Thuya's mummy suggests that she was of Egyptian origin, although it has been speculated that her husband may have had foreign ancestry.

The marked similarity between the names of *Yuya and Thuya, their daughter *Tiye, and *Ay and his wife Tey has prompted the suggestion that they may all have been closely related.

BIBL. Quibell, J. E. *The Tomb of Yuaa and Thuii*. Cairo: 1908; Aldred, C. *Akhenaten, King of Egypt*. London: 1968; Davis, T. M., Maspero, G. and Newberry, P. E. *The Tomb of Iouiya and Touiyou*. London: 1907.

Ti   Court Official   reign of *Niuserre, 2453 - 2422 BC.

Ti, a Court official of high standing, a great landowner, and administrator of the royal funerary temples, lived at the beginning of the Fifth Dynasty. He is most famous for his magnificent tomb at Saqqara which was discovered by Mariette and which is one of the best examples of Old Kingdom non-royal funerary architecture. The tomb originally stood above ground and was designed to incorporate some of the features which appeared in the contemporary mansions occupied by the wealthy when they were alive; these included a portico, two great colonnaded halls, a passage and a store-chamber for possessions.The funerary offerings were presented in the great court, decorated with twelve square pillars, and a passage descended to give access to the second great chamber where Ti was buried and where his sarcophagus still remains.

The mural reliefs in this tomb are amongst the finest examples of Egyptian art extant and they show a far wider range of activities than had hitherto been represented in the tomb context. The scenes show Ti as a great feudal landowner, supervising various activities on his estate, and they provide a vivid insight into the details of daily life at that time. The subjects include agricultural pursuits such as harvesting, market scenes, the fattening of geese and the feeding of cranes. These were intended to supply the deceased tomb-owner with an eternal food supply; Ti is also shown supervising ship-building activities, goldsmiths, carpenters, leather-workers and masons producing stone vessels, as well as receiving the accounts from his officials and inspecting the sacrifice of animals. He is also depicted enjoying various leisure pastimes such as boating in the marshes and, as a most important rite to ensure his continuation after death, Ti also receives the presentation of the funerary offerings. Throughout the scenes, his wife Neferhotep appears as his constant companion and as the joint beneficiary of the funerary goods.

BIBL. Steindorff, G. *Das Grab des Ti.* Leipzig: 1913; Epron, L. and Daumas, F. *Le tombeau de Ti.* Cairo: 1939.

Tiglath-Pileser III King of *Assyria. 745 - 727 BC.

*Assyria, as the great northern power of the Near East, needed to gain access to a sea-coast and to the products of the Levant, particularly timber. Under Tiglath-pileser III, the revitalised and ambitious *Assyrian state therefore attempted to bring the petty kingdoms of that area under its direct control.

In the third year of his reign (742 BC), Tiglath-pileser III advanced into Syria and eventually brought the vassal states there under his influence; however, another rebellion arose amongst them and the *Assyrian king returned to quell the insurrection. By 738 BC, in order to prevent further trouble, the *Assyrians began a policy of direct annexation of the vassal states in Syria, but conflicts resulted in the devastation of Damascus and the deportation of a substantial proportion of the people to *Assyria. Similarly, in Israel, King Pekah was deposed and replaced by Hoshea.

Egypt was drawn into the the combat because the petty kingdoms that had once been Egyptian client states now appealed to her for help. The accounts of Egyptian involvement with *Assyria are only preserved in the Old Testament and in cuneiform texts, but no reference to these events has been found in Egyptian records.

BIBL. Von Zeissl, *Athiopen und Assyrer in Agypten.* Gluckstadt: 1944; Winton Thomas, D. (ed.) *Documents from Old Testament times.* London: 1958.

Tiye Queen reign of *Amenophis III, 1417 - 1379 BC.

Tiye was the daughter of *Yuya, the King's Lieutenant of Chariotry and Master of the Horse, and *Thuya, who was probably a royal lady-in-waiting. She had at least one brother, Anen, who held high offices under *Amenophis III, and it is possible that *Ay was another brother.

As a child, Tiye was married to *Amenophis III, although she was not a royal heiress; this marriage may have been arranged because there was no royal daughter, or because *Tuthmosis IV (*Amenophis III's father) was attempting to limit the traditional powers of the priests of Amun, who had previously played a major role in the selection of the royal heir by giving or withholding the god's approval.

Despite her non-royal origins, Tiye became the Great Royal Wife of *Amenophis III and she continued to exert influence over him and their son, *Akhenaten (Amenophis IV). She was frequently represented with her husband in sculptures, reliefs and inscriptions. In this reign, a new method of broadcasting important events was devisedwith the issue of large inscribed, commemorative scarabs, and on these, Tiye's name (and in two cases, those of her parents) was associated with that of *Amenophis III. One scarab inscription refers to a large lake which *Amenophis III ordered to be made for Tiye; this may have been either a pleasure lake for the queen, or an inundation 'basin' which was flooded so that a substantial harvest could be reaped, which would be credited to Tiye's revenues. On another scarab, Tiye is mentioned as the King's wife at the celebration of the arrival in Egypt of the *Mitannian princess, *Ghilukhepa, who was to enter the royal harem.

*Amenophis III and Tiye lived in the palace complex at Malkata at Thebes, where they would have enjoyed a luxurious and cosmopolitan lifestyle. In his long and affluent reign, *Amenophis III celebrated three jubilee festivals in his regnal years 30, 34 and 37, with great festivities at Memphis and Thebes.

The couple's eldest son (Thutmose) did not survive to inherit the throne, and a younger son became King Amenophis IV. As *Akhenaten, he introduced great changes during his reign, and moved the Court from Thebes to Amarna. It is possible that *Amenophis III and Tiye lived at Amarna during their later years; however, a scene which shows *Amenophis III at this city may simply represent an ancestor-cult rather than indicating that he actually took up residence there. There is little doubt that Tiye, as the dowager queen, spent time in the new capital; she may have had her own palace and temple there, and her state-visit to Amarna, which probably occurred in Year 12, is well-recorded in a tomb-scene.

Tiye's influence on state affairs continued after her husband's death: *Akhenaten appointed her, with *Nefertiti and *Ay, as his advisers; King *Tushratta of *Mitanni addressed correspondence to her, requesting that the good relations the two countries had enjoyed during the reign of *Amenophis III should continue under her son *Akhenaten. This king also wrote to *Akhenaten, advising him to consult his mother, and it is evident that Tiye enjoyed prestige abroad as a wise and shrewd adviser.

Tiye's other children included the princesses Baketaten and Sitamun, and the latter married *Amenophis III, her own father. It is possible that Tiye was also the mother of *Smenkhkare and *Tutankhamun, although it is perhaps more likely that they were her grandchildren, born from the union of her husband and her daughter Sitamun. Tiye was obviously closely related to *Tutankhamun, for an auburn lock of Tiye's hair, enclosed in a small coffin, was found in the young king's tomb.

It is possible that Tiye was originally buried at Amarna in the Royal Tomb; her steward Huya was buried there in one of the nobles' tombs. Her remains were probably later removed to Thebes and buried in one of the large subsidiary chambers of her husband's tomb, situated in the western branch of the Valley of the Kings. When some of her funerary goods, particularly the shrine, were discovered by Theodore M. Davis in Tomb 55 in the Valley of the Kings, this led to much speculation. Davis claimed that the body buried in Tomb 55 must be that of Tiye, although others argued that it was the mortal remains of *Akhenaten himself. Further investigation has shown that the body is male, and it has been tentatively identified as belonging to *Smenkhkare. The presence in the tomb of several funerary items belonging to Queen Tiye has been explained by various theories. After her death, Tiye's funerary cult was continued at Thebes; at Sedeinga in Nubia, she was also worshipped in a cult established for her by *Amenophis III, in which she appeared in the form of the local goddess, Hathor.

BIBL. Fakhry, A. A note on the tomb of Kheruef at Thebes. *Ann. Serv.*42 (1943) pp. 447-508; Gardiner, A. H. The so-called tomb of Queen Tiye. *JEA* 43 (1957) pp. 10-25; Lansing, A. Excavations at the palace of Amenhotep III at Thebes. *Bull. MMA* 13 (1918) March supplement. pp. 8-14; Rowe A. Inscriptions on the model coffin containing the lock of hair of Queen Tyi. *Ann.Serv.*40 (1941) pp. 623-7; Aldred, C. *Akhenaten, King of Egypt.* London: 1988; Davis, T, Maspero, G. et al. *The Tomb of Queen Tiyi.* London: 1910.

Tjehnyu

The Egyptians gave the name 'Tjehnyu' to a tribe who occupied part of 'Libya'. Originally, these people may have been of the same race and shared the same culture as the Egyptians who lived in the western Delta, and they perhaps occupied the oases in the western desert. They were closely related to the *Tjemhu, but the Egyptians distinguished between the two tribes. The Tjehnyu are shown in Egyptian scenes and records of Ramesside times wearing the phallus-sheath and a headdress with upright feathers; their hair is worn in a distinctive style, with a large curl hanging down from one side of the head. The Tjehnyu joined the *Meshwesh and *Libu in harrassing the Egyptians in the Delta during the reign of *Ramesses II, and later, they were swept into the conflict between Egypt and the *Sea-peoples.

BIBL. *CAH* ii, ch xxviii; Edgerton, W. F. and Wilson, J. A. *Historical Records of Ramesses III*. Chicago: 1936; Holscher, W. *Libyer und Agypter*. Gluckstadt: 1937.

Tjemhu.

The Tjemhu are one of the *Libyan tribes who are distinguished in the Egyptian records. In temple wall-scenes commemorating the conflicts between the Egyptians and the coalition of *Libyans and *Sea-peoples, they are shown wearing the phallus-sheath, a hairstyle with a large curl hanging down at the side of the head, and a headdress of upright feathers. They were apparently driven by hunger to attack Egypt during the Ramesside period, in the hope that they would be able to settle in the Delta.

BIBL. *CAH* ii, ch xxviii; Edgerton, W. F. and Wilson, J. A *Historical Records of Ramesses III*. Chicago: 1936; Holscher, W. *Libyer und Agypter*. Gluckstadt: 1937.

Trajan   Roman Emperor   AD 97 - 117.

Trajan was adopted as heir by the previous Roman emperor, Nerva, and he in turn adopted his successor, *Hadrian. Trajan attempted to be an ideal emperor: he was a competent administrator and a lavish builder, who inaugurated such projects as his Forum and the Baths in Rome. In AD 106 he took Arabia, and once the Roman occupation of the area was complete, it was possible to reopen the canal built to join the Nile to the Red Sea, which had fallen into disrepair in the first century BC.

There were also many building projects undertaken in Egypt during his reign. In the Temple of Khnum at Esna, there are important texts on the walls of the hypostyle hall; his name occurs at Denderah, together with that of *Hadrian, in reliefs on the Birth-house built by *Augustus; and at Kom Ombo, in the outer passageway around the temple, the wall-reliefs show Trajan kneeling and sacrificing to the Egyptian gods. A neighbouring scene of the same date shows a unique representation of medical instruments. On the island of Elephantine at Aswan there are the foundations of a small temple which also date to Trajan's reign, while among the buildings on the sacred island of Philae (which have now been moved to a neighbouring island, as part of the programme to save the monuments of Nubia following the construction of the High Dam at Aswan), Trajan's Kiosk remains an outstanding feature

BIBL. Milne, J. G. *A History of Egypt under Roman rule.* London: 1924.

Tushratta   King of *Mitanni   reign of *Amenophis III, 1417 - 1379 BC.

In the early Eighteenth Dynasty, *Mitanni – the great northern Mesopotamian state – had come into direct conflict with Egypt, and *Tuthmosis III had led military campaigns to prevent *Mitanni's further expansion. A diplomatic alliance had then been fostered between the two countries, which was cemented by royal marriages when the *Mitannian king, Artatama I, gave his daughter to become the wife of *Tuthmosis IV, and *Amenophis III received two *Mitannian princesses, *Ghilukhepa and *Tadukhepa, in marriage.

Tushratta, the son of *Shuttarna, became king of *Mitanni after an elder brother was murdered. He was the brother of *Ghilukhepa and the father of *Tadukhepa, and he enjoyed cordial diplomatic and familial relationships with *Amenophis III and his Court. In the archive of letters found at Tell el Amarna, Tushratta's letters have been discovered addressed to *Amenophis III, his widow Queen *Tiye, and Amenophis IV – *Akhenaten. His letter to *Amenophis III, written in five hundred lines of well-preserved text, is the main source for the study of the Hurrian language. In addition to family matters, the correspondence relates how Tushratta sent the image of the goddess 'Ishtar of Nineveh' to his elderly and sick son-in-law, *Amenophis III, in Year 36 of his reign, in the hope that she would bring about a cure for the Egyptian king.

The *Hittite king, *Suppiluliumas, became engaged in military conflict with Tushratta and finally Tushratta was assassinated; he was succeeded by Artatama, the heir favoured by a faction who were supported by the *Assyrians.

BIBL. Mercer, S. A. B. *The Tell El-Amarna Tablets.* (two vols) Toronto: 1939.

Tutankhamun   King   1361-1352 BC.

Tutankhamun succeeded *Smenkhkare as ruler of Egypt when he was still a child of eight or nine years. It is probable that he was the son of *Amenophis III, whom he calls 'father' on one of the granite lions which originally stood in the Temple of *Amenophis III at Soleb and is now in the British Museum. Another interpretation of this evidence suggests that the word is to be translated as 'ancestor', and that *Akhenaten, rather than *Amenophis III, could be Tutankhamun's father. His mother may have been one of the queens of *Amenophis III – *Tiye or Sitamun – or another unknown woman in the king's harem. Medical examination of the mummy of Tutankhamun and of the body found in Tomb 55 (believed to be that of *Smenkhkare) has indicated that these two men were probably full brothers; both had the unusual although not abnormal platycephalic skull that is also present in an exaggerated form in the art representations of *Akhenaten.

Tutankhamun married the third daughter of *Akhenaten and *Nefertiti and originally the names of the royal couple were Tutankhaten and *Ankhesenpaaten, but these were later changed to Tutankhamun and Ankhesenamun when there was a return to orthodox religion. As a child ruler, Tutankhamun was probably advised at first by *Nefertiti and then by the courtier, *Ay; *Horemheb also rose to eminence in this reign as the King's Deputy.

Tutankhamun may have lived for some time at the Northern Palace at Amarna, under *Nefertiti's tutelage, or he and *Ankhesenpaaten may have moved there after *Nefertiti's death. It is unclear when Tutankhamun's Court left Amarna and returned to Thebes, and the extent to which the Aten was replaced by the traditional gods during his reign. In the Amarna archive there are letters addressed to Tutankhamun by foreign rulers and these may have been sent to him while he still resided there.

His Restoration Stela was issued from Memphis, which presumably became his new capital, although the stela was set up in the Temple of Karnak at Thebes. The inscription gives details of the chaos that prevailed in the land and of the steps that the young king took to restore the old order: the gods, particularly Amun, were reinstated, and since no priests could be found (presumably because *Akhenaten had eliminated them), a new priesthood was drawn from well-known persons in all the major towns. The cult of the Aten still retained some importance, for the sun's disc and rays – the Aten's symbol – was represented on the king's coronation throne as the royal patron deity.

Few other details of Tutankhamun's short reign have survived, although in the Temple of Luxor, a great hall was decorated with wall-reliefs that show his great festival of Amun. The king's programme of restoration was obviously curtailed by his untimely death before he reached twenty; examination of the mummy has not revealed conclusive evidence of the cause of death.

Tutankhamun was buried in an improvised tomb in the Valley of the Kings and the entrance to this was later covered over by debris from the tomb of Ramesses VI. Although it was robbed in antiquity, Howard Carter, excavating on behalf of Lord Carnarvon, discovered the tomb in 1922 and found most of the contents intact. The spectacular treasure, crammed into the four small rooms of the tomb, included the funerary goods and the three golden coffins and gold mask that covered the mummy. All these items are now in the Cairo Museum, with the exception of the mummy and one of the gold covered wooden coffins which remain in the tomb. All the other royal burials in the Valley of the Kings had been plundered extensively, so this tomb provided a unique opportunity to study the funerary art and ritual of the New Kingdom.

Two female foetuses were also discovered in the tomb. These were presumably the offspring of the royal couple. Because Tutankhamun apparently had no heir, his throne was inherited by *Ay, a senior courtier, who is shown in the tomb scenes performing the burial rites for the young king.

Since the names of *Akhenaten and *Smenkhkare were not obliterated during the reigns of Tutankhamun or *Ay, but at a later date, it would appear that the destruction of the Aten cult was undertaken by their successors.

BIBL. Carter, H. *The Tomb of Tutankhamun.*(three vols) London: 1923-33; Varille, A. Toutankhamon, est-il fils d'Amenophis III et de Satamon? *Ann.Serv.*40 (1941) pp. 651-7; Aldred, C. *Akhenaten, King of Egypt.* London: 1988; Piankoff, A. *The shrines of Tut-ankh-Amon.* New York: 1962 ; Connolly, R. C. Harrison, R. G. and Ahmed, S. Serological evidence for the parentage of Tutankhamun and Smenkhkare. *JEA* 62 (1976) note on p.184; Harrison, R. G. Connolly, R. C. and Abdalla, A. The kinship of Smenkhkare and Tutankhamun demonstrated serologically. *Nature* 224 (1969) pp. 325-6; Leek, F. F. *The human remains from the Tomb of Tutankhamun.* Oxford: 1972. Reeves, N. *The Complete Tutenkhamun.* London:1990.

Tuthmosis I   King   1525 - 1512 BC

A middle-aged soldier when he came to the throne, Tuthmosis I may have been co-regent with his predecessor, *Amenophis I. His mother, Senisonb, had no royal blood, and his claim to rule came probably through his wife, Princess Ahmose. It is likely that she was the sister of *Amenophis I and the daughter of the previous king, *Amosis I, and his queen, *Ahmose-Nefertari.

Tuthmosis I was the first of the great military pharaohs of the Eighteenth Dynasty who carried forward plans for expansion which could be based on the achievements of the Theban princes of the Seventeenth Dynasty. For many years, only Tuthmosis I's grandson, *Tuthmosis III, was able to emulate his military successes abroad.

His accession to the throne is proclaimed on two stelae from Wadi Halfa and Quban which preserve the text of a letter to Turi, the Viceroy of Nubia. In Year 2, Tuthmosis I campaigned in *Nubia; this is recalled in an inscription which is engraved on the rock near the island of Tombos above the Third Cataract, and in the biographical inscription of his commander, Ahmose of El Kab, who relates how he navigated the king's fleet to *Nubia. Tuthmosis I ultimately advanced Egypt's control in *Nubia to a considerable degree, campaigning as far south as the region of the Fourth Cataract and constructing fortresses in the new territory.

His northern campaigns were even more impressive. An expedition in which Ahmose of El Kab and his younger relative, Ahmose Pennekheb, again took part thrust across the River Euphrates into Nahrin, which was ruled by the king of *Mitanni. Here, a commemorative stela was set up: many of the enemy were slaughtered or taken captive and, on his return home, Tuthmosis I celebrated his victory with an elephant hunt in the region of Niy in Syria. His campaigns displayed military genius and extended Egyptian power as far as it was destined to reach – to the River Euphrates in the north and towards the region of the Fifth Cataract in *Nubia.

Tuthmosis I apparently built extensively at Karnak, but little else is known of his relatively short reign. His eldest sons, Amenmose and Wadjmose, did not live to succeed him, and *Tuthmosis II, his son by the secondary queen, Mutnefer, became his heir. His Great Royal Wife, Ahmose, gave him a daughter, *Hatshepsut, who later emphasised her royal pedigree and her father's support, to justify her seizure of the throne.

Tuthmosis I was the first king to prepare a tomb in the Valley of the Kings at Thebes; quarried by the important official Ineni, its location in a remote and lonely valley was probably chosen in an attempt to deter tomb-robbers. Although it was of modest construction, this tomb established the pattern for later burials in the Valley. The king's mummy may have been amongst those discovered in the cache at Deir el Bahri.

His funerary temple, which established the precedent of separating the temple from the tomb, was probably built on the edge of the Theban cultivated plain, but it has never been uncovered. This king also founded the village at Deir el Medina that housed the royal necropolis workmen and their families, but it was his predecessor, *Amenophis I, who became the patron of the community and received a cult there as a dead, deified ruler.

BIBL. Bruyere, B. *Rapport sur les fouilles de Deir el Medineh.* (sixteen vols) Cairo: 1924-53; Winlock, H. E. Notes on the reburial of Tuthmosis I. *JEA* 15 (1929) pp. 56-68.

Tuthmosis II King c.1512 - 1504 BC.

The son of *Tuthmosis I by a secondary queen, Mutnefer, Tuthmosis II married *Hatshepsut, who was the Great Royal Daughter of *Tuthmosis I by his chief wife, Ahmose. This marriage apparently produced no male heir, for before his death Tuthmosis II confirmed *Tuthmosis III – the son born to him by a concubine Isis – as his successor. This did not prevent *Hatshepsut (who acted as the child's regent after Tuthmosis II's premature death) from seizing the throne in her own right. Neferure, the daughter of Tuthmosis II and *Hatshepsut, was married in childhood to *Tuthmosis III, to confirm his claim to the throne.

Despite his short reign, Tuthmosis II pursued an active military policy: a stela dating to Year 1 of his reign relates that the king overthrew an insurrection in *Nubia and also led a campaign to Palestine. At home, he contributed to the building programme in the Temple of Amun at Karnak; his funerary monuments – an undistinguished temple on the west bank at Thebes and a modest tomb with an unfinished sarcophagus in the Valley of the Kings – indicate that his reign was less illustrious than those of his father or his son.

BIBL. Edgerton, W. F. *The Thutmosid succession.* Chicago: 1933.

Tuthmosis III King 1504 - 1450 BC.

Tuthmosis III, the son of *Tuthmosis II by a concubine named Isis, came to the throne as a minor under the regency of his father's Great Royal Wife, Queen *Hatshepsut. With her impeccable royal lineage and the support of powerful officials, *Hatshepsut was able to seize control, and in Year 2 of her joint rule with Tuthmosis III, she was crowned as Pharaoh with full powers, reducing Tuthmosis III to insignificance. He probably spent most of the years of this co-regency in training with the army, but by Year 22 (1482 BC), when *Hatshepsut died, he was able to gain complete control of the country. His hatred for his step-mother, who had barred him from power for so long is evident in the erasure of her name from the monuments which was carried out in his reign.

During *Hatshepsut's reign, the possessions which *Tuthmosis I had gained in Syria and Palestine had largely disappeared; some princes there had declared themselves independent while others had changed their allegiance to *Mitanni, Egypt's great Mesopotamian rival.

Tuthmosis III was eager to restore these possessions and in Year 23 (the second year of his independent reign), he set out on his first campaign, marching to Gaza and then on to Megiddo, a fortified town overlooking the plain of Esdraelon, where he defeated a coalition of Syrian princes. The king acted with great personal valour and completely routed the enemy; Megiddo was finally taken after a seven-month siege, and this victory was obviously regarded as the basis for his future efforts in Syria and Palestine.

The Kingdom of *Mitanni, thrusting as far as the Euphrates, continued to hinder Tuthmosis III's plans for expansion, and a total of seventeen campaigns were waged in Syria to drive the *Mitannians back across the Euphrates and establish Egypt's supreme power in the area. In the eighth campaign in Year 33, the Egyptians succeeded in crossing the Euphrates and defeating the king of *Mitanni, but conflict continued even after this.

Egypt became the greatest military power in the ancient world and received lavish gifts from the other powerful states of *Assyria, Babylonia and the *Hittites. Her administration of the Syro-Palestine empire centred around the policy of leaving local rulers in charge, but ensuring that they were favourable to Egypt; this was underlined by removing their children or brothers to Egypt where they were educated and retained as hostages. In *Nubia also Tuthmosis III confirmed Egyptian domination as far as the Fourth Cataract on the Nile. He is rightfully acknowledged as Egypt's greatest ruler, and records of his campaigns are preserved in the inscriptions in the Temple of Karnak and on the Armant and Gebel Barkal stelae.

At home, Tuthmosis III pursued equally efficient and beneficial policies and built more temples than any other ruler until that date. At Karnak, his major additions were the Seventh Pylon and the Festival Hall, where unusual plants he brought back from Syria are depicted on the walls. His funerary temple at Thebes is now almost completely destroyed; his tomb in the Valley of the Kings contains wall-scenes representing the Book of Amduat ('What is in the underworld'), and his mummy was amongst those discovered in the Deir el Bahri cache.

Many of his courtiers and officials have fine tombs at Thebes, including that of the famous vizier, *Rekhmire, but the administrative capital was now situated at Memphis. Tuthmosis III had several wives including Neferure (the child of *Tuthmosis II and *Hatshepsut) and Hatshepsut-Meryetre, who was the mother of his heir, *Amenophis II. There were also three queens (who may have been of foreign origin) whose tomb was found to contain some fine jewellery.

In his later years, Tuthmosis III led no further campaigns and probably devoted his attention to building projects. He was remembered as a world conqueror and Egypt's greatest pharaoh and his exploits were emulated by the later rulers *Sethos I and *Ramesses II.

BIBL. Breasted, J. H. *Ancient Records of Egypt: Historical Documents 2: The Eighteenth Dynasty*. Chicago: 1906; Edgerton, W. F. *The Thutmosid Succession*. Chicago: 1933; Faulkner, R. O. The Euphrates campaign of Tuthmosis III. *JEA* 32 (1946) pp. 39-42; Faulkner, R. O. The Battle of Megiddo. *JEA* 28 (1942) pp. 2-15.

Tuthmosis IV   King   1425 - 1417 BC.

The son of *Amenophis II and Queen Tio, Tuthmosis IV was not the heir apparent and probably succeeded because of the death of an elder brother. In the Dream Stela, which dates to Year 1 of his reign, Tuthmosis IV tells the story of how, as a young man, he fell asleep near the Great Sphinx at Giza; subsequently, in a dream, Harmachis (the deity embodied by the Sphinx) prophesied that the young prince would one day become king, but also expressed his displeasure with the sand which engulfed the body of the Sphinx. When Tuthmosis IV became king he therefore ordered the sand to be cleared away, and the stela was set up between the paws of the Sphinx, to commemorate this event.

Little evidence of the king's reign survives. His funerary temple near the Ramesseum at Thebes is poorly preserved; his tomb, sarcophagus and funerary furniture were discovered by Howard Carter, and in 1898, his mummy had been found amongst those in the royal cache in the tomb of *Amenophis II. Medical examination later revealed that he had died as a young man in his twenties.

His foreign policy included a campaign in *Nubia in Year 8 to check an incursion of desert tribesmen, and he also continued military action in the Asiatic provinces. His reign saw a major change in Syrian affairs: here, neither the Egyptians nor the *Mitannians could gain complete supremacy, and so they finally made a peaceful alliance, marking it with a royal marriage between Tuthmosis IV and the daughter of King Artatama I. It is likely that this *Mitannian princess became *Mutemweya, the king's Great Royal Wife. She is shown as the mother of *Amenophis III in the scenes in the Temple of Luxor which depict his divine birth. Because of Tuthmosis IV's early death, it is possible that there was no royal sister to become the wife of *Amenophis III, and he therefore broke the traditional pattern by marrying a commoner, *Tiye.

Tuthmosis IV's reign is also significant because there is evidence that at this time, the Aten came to be regarded as a separate deity; a scarab inscription refers to the Aten as a god of battles. *Akhenaten, the grandson of Tuthmosis IV, was to develop the cult of this god into a form of monotheism.

BIBL. Shorter, A. W. Historical scarabs of Tuthmosis IV and Amenophis III. *JEA* 17 (1931) pp 23-5; Carter, H, Newberry, P. E. and Maspero, G. *The Tomb of Touthmosis IV*. London: 1904.

U

Unas King 2375 - 2345 BC.

Unas was the last king of the Fifth Dynasty, and his pyramid complex at Saqqara has two features of special interest. The pyramid was smaller than those of his predecessors, and nearby there were the tombs of his chief queen, Nebet, and other members of his family and courtiers. The internal structure of his pyramid incorporated several innovative features, but it is best known for the inclusion of vertical lines of hieroglyphs on the walls of the vestibule and the burial chamber.

These were magico-religious texts, designed to ensure the safe passage of the king into the next world, and they are known today as the 'Pyramid Texts'. The appearance of these texts in Unas' monument is the earliest example of their use within a pyramid, but they were later inscribed in the pyramids of *Teti, *Pepy I, Merenre, *Pepy II and Ibi, and in the pyramids of *Pepy II's three queens. They are the oldest religious texts to have been discovered in Egypt and they were evidently compiled from earlier, oral traditions. Altogether, over seven hundred spells are known from these Texts, but they do not all occur in any one pyramid. In the pyramid of Unas there are two hundred and twenty-eight spells, inscribed in vertical lines of hieroglyphs; each incised sign is filled in with blue pigment which makes the hieroglyphs stand out in marked contrast to the background of the white wall.

The other major feature of Unas' pyramid complex is the causeway, which is the best preserved example of its kind; it is seven hundred and thirty yards long. It was excavated by Selim Bey Hassan in AD 1937-8, and later by Abdessalam Hussein. On the inner walls of the corridor, there are the remains of scenes carved in low relief which are of the highest quality; the subject matter is also of considerable interest, showing labourers working on the royal estates, hunting scenes, craftsmen engaged in various manufacturing activities, and bearded *Asiatics arriving in ships, perhaps coming from a trading expedition to *Byblos.

There are also ships that bring granite columns and architraves from the quarries at Aswan for the king's mortuary temple. One scene of special interest is the so-called 'famine relief' which depicts emaciated people who are dying of hunger. There is no obvious explanation for this, although it has been suggested that the people were not Egyptians and that, if the sequence was more completely preserved, it would probably show that they were the recipients of Unas' bounty.

BIBL. Hussein, A. S. M. Fouilles sur la chausee d'Ounas, 1941-43. *Ann. Serv.* 43 (1943) pp. 439-48; Hassan, S. The causeway of Wnis at Saqqara. *ZAS* 80 (1955) pp. 136-9; Drioton, E. Une representation de la famine sur un bas-relief egyptien de la Ve Dynastie. *BIFAO* 25 (1942-3) pp. 45-54; Mercer, S. A. B. *The Pyramid Texts in translation and commentary.* (four vols) New York: 1952; Stevenson Smith, W. *The Art and Architecture of ancient Egypt.* Harmondsworth: 1958 pp. 75, 76 and p. 262 nn. 28, 29.

Userkaf King 2494 - 2487 BC.

The first king of the Fifth Dynasty, Userkaf was perhaps a descendant of a secondary branch of *Cheops' family. He probably strengthened his claim to the throne by marrying *Khentkaues, and was succeeded by his sons *Sahure and *Neferirkare.

In the Westcar Papyrus, the folk-tale mentions Userkaf as one of the triplets born to the wife of a priest of Re, who is destined to exercise the divine kingship in Egypt. Although the story gives an inaccurate description of his parentage, he undoubtedly ushered in a dynasty that gave unprecedented power to the priesthood of Re. The epithet 'son of Re' was first adopted by the kings at an earlier date, but the Fifth Dynasty rulers began to use it as part of their official titulary. On the Palermo Stone it is recorded that Userkaf made offerings and gifts of land to the sun-god.

A new type of monument was introduced by Userkaf; this was a special type of sun-temple which emphasised the close association this dynasty had with the cult of Re, and these temples continued to be built throughout the first eight reigns of the dynasty. Built at Abu Ghurob, some distance to the south of Giza, the sun-temples reflected the lay-out of a pyramid complex, having a valley building, a causeway, and the equivalent of a funerary temple and a pyramid, but here, the king's burial place was replaced by an open court in which stood a squat stone obelisk mounted on a platform. This was supposed to imitate the Benben stone at Heliopolis, where it formed the central feature of Re's temple and probably represented a sun-ray and the god's cult-symbol. At least six kings of this dynasty are known to have built sun-temples, but so far only two of these have been located and excavated, including that of Userkaf.

The sun-temples underlined the royal piety to Re; they provide a contrast with the emphasis that the previous dynasty had placed on the king's own burial place. The kings of the Fifth Dynasty continued to build pyramids for themselves, although these were constructed of inferior materials and, instead of using stone throughout, the core was made of brickwork. Userkaf's pyramid was at Saqqara and resembled those of *Cheops and *Mycerinus in its layout. It was in a ruinous state by the time it was discovered and had been used as a quarry in antiquity. The walls of the court were covered with finest quality reliefs which preserved part of a fowling scene, and in the temple, the head of a magnificent colossal statue of the king was discovered; this was of red granite, and is now in the Cairo Museum. A smaller head of Userkaf was found in his sun-temple.

BIBL. Stock, H. Das Sonnenheiligtum des Konigs Userkaf. *ZAS* 80 (1955) pp. 140-44; Lauer, J. P. Le temple haut de la pyramide du roi Ouserkaf a Saqqarah. *Ann. Serv.* 53 (1955) pp. 119 - 33; Ricke, H. Erster Grabungsbericht uber das Sonnenheiligtum des Konigs Userkaf bei Abusir. *Ann. Serv.* 54 (1956-7) pp. 75-82, 305-16; Dritter Grabungsbericht uber das Sonnenheiligtum des Konigs Userkaf bei Abusir. *Ann. Serv.* 55 (1958) pp 73-7.

Wenamun   Literary character   c.1100 BC.

The 'Story of Wenamun' is preserved on a papyrus which was purchased in Cairo in 1891 and is now in Moscow. It is a major literary source for the later period of Egypt's history and for the decline of her influence in Syria and Palestine. The story is perhaps based on an actual report, and it relates the experiences of Wenamun's travels and trading operations in the eastern Mediterranean when he was sent on a mission to Syria at the end of the Twentieth Dynasty (the papyrus can be dated to a time shortly after this journey was supposed to have taken place).

As the background to Wenamun's adventures, *Ramesses XI had yielded his throne to two rulers – Smendes at Tanis in the north and *Herihor, High-priest of Amun at Thebes in the south. Egypt's former greatness abroad had by now collapsed, and the difficulties which Wenamun encountered with foreign princes and officials illustrate all too vividly that Egypt was no longer feared or respected by other peoples of the Near East.

Wenamun was a temple official who was sent to acquire cedarwood from *Byblos to restore the sacred barque in which Amun's divine statue was carried around during festivals. In order to enhance Wenamun's prestige, an image of the god – 'Amun of the Road' – was sent with him.

This story, set in that period of the New Kingdom when Egypt's empire was lost, can be compared with the Story of *Sinuhe which reflects the political and economic conditions of the Middle Kingdom when Sinuhe in his travels meets with personal success because he comes from a renowned and respected country.

BIBL. *AEL* ii. pp. 224-30; Nims, C. F. Second tenses in Wenamun. *JEA* 54 (1968) pp. 161-4.

X

Xerxes   Emperor of *Persia   486 - 465 BC.

The son of *Darius I, Xerxes succeeded his father as Emperor in 486 BC, and shortly after, he defeated an Egyptian uprising. Unlike his father, he did nothing to improve or enhance conditions in Egypt and inaugurated no building programmes in the Egyptian temples. He was apparently prepared to use the Egyptians to suit his own ends, as when, at the Battle of Salamis (480 BC), he led a large Egyptian fleet against the *Greeks. According to *Herodotus (vii,7), he was cruel and tyrannical to the Egyptians. He was murdered, and Artaxerxes succeeded him in 465 BC.

Apart from the interest which *Darius I showed in Egypt and the exchange of personnel which must have occurred at all levels during the two periods of *Persian rulership in the country, it would seem that the *Persian kings and their civilisation had very little longterm effect upon the Egyptian people, their beliefs, or their customs.

BIBL. Posener, G. *La premiere domination Perse en Egypte.* Cairo: 1936.

Yuya, King's father-in-law, reign of *Amenophis III, 1417 - 1379 BC.
*Tiye, the daughter of Yuya and *Thuya, became the chief queen of *Amenophis III, and they are mentioned as the queen's parents in inscriptions on two commemorative scarabs from the reign of *Amenophis III. Yuya came from the town of Akhmim, where he probably held estates and where he was Prophet of Min, the chief god of the area, and Superintendent of Cattle. He also held important positions at Court as 'King's Lieutenant' and 'Master of the Horse', and his title of 'Father-of-the-god' may have referred specifically to his role as the king's father-in-law.

The tomb belonging to Yuya and his wife was discovered in the Valley of the Kings at Thebes in 1905 by J. E. Quibell, who was working on behalf of Theodore M. Davis. Although it had been entered, the tomb-robbers were perhaps disturbed, and Quibell found the funerary goods and the two mummies virtually intact. The mummy of Yuya showed that he had been a man of taller than average stature, and the anatomist G. Elliot Smith considered that his appearance was not typically Egyptian, which, together with his unusual name, led to speculation that he was of foreign origin. This has never been proved, but it is conceivable that he had some *Mitannian ancestry, since it is known that knowledge of horses and chariotry was introduced into Egypt from the northern lands and Yuya was the king's 'Master of the Horse'.

One possibility is that Yuya was the brother of Queen *Mutemweya, who may have had *Mitannian royal origins, and it has also been suggested that he may have been closely linked with *Ay. They both came from Akhmim, held similar titles, and had names that may show some association. The theory that Yuya could be identified with *Ay and *Thuya with *Ay's wife, Tey, is chronologically impossible, but *Ay may have been Yuya's son and the brother of Queen *Tiye and of Anen (who held a high position in the Temple of Amun at Karnak). Since there is no conclusive evidence, the family connections between these people must remain speculative.

BIBL. Quibell, J. E. *The Tomb of Yuaa and Thuiu.* Cairo: 1908; Aldred, C *Akhenaten, King of Egypt.* London: 1988; Davis, T. M., Maspero, G. and Newberry, P. E. *The Tomb of Iouiya and Touiyou.* London: 1907.

INDEX OF PERSONS MENTIONED
BUT WITHOUT AN ENTRY

Abdi-Ashirta of Amurru, see Rib-Addi.

Abimilki, see Meritaten, Phoenicians.

Achaeans, see Ahhiyawa, Akawasha and Sea-peoples.

Achaemenids, see Cambyses, Darius I, Nebuchadrezzar II.

Achthoes, Chancellor of Mentuhotep II, see Mentuhotep II.

Achthoes II, see Achthoes (Akhtoy).

Achthoes III, see Achthoes (Akhtoy) and Merikare.

Adad-nirari II, see Assyrians.

Adicran, see Apries.

Aeizanes, see Meroites.

Aelius Gallus, see Strabo.

Agatharchides of Cnidus, see Diodorus Siculus.

Ahmose of El Kab, son of Ebana, see Amenophis I, Amosis I, Tuthmosis I.

Ahmose, wife of Tuthmosis I, see Hatshepsut, Tuthmosis I, Tuthmosis II.

Ahmose Pennekheb, see Amenophis I, Amosis I, Tuthmosis I.

Akhet-hotep, see Ptah-hotep.

Alexander IV, see Ptolemy I.

Alexander Helios, see Cleopatra VII.

Amen-hir-khopshef, see Nefertari.

Amen-Re Hornakht, see Osorkon II.

Amenardis II, see Psammetichus I, Taharka.

Amenemope, King, see Psusennes I.

Amenhotep, High-priestofAmun, seePinehas, Pinudjem I, Ramessenakhte,
    Ramesse IX, Ramesses XI.

Amenmesse, see Merneptah, Siptah.

Amenmose, see Tuthmosis I.

Ammenemes IV, see Ammenemes III.

Amorites, see Phoenicians.

Anen, see Tiye, Yuya.

Ankhesenpaaten-sherit, see Ankhesenpaaten.

Antiochus III of Syria, see Ptolemy IV, Ptolemy V.

Apollonius, see Ptolemy II.

Arsinoe II, see Ptolemy II.

Arsinoe III, see Ptolemy IV.

Artatama I, see Mitanni, Mutemweya, Tushratta, Tuthmosis IV.

Artaxerxes III, see Cambyses, Nectanebo I, Persians.

Aryandes, see Cambyses.

Au-ib-re, see Hardedef.

Babylonia, see Ammenemes II, Amenophis III, Apries, Assyrians, Cyaxares, Jews,
    Meritaten, Mitanni, Nabopolassar, Nebuchadrezzar II, Necho II,
    Phoenicians, Psammetichus I, Tuthmosis III.

Baketaten, see Amenophis III, Tiye.

Balbilla, see Hadrian.

171

CHRONOLOGICAL TABLE

PREDYNASTIC PERIOD (c.5000–3100 BC)

Scorpion before 3100 BC

UNIFICATION OF EGYPT (c.3100 BC)

ARCHAIC PERIOD

First Dynasty c.3100–2890 BC

Narmer (Menes)	c.3100 –? BC
'Aha	c.3070 BC
Djer	c.3042 – 2995 BC
Den	c.2985 – 2930 BC

Second Dynasty c.2890-2686 BC.

Peribsen	c.2700 BC
Kha'sekhem	c.2724 – 2703 BC
Kha'sekhemui	c.2703 – 2686 BC

OLD KINGDOM

Third Dynasty c.2686 – 2613 BC

Djoser	c.2667 – 2648 BC
Huni	c.2637 – 2613 BC

Fourth Dynasty c.2613 – 2494 BC

Sneferu	c.2613 – 2589 BC
Cheops	c.2589 – 2566 BC
Chephren	c.2558 – 2533 BC
Mycerinus	c.2528 – 2500 BC
Shepseskaf	c.2500 – 2496 BC

Fifth Dynasty c.2494 – 2345 BC

Userkaf	c.2494 – 2487 BC
Sahure	2487 – 2473 BC
Neferirkare	2473 – 2463 BC
Niuserre	2453 – 2422 BC
Isesi	c.2414 – 2375 BC
Unas	2375 – 2345 BC

Sixth Dynasty c. 2345 – 2181 BC

Teti	c.2345 – 2333 BC
Pepy I	2322 – 2283 BC
Pepy II	2269 – c.2175 BC
Nitocris	c.2183 – 2181 BC

FIRST INTERMEDIATE PERIOD

Seventh Dynasty   *c.2181 – 2173 BC*

Eighth Dynasty   *c.2173 – 2160 BC*

Ninth Dynasty   *c.2160 – 2130 BC*

Achthoes I   c.2160 BC

Tenth Dynasty   *c.2130 – 2040 BC*

Eleventh Dynasty   *c.2133 – 1991 BC*

Mentuhotep II (Nebhepetre)	2060 – 2010 BC
Mentuhotep III (S'ankhkare)	2009 – 1998 BC
Mentuhotep IV (Nebtowyre)	1997 – 1991 BC

MIDDLE KINGDOM

Twelfth Dynasty 1991 – 1786 BC

Ammenemes I	1991 – 1962 BC
Sesostris I	1971 – 1928 BC
Ammenemes II	1929 – 1895 BC
Sesostris II	1897 – 1878 BC
Sesostris III	1878 – 1843 BC
Ammenemes II	1842 – 1797 BC
Ammenemes IV	1798 – 1790 BC
Sebeknefru	1789 – 1786 BC

SECOND INTERMEDIATE PERIOD

Thirteenth Dynasty	*1786 – 1633 BC*
Fourteenth Dynasty	*1786 – c.1603 BC*
Fifteenth Dynasty (Hyksos)	*1674 – 1567 BC*

Auserre Apophis I	c.1570 BC – c.1570 BC
Sixteenth Dynasty (Hyksos)	*c.1684 – 1567 BC*
Seventeenth Dynasty.	*c.1650 – 1567 BC*
Seqenenre Ta'o II	c.1575 BC
Kamose	c.1570 – 1567 BC

NEW KINGDOM

Eighteenth Dynasty 1567 – 1320 BC

Amosis I	1570 – 1546 BC
Amenophis I	1546 – 1526 BC
Tuthmosis I	1525 – 1512 BC
Tuthmosis II	c.1512 – 1504 BC
Hatshepsut	1503 – 1482 BC
Tuthmosis III	1504 – 1450 BC
Amenophis II	1450 – 1425 BC
Tuthmosis IV	1425 – 1417 BC
Amenophis III	1417 – 1379 BC
Akhenaten (Amenophis IV)	1379 – 1362 BC
Smenkhkare	c.1364 – 1361 BC
Tutankhamun	1361 – 1352 BC
Ay	1352 – 1348 BC
Horemheb	1348 – 1320 BC

Nineteenth Dynasty 1320 – 1200 BC

Sethos I	1318 – 1304 BC
Ramesses II	1304 – 1237 BC
Merneptah	1236 – 1223 BC
Siptah, Tewosret	c.1209 – 1200 BC

Twentieth Dynasty 1200 – 1085 BC

Ramesses III	1198 – 1166 BC
Ramesses IV	1166 – 1160 BC
Ramesses V	1160 – 1156 BC
Ramesses IX	1140 – 1121 BC
Ramesses XI	1113 – 1085 BC

THIRD INTERMEDIATE PERIOD

Twenty-first Dynasty c.1089 – 945 BC

Kings (Tanis)		High Priests (Thebes)
Smendes	1089 – 1063 BC	Herihor 1100 – 1094 BC
Psusennes I	1063 – 1037 BC	
Pinudjem 1	1044 – 1026 BC	Pinudjem 1 1064 – 1045 BC
		Pinudjem 11 985 – 969 BC
Psusennes II	959 – 945 BC	

Twenty-second Dynasty 945 – 730 BC

Shoshenk I	945 – 924 BC
Shoshenk II (co – regent)	c.890 BC
Osorkon II	874 – 850 BC
Shoshenk III	825 – 773 BC
Pemay	773 – 767 BC

Twenty-third Dynasty (Leontopolis) c.818 – 715 BC

Pedubast I	818 – 793 BC

Twenty-fourth Dynasty c.727 – 715 BC

Tefnakht I	727 – 720 BC
Bakenranef	720 – 715 BC

Twenty-fifth Dynasty c.780 – 656 BC

Kashta	c.760 – 747 BC
Piankhy	747 – 716 BC
Shabako	716 – 702 BC
Shebitku	702 – 690 BC
Taharka	690 – 664 BC Assyrians in Egypt
	c.680 – 663 BC
Tanuatamun	664 – 656 BC

Twenty-sixth Dynasty 664 – 525 BC

Necho I	672 – 664 BC
Psammetichus I	664 – 610 BC
Necho II	610 – 595 BC
Psammetichus II	595 – 589 BC
Apries	589 – 570 BC
Amasis	570 – 526 BC
Psammetichus III	526 – 525 BC

LATE PERIOD

Twenty-seventh Dynasty   *525 – 404 BC. First Persian Period*
Rule of eight Persian kings including Cambyses, Darius I, Xerxes

Twenty-eighth Dynasty   *404 – 399 BC*

Kings of Sais

Twenty-ninth Dynasty   *339 – 380BC*

Kings of Mendes

Thirtieth Dynasty   *380 – 343 BC*

Kings of Sebennytos, including Nectanebo I (Nekhtnebef) 380 – 363 BC

Thirty-first Dynasty   *343 – 332 BC Second Persian Period*

Rule of three Persian kings

CONQUEST OF EGYPT BY ALEXANDER THE GREAT 332 BC

(Alexander ruled until his death in 323 BC)

PTOLEMAIC PERIOD 323 – 30 BC

Ptolemy I	305 – 283 BC
Ptolemy II	283 – 246 BC
Ptolemy III	246 – 221 BC
Ptolemy IV	221 – 204 BC
Ptolemy V	204 – 180 BC
Ptolemy VIII	145 – 116 BC
Cleopatra VII	51 – 30 BC with Ptolemy XII 51 BC
	with Ptolemy XIII 51 – 47 BC
	with Ptolemy XIV 47 – 30 BC

CONQUEST OF EGYPT BY OCTAVIAN (AUGUSTUS) 30 BC

ROMAN PERIOD 30 BC – c. AD 600

ABBREVIATED TITLES OF BOOKS AND PERIODICALS

AEL i, ii, iii — Lichtheim, M. Ancient Egyptian Literature. (Three Vols) Los Angeles: 1973-1980.

AJSL — American Journal of Semitic Languages and Literature.

ANET — Pritchard, J. B.(ed). Ancient Near Eastern Texts relating to the Old Testament. Princeton:1969

Ann.Arch.Anthr. — Annals of Archaeology and Anthropology.

Ann.Serv. — Annales du Service des Antiquitiés de l'Égypte.

BIFAO — Bulletin de l'Institut Français d'Archéologie Orientale.

BJRL — Bulletin of the John Rylands Library, Manchester.

Bull.MMA — Bulletin of the Metropolitan Museum of Art, New York.

CAH ii — The Cambridge Ancient History. Vol.2. 3rd ed. 1970-5

Chron. d'Ég. — Chronique d'Égypte

Herodotus, Bk ii — Herodotus, The Histories Book 2 (tr. by Waddell, W.G. Loeb Classical Library. London:1939).

JARCE — Journal of the American Research Center in Egypt.

JEA — Journal of Egyptian Archaeology.

JNES — Journal of Near Eastern Studies.

JHS — Journal of Hellenic Studies.

Kienitz, F. K.. Die politischeGeschichte Ägyptens vol. 7. bis zum 4. Jahrhundert vor der Zietwende. Berlin:1953.

Kitchen, K.A. Ramesside Inscrips.Kitchen, K. A. Ramesside Inscriptions. Oxford 1968.

Kitchen, K.A. 3rd Int.Kitchen, K. A. The Third Intermediate Period in Egypt (1100-650). Warminster: 1973; 2nd ed. 1986.

Rec.trav — Recueil de travaux rélatifs à la philologie et à l'archéologie égyptiennes et assyriennes.

ZÄS — Zeitschrift fur Ägyptische Sprache.

Recommended Reading

Aldred, C. *Akhenaten: King of Egypt*: London: 1991
    See pages 5, 27, 71, 77, 92, 144, 152, 155, 158, 167

Bowman, A. K. *Egypt after the Pharaohs, 332 BC - AD 642*. London: 1986.

David, A. R. *A guide to religious ritual at Abydos, c.1300 BC*. Warminster: 1973.

Dunham, D. *The Royal Cemeteries of Kush* (five vols): Boston, Mass.: 1950-63
    See page 79

Edwards, I. E. S. *The Pyramids of Egypt*: Harmondsworth: 1992
    See pages 33, 34, 42

Emery, W. B. *Archaic Egypt*: Harmondsworth: 1991
    See pages 27, 39, 41, 66, 67, 128, 179

Emery, W. B. *Great Tombs of the First Dynasty*. (three vols) Cairo and London: 1949-58.

Emery, W. B. *Archaic Egypt*. Harmondsworth: 1991.

Green, P. *Alexander of Macedon, 356-323 BC*: Berkeley: 1991
    See page 6

Hayes, W. C. *The Scepter of Egypt*. (two vols) New York and Cambridge, Mass: 1953-59; 2nd ed. 1990.

Kitchen, K. A. *Pharaoh Triumphant: The Life and Times of Ramesses II*: Warminster: 1993
    See pages 120, 179

Laming Macadam, M. F. *The Temples of Kawa* (two vols): Oxford: 1949, 1955
    See page 79

Martin, G. T. *The Royal Tomb at El-Amarna*: Vol. 2, *The Reliefs, Inscriptions and Architecture*: London: 1974
    See page 5

Petrie, W. M. F. *The Royal Tombs of the First Dynasty. Part 1*. London: 1900.

Petrie, W. M. F. *The Royal Tombs of the First Dynasty. Part 2*. London: 1901.

Reisner, G. A., Smith, W. S. *A History of the Giza Necropolis,* Vol. 2, *The Tomb of Heterpheres, the Mother of Cheops*: Cambridge, Mass.: 1955
    See page 53

Simpson, W. K. (ed.) *The Literature of Ancient Egypt.* New Haven: 1972.

Smith, G. E. *The Royal Mummies*. Cairo: 1912.

Smith, W. S. *The Art and Architecture of Ancient Egypt*. Pelican History of London: 1958.

A Biographical Dictionary of Ancient Egypt contains more than two hundred entries on important historical and cultural figures, as well as some less well known individuals in Egypt's long history (ca. 3100 B.C.–ca. A.D. 600). Not only are rulers and members of their families listed (Akhenaten, Nefertiti), but also other significant figures who had particularly impressive or interesting tombs (Cheops, Tutankhamun), who showed great military prowess (Sethos I, Ramesses II), or who had special literary or other skills (Ipuwer, Manetho). Also featured are foreigners with whom the Egyptians came into contact (Alexander the Great), and major classical writers (Herodotus) who have left vivid descriptions of ancient Egypt.

The entries are based on original source material noted in the bibliographical references. A brief history of ancient Egypt, a glossary, a chronology of dynasties, and four maps enhance this reference work, which will be useful to scholars and all general readers interested in ancient Egypt.

Dr. A. Rosalie David is Keeper of Egyptology at the Manchester Museum, the University of Manchester. She is the author of *The Ancient Egyptians, The Pyramid Builders of Ancient Egypt,* and *Discovering Ancient Egypt,* among other books. **Antony E. David** is Principal Manager (Collection care), Lancashire County Museums.

Cover design developed by Philippa Parkinson from cartouches
of Tuthmosis III in the temple of Karnak at Luxor

University of Oklahoma Press
Norman

ISBN 0-8061-2822-4

9 780806 128221